Faith, Famine, and Faction

Faith, Famine, and Faction

Religious Conflict in an
Irish Mining Community, 1847-1858

Thomas P. Power

WIPF & STOCK · Eugene, Oregon

FAITH, FAMINE, AND FACTION
Religious Conflict in an Irish Mining Community, 1847-1858

Copyright © 2020 Thomas P. Power. All rights reserved. Except for brief quotations in critical publications or reviews, no part of this book may be reproduced in any manner without prior written permission from the publisher. Write: Permissions, Wipf and Stock Publishers, 199 W. 8th Ave., Suite 3, Eugene, OR 97401.

Wipf & Stock
An Imprint of Wipf and Stock Publishers
199 W. 8th Ave., Suite 3
Eugene, OR 97401

www.wipfandstock.com

PAPERBACK ISBN: 978-1-7252-8334-3
HARDCOVER ISBN: 978-1-7252-8336-7
EBOOK ISBN: 978-1-7252-8335-0

Manufactured in the U.S.A.   September 15, 2020

To My Father and Mother, Richard and Sheila Power,
on their 60th Wedding Anniversary

Contents

Preface ix
Acknowledgements xi

Chapter 1   The Altogether Novel State of Things 1
Chapter 2   The Siberia Even of Waterford 25
Chapter 3   Pioneers of Another Existence to the
             Bonmahonites 69
Chapter 4   Industry and Self-Reliance 99
Chapter 5   Theological Primer 116
Chapter 6   The Stirabout Creed 1847-1855 138
Chapter 7   Burned In Effigy 1855-1858 185
Chapter 8   Facts are Stubborn Things 221
Chapter 9   Conclusion 245

Abbreviations 255
Endnotes 257
Bibliography 305
Index 315
About the Author 323

Preface

In 1979 I published two articles on the Rev. D.A. Doudney and educational establishments at Bunmahon, Co. Waterford. These were reflective of my level of interest and the sources available at the time. Since then, on and off over the years, I have kept the topic on my radar, and now revisit it in the light of more information becoming available.

Except for chapters 5, 7, and 9 chapter titles are taken from contemporary sources including, as follows: Ch. 2: *GM* 53 (1853), 227; *Credentials*, 489; Ch. 3: *GM* 53 (1853), 228; Ch. 4: *Try and Try Again*, 181; Ch. 6: J. Forbes, *Memorandums made in Ireland in the autumn of 1852*, 2 vols. (London, 1853), i, 256; Ch. 8: *Try and Try Again*, 203. See the list of Abbreviations and Bibliography below for full bibliographic references.

Note on Spelling: The modern spelling, Bunmahon, is used in the text except in cases where the older form, Bonmahon, is used in primary sources as quoted.

Acknowledgements

Over the course of writing this book I have incurred a number of debts. I am grateful to custodians of the National Library of Ireland, the National Archives of Ireland, the Representative Church Body Library, Trinity College Library, and the Waterford County Archives for making material available to me. In particular, I would like to thank Harriet Wheelock of the Royal College of Physicians, Dublin, who made available the rich archive relating to the college's property in Waterford. I am grateful to Rev. Gerard Chestnutt for allowing access to the Waterford Diocesan Archives in respect of the papers of Bishops Foran and O'Brien.

I want to acknowledge the study leave and financial incentives approved by George Sumner (Wycliffe College) and Linda Corman (Trinity College) that made the research for and writing of this book possible.

I want to thank Bonnie Kung of the Development Office, Wycliffe College, who was ever helpful and patient with my requests for assistance with images, and Amanda Wagner of ITS, University of Toronto, who assisted with formatting. Thanks to my family, Emily, Brendan, and Marlene, all of whom assisted in various ways in the final stages of preparation.

For their support and encouragement over the years in the enterprise of Waterford studies, I want to thank Des Cowman, Emmet O'Connor, and Julian Walton, the latter of whom generously supplied me with a copy of "Emily's Story."

Finally, I want to thank my father, Richard ("Dick") Power, who inspired in me a love of and curiosity about the Bunmahon and Stradbally area from my early years.

Thomas Power
Wycliffe College
University of Toronto
Toronto
January 2014.

Location of Waterford in Ireland

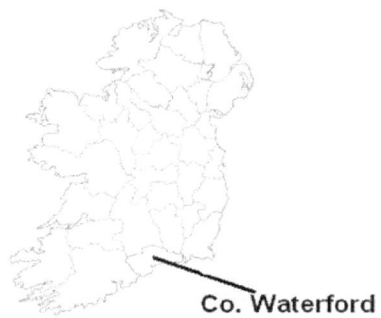

Parish Locations

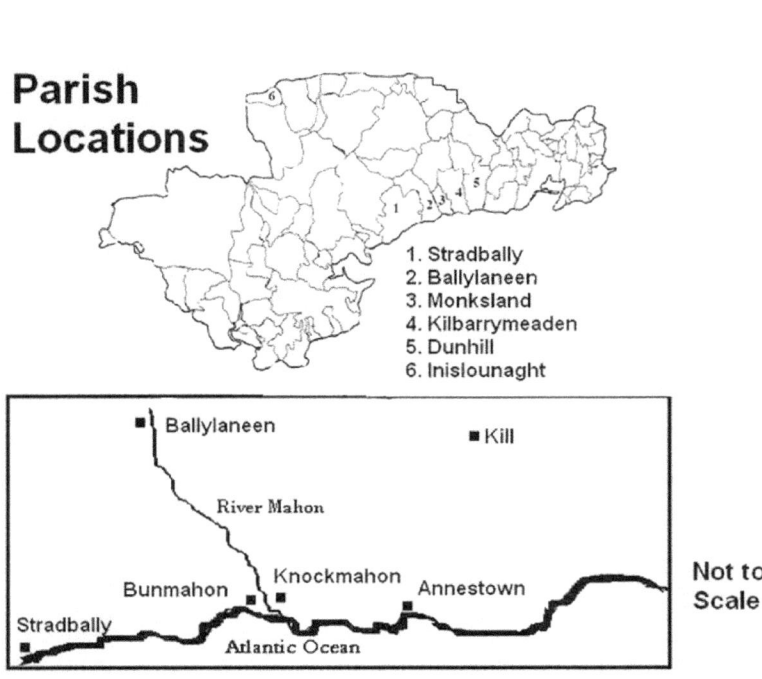

1. Stradbally
2. Ballylaneen
3. Monksland
4. Kilbarrymeaden
5. Dunhill
6. Inislounaght

Chapter 1

The Altogether Novel State of Things

Religious conflict in Ireland has had a long history and has assumed different forms and expressions over the centuries. Its manifestations have veered from benign debates over theological and doctrinal differences, to the more violent expressions of sectarianism.

This book is a case study of religious conflict in the copper mining community of Bunmahon, Co. Waterford, Ireland, in the mid-nineteenth century. The circumstances and events intrinsic to the conflict are intimately and inextricably bound up with the life and character of one man, David Alfred Doudney (1811–1893). In order to demonstrate the influences and life experiences that together combined to make this unique individual, who turned up in Monksland parish as its new curate in the autumn of 1847, this chapter examines three interconnecting aspects of Alfred Doudney's formation. These factors are his religious development, his professional call, and his family circumstances. All three were important formative influences that converged when Doudney came to Ireland from England in 1846, and therefore it is crucial to delineate the constituent elements of each.

A Vital Faith

Information about Doudney's early life is found in the account written of him by his son and daughter entitled, *Memoir of the*

Rev. D. A. Doudney, D.D. first published in 1893 shortly after its subject's death.¹ From it we learn that he was born on March 8, 1811, at Portsea, Portsmouth, Hampshire. The man who was to have such an impact on the mining community of Bunmahon in the mid-nineteenth century came from humble origins, and was raised in a household imbued with a strong religious faith. In terms of faith development, he had parents and grandparents who were committed believers. The family was not Church of England but was either Baptist, Independent, or Congregationalist in background. The young Doudney was influenced in his faith by sermons he heard, while pocket money was spent on the purchase of books, magazines and missionary biographies, though the Bible was the most treasured reading material.² Illustrative of the religious fervor of the Doudney household is that a servant who came to live there with his cousin was in the habit of praying with both boys who also received instruction from other family members.³

Doudney was raised in a household where his father John Doudney (d.1834), though a severe man, nevertheless tended to the faith of his children, and oversaw a home where hymn singing was regular.⁴ It was in situations of his father's anger that Doudney early realized the power of prayer and forgiveness.⁵ Another side to his father was charitableness for, though he was a tallow chandler, he nevertheless took into his household a nephew whose own parents had died.⁶ Thus a strong religious atmosphere pervaded the Doudney household in terms of family influence, charitableness, and reading materials. These were facets that were to be influential in Doudney's life.

When he was a teenager Doudney had a life-changing conversion experience. After leaving home to pursue the printing trade in Southampton —something his father discouraged him from doing, though his mother, Sarah, was supportive —while he took his mother's advice to engage in daily reading of the Bible, if only a few verses, his mind was unsettled.⁷ In this troubled state, his elder brother recommended that he read Phillip Doddridge's, *Rise and Progress of Religion in the Soul* (London, 1744), which was a classic of eighteenth century evangelical spirituality and which served to convict him of his own sinful state.⁸ A spiritual crisis ensued, accentuated by the appearance of a ghost-like figure in a play he attended at this time which caused him to feel that his death and subsequent transporting to hell was imminent.⁹ After agonizing and praying earnestly, words of forgiveness were spoken to his heart and on June 21, 1826 he gained a compelling sense that his burden had lifted and he was free, something that was further confirmed by a sermon he heard in Southampton.¹⁰

However, in typical evangelical fashion, once his internal spiritual conflicts had been resolved, his external situation altered for the worst, in that after he moved to a different printing establishment he found himself surrounded by "sceptics, infidels, swearers, [and] Sabbath-breakers," a situation which made him more dependent on divine providence.¹¹ This negative context was somewhat balanced by the fact that at this period in his life he was involved in teaching Sunday school to children.¹²

Doudney aged about 15 in London with a cousin pointing to a building he would later rent to conduct the printing business.
Source: *Try and Try Again*, 91.

Following the conversion experience, which was a significant event in his spiritual development, Doudney was ever open to

God's provision. For instance, at one time after he had moved from Southampton to London his spirits were so low that he sought peace and comfort, which came in the form of a verse ("For I am with thee, and no man shall set on thee, to hurt thee") which he found on a torn off page from a Bible lying on the ground as he returned to work.[13] Such a realization of the encouragement to be had in the timely provision of God's Word served as a reassurance of God's presence and care for him. This continued through all the anguish occasioned by the loss of three children and his wife in 1840 and 1841.

Doudney's upbringing, faith, and life experience were tangibly interwoven. Every circumstance that presented itself or decision that had to be made was interpreted or considered from the perspective of the Christian faith. Such a process was not easy or self-apparent, as it often involved deep struggle and questioning. But it was permeated by openness to God's leading in all things, which was a characteristic attribute of evangelical faith.

To Doudney and most evangelicals such dependence and openness contrasted sharply with the apparent secretiveness of the Roman Catholic Church and the control it seemingly exercised over its adherents, engendering in him a life-long antipathy to that institution. Thus on a trip to Belgium, probably in the early 1840s after the death of his three children and his wife, he entered a Catholic church in Ostend where, he records, the "indignation I felt against the priests for thus misleading these poor deluded creatures."[14] This stance was to influence his ministry in Ireland.

In 1840 when he acquired the journal, *The Gospel Magazine*, Doudney revealed that he had felt the call to ministry in the Church for about twenty years, but was unable to pursue it because of his business concerns and his growing family. Its realization came about in providential circumstances in April 1845. The fact that his childhood friend, John Doudney Lane, had become a clergyman was a formative influence on Doudney wanting to do the same, though he admitted that it was something he had tried to suppress.[15] More importantly he wished to influence others to come to faith, for, as the

Memoir records: "He had felt for himself the savour and the power of Divine love, and he longed to make it more and more known to others."[16] As well, he was writing editorials for the *Gospel Magazine* that in themselves constituted sermons, which he felt he had the public speaking ability to deliver orally.[17]

Following a period of waiting, a visit from a minister friend, Rev. Arthur Hewlett, prompted in his head the words from the Bible: "The harvest truly is plenteous, and the labourers are few; pray ye, therefore, the Lord of the harvest, that He would send forth labourers into His harvest" (Luke 10: 2). Following a time of reflection, he fixed on following the intent of this verse in whatever situation God would make apparent to him. Intimating this to Rev. Hewlett, the latter shortly afterwards wrote Doudney to know if he (Hewlett) contacted the bishop of Cashel, Robert Daly, would he (Doudney) be willing to go to Ireland. The verse, "And he [Abraham] went out, not knowing whither he went" (Hebrews 11: 8), came to mind and served to overcome his initial dismissal of this proposal, and this was confirmed by other circumstantial (but not coincidental) occurrences, including a providential meeting with the Robert Jocelyn, earl of Roden, who was a subscriber to the *Gospel Magazine* and one of the leading Irish evangelicals at the time.[18]

Doudney contemplates the prospect of going to Ireland.
Source: *Try and Try Again*, 119.

Through a mutual friend, a meeting between Doudney and the bishop of Cashel was arranged. In the course of the meeting, Doudney declared that though he had been engaged in the printing business, for twenty years he had always felt a longing for the ministry, but that he had no formal education that would prepare him for it. The bishop declared that given his age—thirty-four— a university education was not a necessary pre-requisite for Doudney, at any rate Daly made it clear that he was more concerned to discern evidence of godliness, knowledge of the Bible, knowledge of human nature, a missionary spirit necessary for ministry in Ireland, and evidence of following the leading of the Holy Spirit, than mere academic qualification.[19] In not requiring a formal academic training as a prerequisite for entry to the ordained ministry, Daly was merely exercising a traditional episcopal prerogative that had existed for generations.[20] Instead Doudney would engage in private study in preparation for an exam conducted by the bishop. Nothing more transpired at this point and it was to be eighteen months before Doudney's initial aversion to going to Ireland dissipated.

Meantime, on another front, his business affairs were operating to validate his decision to enter the ministry and go to Ireland. Economic circumstances in 1846 caused one of Doudney's largest customers, who had speculated on railway expansion, to default in his payments thereby forcing Doudney to sell his printing business at a considerable loss.[21] The purchaser, W.H. Collingridge, took over the building that Doudney had occupied for his printing business, an arrangement which involved Collingridge producing the *Gospel Magazine* at cost for a number of years without loss to Doudney.[22]

Forced out of business, providentially, within days of these developments Doudney received a letter from Bishop Daly, with whom he had no communication since the initial interviews of eighteen months previously, proposing that he go to Templemore, Co. Tipperary, to assist the rector there with the supervision of the local school and give classes in the vicinity. This arrangement was designed to test Doudney's suitability for ministry and if he proved successful then after three or four months the bishop would ordain him for the Church of Ireland.[23] Viewing all this as providential, given the circumstances of the recent disposal of his printing business, Doudney assented to the bishop's proposal.

However, Doudney's decision to give up the printing trade, remove to Ireland, and seek ordination in the Church of Ireland was questioned by some of his close friends and supporters at least two of whom were former members of that denomination. This occasioned Doudney to respond with a public defence of his decision which was published in February 1847 in the columns of the *Gospel Magazine*. Therein he unequivocally stated that his decision was based on God's leading, that the theological principles upon which the *Gospel Magazine* had been based for eighty years were not compromised by his action, and that its pages were to be open to a wide readership no matter what their denomination.[24] Clearly Doudney felt that the concerns raised by some of the journal's readers were petty given the misery surrounding him in Templemore (where by this time he had removed), for he apologized for writing a quick response, adding that "we are surrounded with too much sorrow— the knock too frequently comes at the door, with its consequent interruption, from some poor three-quarter starved applicant — to permit of a lengthened and well-digested reply."[25]

All of this is to indicate that we cannot hope to understand Doudney unless we appreciate his background and his religious formation which were based on a strong commitment to what the Bible revealed about God. It is apparent that so many of his actions and his interpretations of events were grounded in the Bible.

Printing Trade

Given his general exposure to books from an early age, it is no surprise that Doudney aspired to enter the printing trade. While still a young boy, he and his cousin John Doudney Lane received a guided tour of a printing office and were introduced to printing processes.[26] Doudney himself along with his mother discerned in this a call from God.[27] Against the wishes of his father who wanted him to pursue his own trade of tallow chandler or soap manufacturer, Doudney left home at age eleven, was apprenticed to a printer in Southampton, and made rapid progress in his chosen trade.[28] In 1832 he moved from Southampton to the firm of Jowett & Mills in Fleet Street, London, and within three weeks of starting he had risen to one of the more important positions which he maintained for three or four years gaining much practical knowledge of the printing business.[29]

In tandem with his emerging interest in printing as a career, Doudney had already in 1831 or 1832, made his first foray into authorship with a work entitled, *The Great Importance Of and the Benefits Arising from Seeking the Lord Whilst Young*, which sold 4,000 or 5,000 copies within the first few weeks, though subsequent attempts at authorship were not as successful, at least in the immediate term.[30] Nevertheless his early interest in writing was later to flourish into a lifelong activity.

Doudney's advance in the printing trade was sufficient for him to start his own printing business in London in 1835, a venture that was to last eleven years. He was generous and accommodating in taking on apprentices, one of whom was William Hill Collingridge, who later inherited Doudney's business and came to establish himself as the City Press, which published many of Doudney's later works including those produced in Bunmahon.[31]

Faith, Famine, and Faction • 9

The City Press offices of D. A. Doudney, Long Lane, Aldersgate, London where he conducted business for eight years (1838-1846).
Source: *Credentials*, 67.

Doudney's printing business was a success for in 1840 he was in a position to purchase the copyright and become editor of a periodical called *The Gospel Magazine*, an evangelical magazine first started in 1766.³² He was to be its editor for fifty-three years until 1892.

As alluded to already, economic decline and the default of a major customer in 1846 caused Doudney to discontinue in the printing business and to sell off his machinery and equipment at a loss. Despite the trauma of this failure in business, his newly attained freedom allowed him in time to embark on a new career as an incipient clergyman in Ireland. His familiarity with the printing trade was to serve him in good stead in Ireland.

Family Bereavements

The third formative influence on Doudney prior to his coming to Ireland was his exposure to tragedy and death early in life. Already as a boy he had a number of near-death experiences. When he was very young he had a narrow escape from serious injury even death with a bull, and on another occasion he was knocked down by a horse with a careless rider.[33] There were further near-death experiences including when he was seventeen when, mistaking Doudney for someone else, a man tried to stab him with a knife, an incident which caused him intense headaches. This was followed by a fall from a horse, while his practice of rising at 4 or 4.30 a.m. caused him to be drowsy during the day.[34]

Coupled with these ailments Doudney's family experience was one riven with tragedy, whether previous to, during, or subsequent to his time in Bunmahon. In 1831, when he was in his twentieth year his sister Mary, the youngest in his family, died of cholera.[35] By April 1832 he had been at the death beds of two elderly friends, including one aunt.[36] Shortly afterwards, in February 1834 when Doudney was twenty-three years old, his father died.[37] More happily, by May, 1834, after a long engagement, Doudney married Jane Draper, daughter of Rev. Bourne Hall Draper, a minister in Southampton, and the marriage proved to be a contented one.[38] A year after his marriage, as we have seen, he went into business on his own as a bookseller and printer.[39]

In October, 1835, their first daughter, Mary Jane, was born, and by February, 1840 they had four children.[40] However, in early March, 1840 the first of a series of family tragedies came when the fourteen-month old son, Bourne Hall, died of convulsions.[41] A year later, the three remaining children were all seriously ill with whooping cough leaving two out of three of them near death, while his wife who had been weak for months, was suffering from consumption.[42] Then in early March, 1841, the youngest child, Sarah, aged five and one half years, passed away; and soon after her sister, Mary Jane, and in

May, 1841, their mother had also died, leaving only a son, David, the eldest, then aged between four and five years old.[43] Thus the years 1840-42 were particularly tragic for Doudney for during that short span he lost three children and his wife.

By February 1842, however, Doudney had married again at St. Mary's, Portsea, Eliza (d. c.1873), daughter of William Durkin.[44] Their first child, George William, was born in April 1843, but he only lived six months, dying of whooping cough.[45] Subsequently, they had eight children, two of whom died relatively young, while another (Arthur) was supposedly drowned in Samoa in the South Seas in 1892 the year prior to Doudney's own death.[46] Thus only six of the children survived to adulthood.[47] The impact of these deaths on Doudney must have been significant and must have carried over into the experience he had in Ireland, whence he went initially without his wife and children.

Doudney on board ship crossing to Ireland, November 1846.
Source: *Try and Try Again*, 125.

Thus by 1846 family circumstances, business reversal, and divine call had coalesced to bring Doudney to Ireland in a providential way. Having accepted the invitation of the bishop of Cashel, Doudney arrived in Ireland in November, 1846 to serve as an assistant in Templemore, Co. Tipperary, and the bishop agreed that if he was satisfied with his work there then he would ordain him to the ministry within a year.

Preparation in Templemore

Doudney set out for Ireland with only £14.[48] Although he approached his new assignment with a certain apprehension, expressive of which was his mentioning "Newspaper accounts had caused me to shrink from the Irish character, as of the most despicable and savage caste," he took solace in the firm belief that he would have God's protection.[49] At any rate his apprehensions were soon dispelled as he was struck upon arrival by the beauty of the landscape and the "attention, and the greatest possible civility" of the people.[50] While he dreaded the prospect of what to expect in Tipperary because of its reputation for agrarian unrest, yet travelling there by train from Dublin through observation of the countryside and the condition of the people, he readily gained sympathy for their plight. Articulating potential solutions to the latter, he surmised that instead of the English parliament voting large sums for the abolition of slavery or English people generally contributing funds for missionary endeavours among the heathen, that they might have demonstrated a concern for Ireland especially in the area of housing.[51] Such expressed concern on Doudney's part was no doubt influenced by his modest origins and his experience of self-improvement and opportunity.

His destination in Ireland was Templemore, situated in the northern part of Co. Tipperary. At the time it was a town of about 3,000 people (three-quarters of whom were Roman Catholic), including an army detachment of 600 or 700 men.[52] It had been developed as an estate village in the eighteenth century by the local family of Carden, who centred their efforts on the military barracks as an inducement to attract Protestant settlement. It had an impressive church which scheduled an early morning service on Sunday to accommodate the town's significant detachment of soldiers.[53]

Doudney arrived in Templemore when the famine was occurring. He had been exposed to suffering and poverty on the streets of London during his fourteen years residence there, but it was something he tried to avoid because of his "sensitive temperament."[54] But in Ireland he was brought face-to-face with the most acute suffering something that at one level he could empathize with given his own family losses.

Within a day of his arrival in the town, Doudney became involved with a relief committee whose remit was meeting the needs of the poor in the area. The public works were operational in the town whereby employment was available for the able-bodied at the rate of 10d. or 1s. per day. The money earned was intended to go towards the purchase of meal which was sold at a reduced price and on credit.[55] Witnessing the condition of the people who came for food, Doudney was struck by how inconsequential his own trials and complaints about coming to Ireland were in comparison, prompting him to ask: "What was my trial compared with the scene now before me? Nothing, comparatively nothing."[56]

He was impressed by the fact that those whose names were not accepted for the public works passively submitted when they were refused food in the line up, in contrast to what would have been the likely reaction, in Doudney's view, of a similar outcome in London. So struck was he by this submissiveness that he "wept and could not help it, so touching was the spectacle, so spirit-broken were the people, so evident their resignation to their desperate fate."[57] Although he tried to keep suppressed the information that he was distributing meal tickets, eventually the whole town found out, and on one occasion twenty or thirty starving women came to his door during the course of one day.[58] These experiences considerably impacted Doudney's sensitivity to human suffering and need.

Famine scene in Templemore.
Source: *Try and Try Again*, 138.

Doudney's ministry in Templemore, which was under the aegis of Rev. William Sandford (b.1814), the military chaplain and the newly appointed curate of Templemore (1846–1853), also included teaching and instruction of the inhabitants in outlying parts.[59] How this was to be carried out was not immediately obvious compared, for instance, with being part of the committee attending the needs of the poor described above. However, shortly after becoming familiar with the locality, he found himself alone, distant from his family, and troubled, but suddenly the verses of Luke 18: 28–30 were brought to his mind.[60] Addressing his situation appropriately, these verses were: "Peter said to him [Jesus], 'We have left all we had to follow you.' Jesus said to them, 'I tell you the truth, no one who has left home or wife or brothers or parents or children for the sake of the kingdom of God will fail to receive many times as much in this age and, in the age to come, eternal life." Inspired and encouraged by this assurance he set forth in the expectation that he could do some good.

Journeying into the mountains four miles outside the town, he visited a cluster of small farms where the people held land on lease, grew corn and potatoes, as well as raised pigs and poultry to pay the rent, all of which allowed them to survive in normal times. Entering a house, he found gathered there up to twenty-five half-starved persons out of 40–50 of the total Protestant population of the district.[61] Doudney led them in a reading from the Bible, prayer, and hymn-singing, for all of which they expressed their hearty gratitude.[62]

On another occasion, he visited a school housed in a barn next door to a cottage about five miles from the town. He was presented with a group of children, "dirty, ragged, and neglected," ranging in age from sixteen or seventeen, down to three or four years old, who had been recently taken in hand by the rector, Rev. Edwin Ormsby, and were making progress.[63] Other visits brought him to different cottages occupied by Protestants where he gave weekly classes.[64] On one occasion, his visit to the cottage of one poor family named Davis occurred just after six of his sheep had been stolen. Doudney used the event to reinforce the lesson that while the loss of the sheep was severe for the family, ultimately they were to have greater security in the hands of the Good Shepherd, and prayed that either the sheep would be found or the loss made up in another way, the former of which occurred within a day or two.[65] News of the return of the sheep spread and opened new doors to Doudney's ministry in the area.

At that stage he had only been in the country for a month or five weeks. Given the contemporary virulence of sheep-stealing, the above instance of the recovery of sheep was in the view of many, a miracle, and in communicating the fact to a friend in England, Doudney by return was the recipient of £15 for the poor. Using that amount he and the curate of the parish went from cabin to cabin distributing Indian meal tickets. In the course of this work he recorded the situation of each family, its name, the number of its members, their means, and any particular circumstance present.[66] While this record was written primarily and initially for the benefit of the person who had donated the money, when read by a second person it was suggested that it be printed in the *Gospel Magazine*, as result of which readers of that publication donated almost £700 which Doudney used for more extensive famine relief.[67] It was stipulated that this money was not to be used to supplement any local funds but was to be at Doudney's sole disposal in order to dispense meal and soup. This requirement was the source of some conflict with the local relief committee whose members wanted Doudney to add his fund to the general relief fund, which he declined to do.[68] The money could not have come at a better time for the famine continued to ravage the population. Its attendant sufferings were to have a profound impact on Doudney, indeed the famine experience was to change his life.

Attending to the needs of the poor caused him to neglect his study of Greek in preparation for his ordination.[69] Indeed by April 1847 Doudney conceded in a letter to a correspondent in England that his ordination would have to be postponed because of "the unceasing, day-and-night solicitations of these poor, starving people. Such have been their claims upon my time that my ordination is considerably delayed, my time for reading and study being so trespassed upon."[70] He used the £700 raised by readers of the *Gospel Magazine* for the relief of famine-stricken victims in Templemore to distribute meal tickets (250 tickets for 7 lbs. of meal per family) for local relief, and by June 1847 he had distributed twenty tons of meal.[71] This undoubtedly saved many from starvation. Although he tried to do this anonymously, soon the word got out resulting in crowds of starving people turning up at his door, making him want to visit them in their cabins instead, in one day, December 19, 1846, visiting about forty families in this way.[72] On one such visit Doudney met the elderly Jack Moriarty, the town crier of Templemore, who declared that it was his eternal soul rather than food that concerned him, in response to which Doudney was able to share "the simple way of salvation" to his host's "warmest thanks."[73] These were typical experiences for Doudney in Templemore in 1846–7.

Faith, Famine, and Faction • 17

In January, 1847, Doudney visited the public works site in the town where the men had been reduced to only three or four days work, and persuaded the inspector to allow the men to finish early in order to have some soup and bread which he provided and distributed to 120 of them who in turn brought it home to their families.[74] In the midst of such great deprivation, Doudney was struck by the gratitude and deference of the people when he distributed meal tickets to them.[75] Nevertheless, he also experienced personal loss, for in April, 1847 there occurred the death in his thirty-fifth year of his childhood friend, John Doudney Lane, thus adding to a long tradition of family loss, a circumstance reinforced by the famine-stricken scenes around him in Templemore.[76] Although he suffered in health while in Templemore and was exposed to the fever numerous times, yet Doudney survived.

Doudney ministering to a family in famine-stricken Templemore.
Source: *Try and Try Again*, 148.

From the many examples of visitation, the following extract is chosen as illustrative of the kind of suffering he came in contact with in Templemore in 1846–7. For April 18, 1847, he recorded in his diary:

> "Went this morning, after the first service, to a distressed house in Mary Street. In an upper back room (a mere hovel) lived a poor man, his wife, and two children, whom I had been in the habit of visiting and relieving. The wife had recently died—then a child—and I found the poor man himself was dead. He died of fever and in a state of raving. As only three of the inmates of that hapless house were free from fever, which I found was raging in it, no one, it appears would enter it to do the last sad offices upon that poor man, although he had been dead upwards of four-and-twenty hours. Two hale women had just begun to wash the body as I entered; and, as he there lay a most pitiable object, for the safety of their own lives, as well as the lives of others, I besought them to desist, urging them quickly to place him in his coffin, and have him buried. [One of these poor women, strong as she then was, took the fever, and has since died.]
>
> Below-stairs I found a mother and child, in one bed, in fever. [The child is since dead.] In another bed, in the same room, were two children, both sick, and, I believe, in fever. In a back room were a man, his wife, and sick children, the merest skeletons; just the bare frames of skin and bones, in which it would seem impossible that life could exist. They had lately come from a distant part of the parish. This has certainly been the worst scene I have witnessed. It has thoroughly prostrated me this day. [Four of these children have since died.][77]

These were the kinds of direct experiences of Ireland Doudney first had when he came there in November 1846. Although raised in the evangelical tradition of Christianity, he had experienced professional loss through the demise of his printing business and family bereavement through the loss of children and his first wife. Such circumstances would have stretched a person's resilience to the limit. But such was Doudney's faith in the providence of God that he followed obediently the call to go to Ireland. There in Templemore he had to confront famine and fever conditions, circumstances he responded to through an appeal for funds which he used for relief purposes.

Formative Experience

Doudney's period in Templemore, which lasted about six months from mid-November 1846 to May 1847, was a formative one in terms of his future for it provided him with his first experience of working closely with Irish people in the context of deprivation, sickness, and starvation. His tasks were diverse, from administering relief directly, preaching at the military barracks, visiting hospitals, to speaking twice or three times weekly to Protestant families in the outlying mountain areas.

In carrying out such tasks he came to appreciate the friendliness of the people, overcoming his own pre-conceived notions of an inherent hostility on their part. He conceded that "there is a feeling, a sensibility, a kindness, about the real Irish character which one cannot but admire."[78] From a position of fear about Ireland he progressed to having a real concern about the condition of its people. It was, therefore, a time of personal growth and a formative period, more especially because the famine was prevailing and attaining its full virulence.

Secondly, Templemore also provided him with an insight into Catholic attitudes and opposition to his efforts, which pre-figured his experience in Bunmahon. On occasion Catholics were present within audible distance (often in the adjoining room) when he gave classes in Protestant households in the outlying mountainous areas.[79] On one occasion thirty to forty Catholics were present when he lectured.[80] He also gave lectures in the barracks once a week, and also visited and taught in the two military hospitals in the town, until Catholic clerical opposition halted the latter practice.[81]

Doudney also gained an insight into the relationship between the Catholic priest and his flock that was later to be of value to him when he moved to his new position in Waterford. In Templemore specific opposition arose around the funeral of a middle-aged Protestant soldier who died of apoplexy. A funeral march through the town with drums and martial music was followed by a solemn burial service with a eulogy by the Protestant clergyman to a mostly Catholic assembly. Subsequently the presence of Catholics at the funeral occasioned a stern denunciation from the altar by the priest about members of his flock attending such events, but those concerned persisted leaving the priest to cease his denunciations.[82] In another case, a man who was near death and was anointed by the local priest was later visited by Sandford and Doudney but when the priest heard of this he came to the house, castigated the occupants, and declared that the anointed man was damned in hell.[83] Such pointed behavior anticipated what Doudney would experience in Bunmahon.

Converts and Proselytism

By February 1847 Doudney's visitations became the focus of the priest's sermons, the substance of which was that Doundey had a meal or soup ticket in one hand and a shilling in another, the implication being that he was trying to make converts to Protestantism.[84] There is no evidence of this. Doudney, who was not yet ordained, was confident that while nominal converts could be had in large numbers, there were no bribes offered and he defied the priest to prove the veracity of his assertions.[85] As we shall see, similar circumstances and responses were to obtain in Bunmahon. Doudney was not concerned to make nominal Protestants, but simply to proclaim the gospel truth as he understood it. This was to be his response when similar charges arose in Bunmahon.

Basing his inspiration on the verse that "man does not live on bread alone," as he went about the cabins of Templemore distributing meal tickets and offering comfort, he had the opportunity to speak to people on matters of eternal import. Visiting a dwelling in Church Street he talked with those present and recorded the reaction: "One wept much as I spoke of sin—its consequences— and the delusion of looking to Peter, to Mary, or the saints, or any being short of the Lord Jesus Christ, for pardon and help....The sick woman responded heartily, and again and again exclaimed, 'It is all truth —it is all truth —what you say, sir.'"[86] In another cabin he found that the assembled group all "listened with peculiar interest, and one of them wept much." As he moved on, a group ran after him and he was able to offer a "short statement of truth." In Gaol Street he visited an old woman and her two daughters (who were thankful to receive the meal ticket), a shoemaker and his family (his wife "wept much"), along with others all of whom Doudney noted, "acknowledged the truth of one's observations."[87]

While Doudney was not interested in overt proselytism, as a prospective clergyman he was naturally concerned about people's eternal souls, especially those near death. Illustrative of this was one occasion before Christmas Day, 1846 when he visited a man dying of dropsy. Doudney recorded the experience in his diary: "Talked to him about his poor soul and found a precious freedom in saying a few brief sentences to him, and to those by whom I was surrounded, about the love, the blood, the all-sufficiency of Christ."[88]

Such experiences are illustrative of the fact that Doudney believed that the famine had opened up the possibility of communicating such truths to Catholics and nominal Protestants in this way. Given the famine conditions, there was an openness and interest which might not otherwise have been the case. Most contemporaries believed the famine to be a disaster, but contrary to this Doudney claimed it to be "among the greatest benefits that could have befallen Ireland."[89] By this he did not mean that it was a good thing that so many suffered, died, or emigrated, as his actions in assisting those in need bore witness. Rather he asserted that the famine had two beneficial results: "It drew off the cottar from his hereditary and indolent dependence upon the potato crop, and it placed Protestantism before him in a light in which he was never wont to regard it."[90] It is in this context that his comment about the famine must be understood.

It was clear that the famine provided the means of access to Catholic households to dispense relief, an access which in normal circumstances would not have existed. In this regard, Doudney commented on one such situation: "These poor Roman Catholics listened to me this day with peculiar interest; and, as they pointed to the relics of the meal, and to the poor children that stood around, saved from starvation, exhibited the most pleasing gratitude."[91]

There was clearly a providential element in the attitude of the local people. The activities of Revs. Sandford and Ormbsy as well as Doudney in providing relief to those in need, operated to change attitudes to Protestants. This is illustrated in a report Doudney made of one experience of handing out meal tickets to grateful people. "The neighbours surrounded Mr. Sandford and told him of the family's pitiable state. Here a meal ticket proved that the once despised Protestants —the 'heretics' as they were wont to be called— had some feeling for Roman Catholics. Numberless times have I been told by them: 'But for Mr. Ormsby and Mr. Sandford, we should not have been alive now; and surely it was the great God sent you here at this time for, if you had not come, many in this town of Templemore would have starved.'"[92] In Doudney's view all this benevolence was in addition shaking people's confidence in the priests as their traditional source of provision at such times of need.[93]

Given these involvements and the effect of his charitable work, Doudney left Templemore with some reluctance, and his departure was regretted by those to whom he had ministered.[94] It was clear also that the experience of such privation and death had an effect on him, and he had to caution himself against an over-familiarity with scenes of death, commenting on one such in January 1847: "God forbid that any familiarity with a sight of these death scenes should in any measure make me indifferent to them."[95] It was the tradition in his family that he had given greatly of himself in the cause of relieving the suffering poor of Templemore, for his daughter Emily recorded of this time: "My father worked so hard at relieving the cases, working amongst them himself — and he was a most tender-hearted man— that his hair went white that winter with the scenes he witnessed."[96] The cumulative experiences Doudney had in Templemore were to be formative in terms of his tenure in Bunmahon.

Curate of Monksland

Evidently Bishop Daly was sufficiently satisfied with Doudney's achievement in Templemore to fulfill his undertaking to ordain him which he did in Christ Church Cathedral, Waterford in June1847, following an ordination examination conducted nearby at the Bishop's Palace.[97] His ordination was not regarded with universal unanimity by his former Baptist and Independent friends and congregations in London who suspected that his entry to ministry in the Church of Ireland would occasion some judgement upon himself.[98] However, his ability to move from his former church affiliation to the Church of Ireland displayed his focus on ministry, service, and God's leading rather than a narrow denonomiantional allegiance for its own sake.

Nevertheless, following a short visit to see family in England, Doudney preached twice in Bunmahon in September 1847 and soon after removed from Templemore to take up his first curacy in Annestown but then more permanently in the parish of Monksland, Co. Waterford. They resided initially in the village of Annestown, some four miles east of the parish, because no accommodation was available locally, though by early 1850 they had removed to Bunmahon.[99]

Monksland was part of a parochial union that also included the parish of Inislounaght or Abbey west of Clonmel, Co. Tipperary, with the former being the smaller of the two. This circumstance of a parish with two parts distant about twenty-five miles from each other, derived from medieval ecclesiastical arrangements revolving around the existence of property owned by a Cistercian monastery in both areas, property that was inherited by the Church of Ireland at the dissolution of the monasteries in the 1540s.[100]

At the time of Doudney's elevation to Monksland, the rector of the parish was Rev. Richard Maunsell who resided at Inislounaght, and who delegated his responsibilities for Monksland to Doudney as curate.[101] Doudney's experience in Monksland, which spanned eleven years from 1847 to 1858, was to be very different from what he had in Templemore.

CHAPTER 2

THE SIBERIA EVEN OF WATERFORD

ALTHOUGH THE AREA WHERE DOUDNEY was to spend eleven years of his life was known as a bathing place —Dorothea Herbert, author of *Retrospections*, records spending summer vacations there with family members in the late eighteenth-century[1]— the aspect that struck visitors most about Bunmahon was its remoteness. Many accounts testify to how relatively inaccessible the area was until after the mid-nineteenth century. In August 1854, a visitor from England, Peter Sibree, who wanted to visit the schools established by Doudney, was stranded in Waterford for a period because he found it difficult to obtain transportation to Bunmahon owing to the regular car being full, making him go via Kilmacthomas from where he had to hire a conveyance to bring him to Bunmahon.[2] The emergence of a copper extraction and processing industry in the 1820s, however, was to open up the area to more outside influences and hence relatively greater accessibility.

The largest concentration of people in Monksland parish was in Knockmahon. Bunmahon lay on the west of the River Mahon, while Knockmahon was to the east of the river. The original mine operations were in the townland of Knockmahon, located in the civil parish of Kill (or Kilbarrymeaden), while the majority of the mine workers lived across the River Mahon in that part of Templevrick townland called Bunmahon, in the civil parish of Ballylaneen.

The College of Physicians of Ireland owned 3,000 acres in County Waterford and was a major landowner in the area west of the River Mahon. It had a rental in 1841 of over £600 from its 75 tenancies or holdings covering 324 acres in Bunmahon alone, in 1847, £1500 annually in income from its lands in and around Bunmahon, and £1684 in 1850.[3] Its property included Bunmahon, Ballinarrid and Templevrick, Bunmahon itself being leased to Richard Power-O'Shee of Gardenmorris north of Knockmahon near Kill, for £427.5s. under a 31-year lease.[4] Power-O'Shee reserved Bunmahon for development as a bathing place, built cottages, and set them out to different individuals, while he sublet Templevrick and Ballinarid into farms, thus making his family into substantial middlemen in the area.[5] The absence of an immediate landlord presence meant that the middleman system became predominant in the area, a system characterized by subdivision and a profusion of smallholdings.[6] However, the property was neglected and by 1816 Power-O'Shee's rental arrears to the college stood at £4,000, a level still high at £3,779 in 1822, a consequence of the post-1815 economic slump.[7] Despite Power-O'Shee's plans for Bunmahon, little development occurred until the 1820s with the discovery of a rich lode of copper ore in nearby Knockmahon.

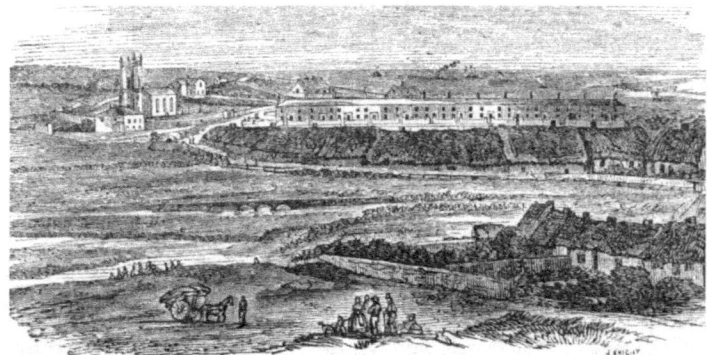

Knockmahon c.1850 showing from left the national school, Monksland parish church, scriptural school, and terrace of houses.
Source: *Memoir*, 121.

Mines and Mining

The mining rights in the area were originally held by the Butlers, earls of Ormond of Kilkenny Castle, an ancestor of which family in the early eighteenth century sold the property to Sir Patrick Dun who in 1748 bequeathed them to the College of Physicians; and other mining rights were held by Lady Osborne and other lesser interests.[8] Serious exploitation of the mining resources of the area only began in the 1820s, with one company estimating that its investment of £15,000 could employ 100–150 men in the first year.[9] In 1825 Richard Power-O'Shee, in consideration of £1,000, sublet the mining rights to the Mining Company of Ireland in return for one-twelfth part of all ore raised.[10]

In 1830 the Mining Company of Ireland—the founding of which had been inspired in part by Quaker philanthropy— announced its discovery of significant copper deposits in the locality.[11] By 1835 the development work for the mine was complete and significant employment prospects were forthcoming. In response to a sharp increase in copper prices, further enhancements occurred in following years including the arrival of a large pumping engine (1837) and the laying out of a railway for transporting ore (1838), all these developments contributing to the emergence of a major industrial operation.[12]

The leasing by the Osbornes of mining rights on its lands in Monksland parish was part of a broad improvement initiative by the family which, as will become apparent below, was to include housing, schools, a church, and a temperance hall.[13] It was the Osborne family that possessed the broader social vision as regards development of the area, whereas the College of Physicians as an institutional property owner was satisfied with the rental income obtained primarily through head tenants like Power-O'Shee and others.

So far as the extent of the mines is concerned they stretched three miles inland and four miles along the coast and were located primarily in the four townlands of Knockmahon, Kilduane, Templevrick, and Ballinasissla. For their extent and richness, along with their favourable location near the sea, which allowed for easy access and transportation of the ore to Swansea in south Wales for smelting, and advanced machinery used in extraction and processing, the mines were particularly profitable.[14] Production increased from 3,588 tons (value £33,166) in 1836, to 7,875 tons (value £63,000) in 1840, to 9,100 tons (value £63,000) in 1843.[15] By 1840 the mines were making an average annual profit of £15,000, and by 1849 production had reached 4,000–5,000 tons valued at £9 per ton equivalent to £36,000–£45,000.[16] In the period 1834–1847 one company made a total profit of about £154,300 from the Knockmahon mines.[17] Clearly production was on a significant and extensive scale.

Production in the mines reached a peak in the early 1840s before Doudney's arrival in the area. In the 1840s overall production fell due to flooding coupled with the depletion of the vein extending inland from Knockmahon, developments which are dateable to 1843–4 thus pre-dating the arrival of famine conditions in the area. The result of this downturn was that neither high wages nor employment levels that obtained previously could be sustained. In consequence, the skilled English miners and supervisors who had been brought over from Cornwall left the area, temporarily as it turned out.[18]

However, the post-famine years saw new investment in improvements to the mining operations (£1,600 in 1848, for instance), though no dividend was issued to share-holders.[19] Though there was a brief recovery in the early 1850s characterized by the discovery of new sources of ore, a rise in the price of copper, increased output, and an upsurge in profits (a 10% dividend was payable to shareholders at the outset of 1856), all this reached a peak in the early 1860s; thereafter the long-term trend being one of decline such that by 1880 significant employment in the mines had ceased and emigration from the area was well established.[20] Thus the overall pattern is clear: an initial period of prosperity that prevailed until the early 1840s, followed by decline, a temporary renewal of prosperity in the early 1850s, and final decline from 1860 onwards. The renewed temporary prosperity of the mines in the 1850s coincided with Doudney's presence in the area.

Mining Operations

Work in the mines was based on a contract system imported from Cornwall, whereby the miners did not earn set wages rather they formed teams, often comprising family members and relatives, which would bid against each other for the right to remove a section of the copper ore. When the contract period expired and all costs associated with tools, candles, explosives and other necessities were deducted, only then would the teams be paid.

Work in the mines involved members of the teams descending by ladder down the different shafts to the galleries. From there the ore was brought up by steam conveyance and then transported in narrow gauge containers to the dressing floors in Knockmahon where it was sorted mostly by women and children who separated the high grade ore from the rock residue.[21] As to working conditions, the very nature of work in the mines itself was conducive to declining health once miners reached middle age.[22] Surprisingly, serious accidents as such were few at Knockmahon those occurring being associated with problems of ventilation and depth.[23]

Apart from the specialist skills of the Cornish miners who were responsible for planning operations, there was employment for skilled craftsmen notably carpenters and blacksmiths, along with an army of casual labourers. The labour force included migrant workers the majority from the hinterland but also some from the Allihies mines in west Cork, who intermarried locally but who also, on occasion, were the objects of hostility because they undercut local wage rates.[24] The nature of the mining operations, therefore, brought together a diverse group made up primarily of locals, supplemented by elements from Cornwall and west Cork. This diverse group was attracted to the area by the availability of skilled and non-skilled employment and the relatively high wages to be obtained for mining work.

Economic Impact

The economic impact of the mines on the locality was significant. An index of the economic impact is the growth in employment numbers, for almost the entire population of the area came to be supported directly or indirectly by the mines. Before the mining expansion, Bunmahon in 1821 consisted of 357 people in 76 houses, but by 1836 the workforce in the mines was 1,000, and by 1840 it was computed that there were around 1,100 people employed in the mines, only a minority of whom were actual miners the vast bulk being labourers.[25] In 1844, the mines gave constant employment to 1,200 people (including 140 women who worked cleaning the ore) whose total monthly wages amounted to £2,500.[26]

As well as significant wage levels another indicator of the prosperity of the mines is house building. There was an expansion in the housing stock to accommodate those who came to the area for employment in the mines. For example, by 1841, 250 new houses had been erected on the College of Physicians property in Bunmahon, rents from which along with adjoining lands amounted to £1,000 annually.[27] Another indicator of the prosperity of the mines in the pre-famine period was that property values increased sharply. In 1841, the agent of the College of Physicians, Thomas McDonagh, reported that: "The demand for land there [Bunmahon] is very great indeed, consequently exorbitant prices are given, in some cases from £6 to £10 per acre for town parks and gardens."[28] Clearly the main landowner was benefiting from increases in property values before the mid-1840s.

However, when the mines went into decline in 1843–4, the result was unemployment, depopulation, insolvent tenants, falling incomes, and declining property values. Many of the management personnel, including those from England, left the area, leaving the village to be dominated by the laboring class. The "ruinous and dilapidated" state which the village was said to have reverted to was not attributable to the Mining Company of Ireland solely but, in addition to the general decline in the mining operations, to the practice of tenants under the college not being willing to sustain a loss for their houses or to hold the house at a higher rent than the former solvent tenant did. As a result houses were left vacant, and because they were built of inferior materials, they soon fell into ruin; while others deliberately allowed their houses to fall into decay in order to negotiate lower terms with the college.[29]

In this situation, the availability of alternative sources of employment and income to the mines were critical but, in the circumstances, limited. Some labourers could fall back on employment in agriculture. This was because many labourers employed in the mines were seasonal workers, who worked part-time in agriculture, a circumstance which accounted for the reduced workforce in the mines at harvest time. The 1841 census indicated that one third of the area's inhabitants were categorized as being engaged in agriculture, while another third were engaged in providing food and lodging.[30] The attraction of the mines for labourers was that they provided double the wages of farm work and employment in them was more regular.[31] However, when the mines went into decline in the early 1840s these advantages disappeared and labourers were obliged to fall back on the more irregular employment given in agriculture.

What made such a prospect a perennial challenge was the fact that the land quality in the hinterland was not good. Another option was fishing but the prospects for this as an alternative were not auspicious given the absence of a harbour for boats, though the sea yielded seaweed which was much in demand for growing potatoes.[32] Indeed, the reliance by those who worked in the mines on the potato crop is indicated by its high price in pre-famine times. In 1841, it was reported that the occupying tenants on College of Physicians' holdings were able to "obtain high prices from the workmen of the Mining Company for the culture of potatoes."[33] Such practices may account for the fact that commodities and supplies were more expensive in the locality than elsewhere.[34] Taken together these factors serve to indicate that the welfare of Bunmahon's population was all too closely tied to the fortunes of the mines.

Living Conditions

In the pre-famine era living conditions in Bunmahon were intolerable, reflective of a sharp increase in population combined with inadequate housing in terms both of quality and number. As people flooded into the area in the 1830s in search of employment, settlement was concentrated on the western side of the River Mahon in Bunmahon as the ground on the Knockmahon side was generally unsuitable for extensive habitation. In Bunmahon some of the mine workers erected cottages and hovels on property for which they paid high rents at affordable levels because of the high wages they were paid. The demand for accommodation was so high, however, that speculators built inferior houses and subdivided them into six or eight parts and set them out to families.[35] Replicating this pattern, farmers, wherever their holdings had roadside frontage, sublet them at high rents (£4, £5 or £6 per acre), and on them sub-standard dwellings or hovels were erected by the tenants.

View of Bunmahon about 1850. Source: *Memoir*, 118.

Such practices and conditions were already prevalent by the time that the Power-O'Shee interest in the College of Physicians property in Bunmahon village ultimately passed c.1838 to the Mining Company of Ireland. The company itself, therefore, was not responsible for creating the crowded living conditions that prevailed; rather it was the speculators and farmers who took advantage of the high demand for plots and accommodation who were culpable. However, the patchwork pattern of house property thus created, whereby multiple landlords derived a profit from the one holding, caused problems when the downturn in the mining operations started in 1843–4.

There was a depreciation in the value of holdings for the sub-tenants were no longer able to pay the high rents they previously had, making their head landlords unwilling to sustain a loss from the holdings or pay the high rent for which they were liable to the College of Physicians. In this situation the houses affected were left uninhabited and because they were made of inferior materials, the landlords allowed them to fall into decay in the hope that the resultant fall in their value would be to their advantage when they came to renegotiate terms with the college.[36]

In good times when demand for land was high and sub-tenants were able to pay, the head tenants of farms sublet portions of their properties as dairy land or potato ground at £6, £8 or £9 per acre, and were thus able to live rent free of their obligations to the Mining Company. However, with the downturn of the early 1840s these sub-tenants were no longer able to meet their rent obligations, thus making it impossible for the head tenants to pay their rents to the college, a situation that was exacerbated when the first failure of the potato crop occurred.[37] Thus even before the famine arrived in the area the local population was highly vulnerable given its dependence on the profitability of the copper mines. In good times from the late 1820s to 1843–4 high wages allowed them to pay the high rents for their holdings, whereas in the decade from the early 1840s to the early 1850s, a downturn in the mining operations impacted the ability of sub-tenants and head tenants alike to meet their rent obligations, leading to the accumulation of arrears.

Vulnerability on this score was exacerbated by the increase in population evident in the pre-famine period. The population of Bunmahon village increased from 357 in 1821 to 972 in 1831 to 1,771 in 1841, representing almost a doubling between 1831 and 1841.[38] Upon his arrival in 1847, Doudney had estimated the population of Bunmahon alone as 100–150 cabins with 1,000 inhabitants.[39] Growth in the housing stock was not commensurate with the growth in population, for the number of houses increased from 76 (1821) to 120 (1831) to 158 (1841), with the average number of persons per house increasing from about 5 (1821) to 8 (1831) to 11 in 1841.[40] These figures indicate that overcrowding was one of the most prominent social evils in pre-famine Bunmahon.

The houses referred to were permanent dwellings and their number did not include the considerable stock of single-roomed mud hovels the number of which stood at 39 in 1841, each containing more than one family, with an additional 50 of such located in the sand dunes.⁴¹ The resultant squalor created by such conditions is well described by an English visitor who came to the area for employment in October 1851:

> "Bonmahon presented a miserable picture. The cabins were of the true Irish type —one room open to the thatch—little or no window —a hole in the roof served as chimney— swarms of half-naked children thronged the doors— idleness, with its associates, wretchedness, penury, and misery, seemed predominant."⁴²

Knockmahon town, across the River Mahon from Bunmahon, had a much smaller population largely because it was the area where the work was conducted and hence inhospitable for dwellings. Nevertheless, in 1841 Knockmahon had 255 people living in 36 houses, an average of 7 per house. The Mining Company did erect houses at various dates for the miners, but the number was insufficient.⁴³

Temperance, Health, and Improvement

Overcrowding was one social evil prevalent in the area. Another was insobriety as it was more broadly in Irish society at the time. The cause of temperance was championed in Waterford by Bishop Nicholas Foran. It was he who in December 1839 interested the pioneer of total abstinence, Fr. Theobald Mathew, to come to Waterford City, which he did. Mathew attended a meeting of the teetotal society at Mount Sion, and for two days administered the pledge at the court house to a number reportedly in the thousands. The legacy of Mathew's visit was tangible in that the city newspapers gave the movement their support, a significant number of employers in the city were named who employed teetotalers, and the movement gained momentum under Foran's leadership.⁴⁴

The teetotal movement in time reached the Bunmahon mining community, among whom drunkenness was commonplace. Payday in the mines, according to one writer, was the occasion for "strife and drunkenness" requiring the intervention of the police, the closing of public houses on Sundays, and sometimes putting the lives of the supervisors of the mines in danger.[45] The Rev. James Veale, Catholic priest of Kill, who was an advocate of temperance, called a meeting in Knockmahon to advance the cause of temperance in the area.[46] A proposal to erect a temperance hall ensued.

The temperance hall cost £1,000 and its construction was undertaken at the initiative of the Lady Catherine Osborne with the support of the mine manager, John Petherick, who was a supporter of the Fr. Mathew's temperance movement and who with Rev. James Veale and Rev. James Power were trustees. Donations from the miners were forthcoming with £400 being collected locally, and contributions from overseas (£600 raised by Rev. James Power) were also made. The hall was later used as a fever hospital and for school rooms for the education of children.[47] The erection of the temperance hall resulted in a sharp decline in excessive drinking. In consequence workers, formerly dissolute, became more productive and were able to collectively save £300 monthly more of their wages than previously.[48] The abstinence movement is likely to have impacted sections of the local population beyond merely the employees of the mines, though in some cases like Patrick Morrissey, a bailiff to the College of Physicians, this is likely to have been done under duress.[49] Overall, as well as productivity increasing, order was restored, and savings increased markedly.[50]

In terms of medical provision to the expanding population, attempts had been made since the mid-1830s to have a dispensary in the area. The mining company had its own medical staff made necessary because of the many injuries and accidents incumbent on the mining operations. There were demands that this should be supplemented by having the main landowner, the College of Physicians, contribute to the establishment of a dispensary for the needs of its tenants in the area, something other local proprietors were prepared to do.[51] The college declined such solicitations, as it did also in 1846 to an appeal from Bishop Robert Daly to support his school in Bunmahon.[52]

Indeed, general improvement in the area as a whole was inhibited because the College of Physicians as an institutional property owner was prohibited by its charter of foundation from granting leases for more than 31 years which would have allowed tenants to engage in improvement efforts.[53] A related problem was the subdivision of holdings, and the degree to which this occurred is evident in the comment of the agent of the College of Physicians who in 1848 remarked that he despaired of "being able to unravel the complicated state of subdivision into which the land has fallen."[54] Despite such expressions of despair, generally the college was unsympathetic to the needs of tenants and under-tenants on its property in the locality.

Church Provision

Other areas of infrastructure —human, service, and institutional— were in the process of development. In institutional terms, Bunmahon and Knockmahon were part of the Catholic diocese of Waterford and Lismore. The bishop of the diocese since 1837 was Nicholas Foran (1784–1855) who was succeeded in 1855 by Dominick O'Brien (1855–73). Foran was a native of Butlerstown, Co. Waterford, was ordained in 1808 at Maynooth, and was made president of the new diocesan college, St John's College, Waterford, in 1814. Having declined the presidency of Maynooth College and the bishopric of Galway, he became parish priest in Lismore (1824–28), and Dungarvan (1828–37), prior to being made bishop in 1837.[55]

Politically Foran supported Daniel O'Connell, intervened in elections in order to advance the interests of O'Connellite candidates, and favoured the repeal cause.[56] On other issues of the day and in common with his episcopal colleagues, Foran favoured the national system of education (1831), the Maynooth act of 1845 (which provided for a capital grant and an increased annual grant), and opposed the colleges act of 1845 which provided for the foundation of new university colleges, a proposal opposed by the bishops as potentially injurious to the faith and morals of Catholic students.[57] As noted above, Foran was also active in promoting the temperance cause locally.

In 1845 the diocese Foran administered had a complement of 36 parish priests, 70 curates, and 76 churches.[58] Although this number of parish priests was comparable to other dioceses in Ireland, the complement of curates was fairly high. In terms of the remuneration of clergy, it is informative to compare Catholic and Protestant levels. In 1833 the Church of Ireland curate of Monksland was Rev. George Edmondson who had a salary of £75, which appears to have been a fairly standard amount for curates in the diocese at the time.[59] In 1848 Doudney's income as curate was £75 (considered the minimum payable to a curate), and in 1852, £80 or £85, a third of which (or £35) went towards rent, and he claimed that the Catholic priest (whether the parish priest or the curate is unclear) had three or four times that amount.[60] This latter assertion is inaccurate, for, although we do not have figures for the income of specific parish priests or their curates in the area, we do know from a survey of clergy incomes in the first half of the nineteenth century that the income of the majority of Catholic parish priests in Ireland was in the range £50–£100, as it was for parish priests with one curate.[61] Catholic curates in the Diocese of Waterford and Lismore in the 1820s eked out an existence on a miserly £10, though, overall, clerical incomes as a whole rose in the early nineteenth century.[62]

Despite the apparent strength in terms of human resources that the complement of clergy in the diocese evinces, the Catholic Church was remiss in responding rapidly to emergent pastoral needs. The locality had churches at Kill (built in 1800 on ground donated by the Power-O'Shee family), at Stradbally (c.1830), at

Ballylaneen (1824), and, though more distant, at Newtown (built in 1835, and rebuilt 1839).[63] Thus while there were churches and pastoral provision in the surrounding area, in 1840 there was no Catholic church or chapel in the immediate area of Bunmahon or Knockmahon. This was despite over ten years of industrial mining activity that brought a large influx of people into the locality and by that date employed over one thousand people who did not have ready access to church services. As a result Catholics in the area were obliged to go to Ballylaneen (where a church had been erected in 1824) for their chapel services, the other options being Stradbally or Kill, both of which were further in terms of distance. There was an older mass house at Faugheen in the townland of Ballyristeen, but it lacked the space to accommodate large numbers.

Provision of a chapel only materialized from the change in function of the temperance hall. In 1847 the hall was sold to the Mining Company of Ireland for £100 (most of which was used to pay off debts on the building incurred by Petherick), and in November 1854 the lease of the building was re-assigned by the company to Rev. Roger Power of Kill (successor to Rev. James Veale as parish priest of Kill and Newtown) on payment of £150. The building was opened as a chapel in December 1854, was enlarged in 1855, and could accommodate a substantial number of people.[64]

As part of their improvement plans for the area, the Osbornes in 1830 donated land for the erection of a church for the Church of Ireland population of the area, under a law that allowed proprietors to make grants of land for such a purpose.[65] It was built to accommodate 180 persons.[66]

Near the Church of Ireland church and adjoining a row of two-storey houses—originally built to accommodate mine supervisors and management from Cornwall who came to work in the local mines— was a post office and a police station, and in 1848 proposals were in hand to expand housing for the coast guard.[67] Bunmahon and Knockmahon had the services of a doctor (George Walker), a midwife, butchers and a slaughterhouse, public houses (nine of which were licensed), a forge, postmaster, along with drapers, shopkeepers, tailor, nail-maker, cabinet-maker, shoemaker, bakers, a pawn-shop, and the more specialized pursuits of clock-maker and optician.[68] This catalogue of occupations is indicative of how the mines acted to stimulate a range of services, trades and facilities to meet the needs of the local population. Complementary to this range of services was the vital but often contentious one of education which emerged to prominence in the early nineteenth century.

Education: Knockmahon Schools

The provision of educational services was one of the most important developments of the early nineteenth century. The emergence of formal educational facilities was to be foundational in the infrastructure of localities. Education was also to be an issue of contention between different interest groups. This was the case locally even before Doudney arrived there in 1847.

In an official report of 1826 there are no schools mentioned for Bunmahon or Knockmahon. But the 1830s was a decade in which a number of initiatives resulted in schools being established locally. The key figure in this development was Lady Catherine Osborne (d.1856). Although her home property was located at Newtown Anner near Clonmel, Co. Tipperary, a distance inland of about 30 miles from her coastal property at Knockmahon, Lady Catherine took a keen interest in the situation of the latter as part of a broad interest in social and economic improvement stimulated by the discovery and exploitation of the minerals on the property.

Her interest was representative of those liberal Protestant landlords who as a result of the Catholic emancipation act in 1829 became more cognizant of being proactive in the cause of bringing the denominations together. Although she expressed ambivalence towards Catholic emancipation itself, saying "my reason is for it and feelings against it," she became a firm supporter of non-denominational education that emanated from the establishment of the National Board of Education in 1831.⁶⁹ In time the national system of education essentially provided state-funded schools under the local auspices of Catholic clergy.

At the time that the land was donated for the erection of the new Church of Ireland church, ground had already been allocated for the erection of a school house.⁷⁰ By 1832 Lady Osborne had established a day school, rent free, in the parish of Monksland at Knockmahon, adjoining the church "near the copper mines."⁷¹ It was originally connected with the London Hibernian Society (a body founded in 1806 for the purpose of establishing schools and disseminating the Bible in Ireland) though by 1839 this association had been severed and it had received no aid except some books. In 1835 we know that the school was kept by one James Howe, supported by Lady Osborne who gave £21 per annum for the upkeep of the school and for the teacher's residence. The children, whose average daily attendance was 18 to 20, paid 1s. to 1s. 6d. per quarter and they were instructed in reading, writing, arithmetic and needlework.⁷²

In 1837 when there was an application for aid from the National Board of Education, the building measured 42 ft. by 24 ft., contained accommodation for the teacher and 40 children, and contained one classroom with 3 desks and 5 seats.⁷³ The school operated five days per week and was open from 10 a.m. to 4 p.m. daily. The teacher's salary of £21 continued to be paid by Lady Osborne and it was supplemented by contributions from the pupils which amounted to 2s per quarter.⁷⁴ As to religious instruction, the regulations of the board required that it be after school hours and provided by clergy to their respective denominational members, though parents had liberty to withhold their children from such instruction if they chose.⁷⁵

The supporters of the school were Lady Catherine Osborne, George Walker, John Petherick, John Richards, and Richard English, all Protestants; and John Power-O'Shee, James Barron, James Vaile (Veale), (parish priest of Kill and Newton), John McGrath (curate of Kill and Newtown), James Power (curate of Kill and Newtown), Lorenzo Power (a head tenant on the College of Physicians estate), Thomas Quin, Thomas Slattery, Michael Power (parish priest of Stradbally and Ballylaneen), and John Sullivan, all Catholics.[76] It was due to their collective representations that the school in Knockmahon was admitted to the national school system.

Notably absent from this list of supporters was the signature of the local Church of Ireland curate, of whom it was said in 1839: "The protestant clergyman [at the time, Thomas Garde Durden] refuses to assist in the establishment of the school, being opposed to the adoption of the National Board."[77] This lack of support was repeated in the case of the Knockmahon female school which had been established in 1840 and continued by Durden's successor as curate, Thomas Power, while an inspector's report on the schools in the area in 1848 stated that: "The Protestant clergymen are opposed to the N[ational] schools."[78] Reluctance on the part of the Protestant clergy to support local initiatives to establish schools that were under the auspices of the National Board derived from their opposition to a system which, in their view, excluded an education based on Scripture.

Such opposition gathered momentum after 1838 with the foundation of the Church Education Society, a Church of Ireland body established in opposition to the National Board and intent on founding its own schools in which a scripturally-based education would be operative. Robert Daly, the new Bishop of Cashel, Waterford and Lismore, and resident in Waterford City, was a champion of the society and became patron of its local diocesan branch. There was some support for the Church Education Society in Waterford with about 30 schools connected with it in existence by 1843, 41 in 1849 and 38 in 1853, with 1,527 pupils on the rolls in 1847, but there is no evidence that any school in Monksland was part of, or affiliated with, the society, although attempts were initiated to create such an association.[79]

Daly was unhappy with a situation whereby, because of prevailing local circumstances, Protestant children were forced to attend a national school where they would be exposed to instruction in Roman Catholic teachings. Clearly this practice would have been a cause of dissatisfaction to Protestant parents and concerned clergy, for it went against the rules of the National Board, which specified that religious instruction was to take place outside of school hours by clergy of the different denominations. This was the situation prevailing in Monksland in 1843 when Rev. William Mackesy, whose normal duties were in Clashmore in west Waterford and who was a supporter of the national system in his own area, was given temporary responsibility for Monksland while the curate was away. Mackesy's support for the national system was to be modified given the novel situation he found in Monksland.

On May 30, 1843 Mackesy reported to the rector of the parish, Rev. Richard Maunsell, who was in Clonmel, that a "great many" Protestant children attended the Knockmahon national school, that nothing was being done to enforce the rules regarding separate religious instruction, and that for these reasons he recommended that a scriptural school under the auspices of the Church Education Society should be established.[80] As rector it was Maunsell's responsibility to communicate these concerns to the bishop of the time. However, nothing appears to have happened until Daly was made bishop, after Mackesy's responsibilities in Monksland had ceased, and until Rev. Thomas Power was appointed curate. It was then that a formal application was made to Daly for a scriptural school to be established in Monksland and it became clear that Daly's preference was to have one under the auspices of the Church Education Society.[81] His hope was that the school would be built in the grounds of the Church of Ireland church in Monksland and be of sufficient size to accommodate about 70 Protestant children, who as matters stood were meeting temporarily in the church building.[82]

In pursuit of this objective Daly was prepared to pay Lady Osborne a higher rent than normal for the ground and to expend over £100 on the school structure. This proposal led to a major controversy in early 1845 between Daly and the Osbornes. As landowners they objected to the fact that the grounds surrounding the church were to be used to erect a scriptural school, contrary to the stipulations in the deed of 1830 which stated that the grounds were to be for the erection of a new church and "for and upon no other use, trust, intent, or purpose whatsoever," and in opposition to the nearby national school that Lady Osborne had promoted through granting a site and funding.[83]

The school established by Lady Osborne, her son-in-law Ralph Bernal (1808–1882) (he had married her daughter, Catherine Isabella, in August 1844, when he also adopted her surname) pointed out to Daly, had not occasioned any opposition prior to Daly's elevation as bishop in 1843, rather Protestants had attended it "readily and without scruple."[84] In fact, Osborne maintained that between 40 and 50 children had attended with the approval of Daly's predecessor as bishop, Stephen Creagh Sandes (1839–42), making the school effectively an exclusively Protestant one before it was placed under the control of the National Board. The English mining families had in the interim sent their children to the largely Catholic school in Bunmahon. It was these children (40–50) who now made up the majority of the 67 or so for whom Daly proposed to erect a scriptural school in the grounds of Monksland church.

Daly strongly opposed the national school system because, like many other Protestants, he believed the Church of Ireland as the state church had the right to oversight of any system of national education, in particular that it be scripturally-based. In contrast, the Osbornes were keen proponents of the national system of education because given its non-denominational ethos they believed it would serve to reduce religious animosity in Ireland. They were related to the Archbishop of Dublin, Richard Whately, who in addition to his episcopal role, was a commissioner of National Education, and hence had a different position on education than Daly.[85] It was on the basis that he did not wish to see sectarian division arise in

Knockmahon that Ralph Osborne refused to make a site available for a scriptural school. As an MP, Osborne provoked the ire of status quo Protestants like Daly on other issues like state support for Maynooth and the reform of the Church of Ireland.

Osborne's position accorded with that of John Petherick, the mine manager since 1832, already known for his support of the O'Connellite cause, who asserted that opposition to the national school system was attributable solely to Daly. Daly, however, was a fervent opponent of the national system and he was anxious to promote scriptural schools under the model of the Church Education Society, of which he was the local patron and advocate. Since it received no state funding, fundraising sermons were preached in Waterford City churches in support of the society.[86] Other local supporters of the society included Rev. Robert Bell, archdeacon of Waterford, who authored a pamphlet supportive of scriptural education.[87] Given the formidable array of personages on each side, the battle over the provision of a scriptural school in the grounds of Monksland church was likely to be intense and protracted.

Information from the locality available to Ralph Osborne suggested that the demand for a scriptural school had not emanated from the parents of the children, but rather that they had been encouraged in making this demand by the curate of Monksland, Rev. Thomas Power, who under Daly's prompting, it was alleged, turned the minds of the parents against the national school and had them withdraw their children from it. In Osborne's opinion this action was "highly injurious to introduce sectarian distinctions, *heretofore unknown* in that part of the diocese of Waterford, by the establishment of a school founded on principles professedly hostile to the feelings and opinions of the great majority of the parishioners."[88] Daly dismissed the charge entirely, asserting that he had not influenced Rev. Power in the way Osborne alleged (a charge Power also denied), rather the demand for a separate school had arisen from the Protestants of the area themselves who applied to Daly for that purpose.[89]

In support of this position Power produced two pieces of evidence. The first, intended to show that the demand for scriptural education pre-dated Daly's arrival in the diocese and Power's assumption of the curacy, was a letter of December 1838 from Lady Osborne on the issue of the national system of education, addressed to William James of Knockmahon (a parent and church warden, and likely one of the petitioners mentioned below). In it Lady Osborne acknowledged the declared preference of the Protestants of the area to continue the old system of education in preference to the new one under the National Board.

The second piece of evidence was a petition dated January 22, 1845 addressed to Osborne with twenty seven signatures of Protestants engaged in the mines who were the parents of 73 children attending the school in the church building, requesting that he make a site available for a scriptural school. The following were the signatures:

W[illiam].H. James	Samuel Pope (church wardens)
Benjamin Blewit	Francis Gill
John Lathbean	Peter Eddy
James Gill	Edward Bateman
John Bateman	Thomas Reynolds
Benjamin Inch	William Inch
William Barkla	Henry Adams
William M'Crea	Richard Curnew
James Bennett	William Ralph
William Dunfoy	James Attridge
William Woodcock	James Coonbes [Coombes]
William Curry	John West
Richard Kinsman	John Coombes
James Clunes	

The petition was signed by Robert K. Atkinson, teacher.[90]

The memorial referred to the fact that the parents were "deeply interested in the spiritual as well as the temporal welfare of our children, and anxious to have them educated upon scriptural principles" and that they had "strong conscientious scruples as well as other objections against the national system of education."[91] Ralph Osborne refused the request of the petition arguing that he saw no reason for the children to be withdrawn from the national school since the rules of the National Board allowed for voluntary religious instruction in the school by clergymen of the different denominations either during regular school hours (so long as the regular school instruction in other subjects was not affected) or otherwise, which typically meant after school hours and/or on Saturdays.

Already in 1838 Lady Osborne had given reassurances on this score to the Protestants of the area when in a letter to William James of Knockmahon (one of the petitioners above), she wrote that in the national schools, "the bible, your own bible, may be read for an hour every day."[92] On the basis of such prior assurance, Ralph Osborne maintained that the onus was on the clergyman—in this case Power—to avail of the opportunity of giving religious instruction within the national school as allowed by the rules.

Further, Osborne pointed out that those who signed the petition soliciting the scriptural school were not representative since they were not permanent residents of Knockmahon for, as employees in the mines, their presence in the area was uncertain given the fluctuating nature of mining activities. If they were excluded from consideration, Osborne maintained, none of the permanent residents would want scriptural education. However, if there were 180 Protestants (including children) then the petitioners (numbering 27) and their children (numbering 73) amounted to 100, then those favouring it were in a majority (not counting the spouses of the petitioners who might have accounted for 27 more), even though they were semi-permanent residents of the area.

The controversy continued with charge and counter-charge between bishop and landowner, and the local curate. The scriptural school was eventually built in the grounds of the church yard, and was attended by all Protestant children.[93] Although average attendance at the school started at 73 in 1845, it fell sharply thereafter, likely due to the effects of the famine, reaching 63 (1846), 40 (1848), 33 (1850), 50 (1852), and 24 (1860), and 21 (1863).[94] The school became part of Doudney's responsibility when he arrived in the parish in 1847.

In a separate development the Knockmahon school, which had come under the National Board in 1839, had by the time of the above controversy, closed due to the death of the teacher, Robert K. Atkinson, and was functioning as a private school under its teachers Michael and Mary Kelly, who were supported by financial contributions from parents.[95] This happened at a time when the scriptural school was being constructed. One result of the controversy was to motivate Lady Osborne and her fellow patrons (though Rev. James Power was dissentient) to reapply to the National Board to have the school which was run privately by the Kellys, readmitted to the system.[96] The subsequent fortunes of the Knockmahon Male School show that it continued through the 1840s and 1850s to be under the patronage of Lady Osborne (until her death in 1856 when she was succeeded by her daughter Catherine Isabella Osborne, d.1880) with John Petherick as local correspondent, and that it received grants towards supplies, repairs, and salaries from the National Board.[97]

Meantime, in 1840 the Knockmahon female school was founded and came into connection with the National Board. Local correspondents for the school were appointed including Rev. James Power of Kilmacthomas (1844–49) and John Petherick (1849–59) under Lady Osborne's patronage.[98] The Osbornes continued to support the school into the 1850s and after.[99] By 1856 with Osborne as patron and Petherick as manager, there was no control by the local Catholic clergy over these schools. Yet this did not cause a difficulty. As Rev. Roger Power reported to the newly appointed bishop, Dominick O'Brien, in June 1856: "they are conducted in the same way as the other National schools and there is nothing in the system of instruction to which the parochial clergy can object. The teachers are Catholic and good moral persons."[100]

What ensued from all this is that there was a legacy of bitterness between the Osbornes and Daly over educational preference and provision. It was to provide an important backdrop to Doudney's arrival in the area in 1847, Daly's expectations of him, and to Doudney's own educational initiatives in the 1850s. In the short term, although Rev. Power denied that he was pressurized into taking the stand that he did under threat from Daly that he would transfer Power out of Monksland, the fact was that Power was subsequently moved far from Monksland to west Waterford to be vicar of Clashmore (to 1868), and he ended his days as rector of Templeree in the diocese of Cashel (1868–90).[101] These developments are perhaps indicative of a reward on Daly's part to Power for his part in the scriptural school controversy and a reprimand to Mackesy whose place he took.

All this had taken place prior to Doudney's arrival. Perhaps Daly believed that Doudney, being an Englishman, would be more resolute with the local population than Power who was from Co. Waterford, and hence might have been compromised by local sympathies. Born c.1813, Thomas Power, son of William Power, had entered Trinity College, Dublin in 1829 and obtained BA (1835), MA (1868), was ordained in 1842, and was curate of Monksland from 1843–47.[102] Or it may have been Daly's hope that Doudney might achieve more acceptance among the Cornish miners than Power and therefore be able to direct them according to Daly's wishes. The next decade was to show that if these were Daly's hopes they were, if not entirely dashed, then at the very least taken in a new direction by the initiatives that Doudney took to give educational provision in the area an entirely new expression.

Education: Bunmahon Schools

Across the River Mahon in Bunmahon, a second initiative in educational provision came in the summer of 1836 with the establishment of the Bunmahon school in the townland of Templevrick west of the main village.[103] At the time of its foundation it was unconnected to any society nor was it erected on any chapel or church ground, nor was it connected with any religious body. Hence it was not embroiled in controversy like its counterpart in Knockmahon.

Public subscriptions contributed to the expense of its erection and the Rev. Michael Power, the parish priest of Stradbally and Ballylaneen, was the school manager who also paid the rent.[104] The building, built of lime, mortar, and stone was thatched, measured 58 ft. by 16 ft., and could accommodate 120 pupils.[105] It came under the National Board in April 1839, the same year as the Knockmahon school. Despite these auspicious beginnings, however, the school experienced a succession of largely incompetent teachers.[106] It closed in March 1847 due to the prevalence of fever in the area, though it reopened later.[107] In September, 1849 Knockmahon male school had 135 pupils on the rolls, supervised by one teacher. Knockmahon female school by September 1849 had a total of 62 pupils instructed by one female teacher. In 1856 the male school had 138, and the female 107.[108] The patroness of the two schools was Lady Catherine Osborne who paid £22 to the male teacher, and £12 to the female teacher.[109]

In September 1852 the Bunmahon Female school was established, separate from the original school. Erected by local funds, it was again under the management of Rev. Michael Power, in whose parish it was located, had an initial enrollment of 55 girls, and the teacher was Alice Barron.[110] By September 1849 the Bunmahon school was catering for 105 pupils, two-thirds of them boys, and the teacher was paid £10 a year.[111] As with the other schools connected with the National Board, both these Bunmahon schools, in varying degrees, benefited from the supply of books and from board contributions to the teacher's salary.[112]

While the National Board eschewed denominational considerations in the granting of aid to the schools, requiring that any religious instruction be outside school hours, in practice religious affiliation was a determinant to a mixed attendance of pupils. The Bunmahon school, as we have seen, was under the management of Rev. Michael Power, while it was noted in 1838 of Lady Osborne's school at Knockmahon that "the neighbouring poor receive very little benefit from the school as it is considered exclusively Protestant."[113] This was because of the circumstances described above whereby because there was a concentration of Protestants in Knockmahon, the school there was almost exclusively Protestant. In the course of time, then, denominationally-specific education became the norm, at least at official level. A gathering of Catholic bishops at the synod of Thurles (1850) declared its desire to have religious education in the national schools based on denominational considerations, and from 1853 official government policy was to have religious education in the national schools for Catholic children based on the Catholic catechism.[114]

Literacy

Another more serious restriction, however, was that most of the children of the area, could not benefit from the schools because from an early age they went to work in the local mines. A report of 1842 into the employment of children in the mines gives some revealing details of their educational standards. The judgement of one individual was that "there is a much smaller amount of education amongst these people than anywhere I have yet found; there are but very few instances indeed amongst the young persons and children of being able to read even." Some of the children employed in the mines were brought before the commission of enquiry to answer questions as to their living and working conditions. Their evidence is indicative of the low level of popular education at the time. Maurice Cuddy aged 11 years told the commission: "I have never been to school; I go to chapel on Sundays; I cannot read or write." Most of the other children questioned replied similarly, though there were the exceptions like Helen Hawke, a Protestant aged 13 who said "I can read pretty well, but not write" or Jane Pollard aged 13 who said "I used to go to the national school close by here, I there learned to read; I cannot write."[115]

So by the time Doudney arrived in 1847 there were three schools operative in Bunmahon and Knockmahon, along with the scriptural school in the grounds of Monksland church. Despite these developments the 1861 census indicated that levels of illiteracy were still high with an estimated two-thirds of the working age population of Bunmahon and three quarters in Knockmahon in that state.[116] Attendance levels, academic attainment, and quality of teachers continued to be defective features of the local schools.[117] All this provides the context within which Doudney embarked on some educational initiatives which, as we will see in Chapters 3 and 4, were to extend educational offerings particularly in the practical sphere.

Faith, Famine, and Faction • 53

English	Irish	Pronunciation
Weeping (4)	ʒul	gūl
Will	toıl	thĕl
With us (5)	lɪŋ	ling
With you (5)	lɪb	liv
a Week	ſeactmaıɲ	shac-thin
Winter	ʒeımɲead	gĕt-rĕ
a Wart	κnıtɲe	foinĕ
Walls (sing. balla)	ballaıð	boll-ĕiř
an Old Woman (2)	caılleać [ɾeoch]	/kill-ac
a Wake	toɲɲ'am	thōr-ruw
Wilderness	ſáɲać	fos-ac
Wheat	cɲuıtɲeact	crū-nact
a Wafer	ablan	ow-ling
Writing	ſʒɲıbıɲ [ɾcɲiov]	sgreev-ing
Wild	fıadaıɲ	fē-an
Wide	faıɲɾıɲʒ	for-shing
Water	uıʒe	uish-gĕ

Translation notes made by George D. Doudney in learning the Irish Language. Source: *Recollections and Remains* between pp.42 and 43.

Language

While the area was the repository of Gaelic culture represented by the fact that two poets —Tadhg Gaelach O'Suilleabhain and Donncha Ruadh MacConmara —were buried locally and the fact that the Irish language was still commonly spoken (and for many it was their only language), it is likely that the local population was increasingly conversant in both languages.[118] Two population groups added to the linguistic mix. The Cornish miners would have been English-speaking with a host of technical mining terms in their repertoire with which the local population had to become familiar in order to become employable and functional. As a group they would have been added to by the influx of other service functionaries associated with the coast guard and the police force. Secondly, there were the Bearachs from west Cork who were likely to have been monoglot Irish speakers.

Cumulatively over time, outside English influences are likely to have contributed to the decline of the native Irish language. On this score it is perhaps no coincidence that the attempts by Phillip Barron to establish a college in the locality devoted to the revival and study of Irish language and culture, date to the 1830s when the mining operations and the influx of English-speaking outsiders became prevalent.[119]

One reporter spoke of the local population "using the native Irish tongue in the common intercourse of life, many speaking no other."[120] While the liturgy of the mass was in Latin, some of the altar denunciations from the priests against Doudney and his schools were delivered in Irish, though the fact that this was noted suggests its novelty of use and hence that the normal delivery was in English.[121] Doudney himself, although a proficient communicator in his own right, was less forthright in trying to understand Irish. He regretted not knowing Irish because, as he wrote in 1848, "much pleasing intercourse is denied us."[122]

Illustrative of the survival of Irish in the area is the following instance in which Doudney's first cousin and brother-in-law, George

David Doudney (1811–1865), who after graduating from Cambridge came to Bunmahon in December 1848 and for a few months received instruction in the Irish language from a young local man named Foley, who had converted to the Church of Ireland.[123] This is likely to be Rev. Daniel Foley (1815–1876), who was born in Kerry, educated at Trinity College Dublin (BA 1843, BD 1854, DD 1858), was professor of Irish there in 1849–61, and who was appointed curate of Dunhill and Guilcagh in 1844. In 1851 he was appointed family chaplain to Lord Donoughmore whose estate lay around Knocklofty in south Tipperary. In addition to producing an English-Irish dictionary (*An English-Irish dictionary: intended for the use of students of the Irish language*) in 1855, Foley was in the employment of the Irish Society for Promoting the Scriptural Education and Religious Instruction of the Irish-speaking Population Chiefly Through the Medium of their own Language (more commonly known as the Irish Society). Established in 1818 with Rev. Robert Daly as one of its two main founders, the Irish Society employed Foley to go on speaking tours around the country, mostly in the west and south-west.[124] It is likely that either Bishop Daly through his association with the Irish Society or David Alfred Doudney (Foley's portrait was featured in the July 1850 edition of *The Gospel Magazine* then being edited in Bunmahon) brought Foley to the attention of George Doudney.

Rev. Dr. Daniel Foley (1815-1876), curate of Dunhill,
and professor of Irish, Trinity College Dublin (1849-61).
Source: *GM* July 1850 (frontispiece).

As a result of Foley's tutoring George Doudney became proficient in Irish, as a test of which Bishop Daly (whom George Doudney heard in Cambridge making an appeal on behalf of the Irish Society for men to come and minister in Irish-speaking districts) had him preach a sermon in Irish on Ephesians 2:8 before a gathering of Gaelic scholars at the Bishop's Palace in Waterford.[125] Despite his impressive performance, Daly was reluctant to ordain Doudney unless he would give a commitment to remain in the diocese, which Doudney could not undertake to do as he had a previous commitment to serve under the Irish Society in an Irish-speaking area, Dunlewey, Co. Donegal (the patroness of which, Miss Courtenay, had promised him the curacy of the parish, where he had a congregation of 24 people), something that eventually materialized, though Doudney shortly after took up a position in Plymouth.[126]

All this is to indicate that it is likely that the majority popuation in Bunmahon had a preference for speaking Irish among themselves, though they could understand and speak English for the conduct of their employment and daily affairs.

Part of the text of a sermon in Irish on Ephesians 2: 8 delivered by Rev. George D. Doudney, 3 July 1848. Printed on his own lithographic press. Source: *Recollections and remains*, facing p.77.

Famine

What made the event of the famine in the Bunmahon area particularly disastrous was that it was preceded by a decline in the local mining industry. In 1844 the industry was negatively impacted because of the advent of cheap ore from Cuba on the Swansea market, and by 1849 production was more than halved.[127] In addition, from as early as 1840 the main vein of copper proceeding inland from Knockmahon was becoming exhausted, reaching complete depletion by 1845.[128] In the more seaward part of the vein increasing seepage became evident from 1845 and by 1849 it became unworkable because of seawater flooding.[129] The fall in the price of copper, which became evident in 1848, meant that from that year mining operations were being conducted at a loss. The layoff of workers that emanated from these developments was exacerbated by food shortages that had become increasingly evident from 1841 onward.[130] Taken together these circumstances meant that there was increasing inability on the part of the mining company to provide stable employment and also its ability to respond meaningfully in terms of relief provision once the famine arrived, was curtailed.

Arrival

There was a partial failure of the potato crop in 1845, leaving a sufficiency to carry over into 1846. Returns for May 1846 indicate that locally the extent of land devoted to potatoes only improved marginally between 1844 and 1845, and that oats and barley were being substituted for the potato crop.[131] However, in 1846 the quantity of potatoes planted in the area was one-third less than normal, a situation compounded by the appearance of blight which affected the whole crop, and what early potatoes were dug were used to feed pigs.[132]

In February 1846 high levels of fever were reported in the area, accompanied by high food prices with hundreds unemployed in Bunmahon itself, and by May 1846 the mining population of the entire area (by then said to number 3,000) was said to be in a "state of great destitution."[133] By that stage the adjoining parishes of Kill and Newtown were no longer supporting the mining population in their distress, something that caused Lorenzo Power (a head tenant on the College of Physicians property) and Richard Purdy, the mining company secretary, to make appeals in Dublin for emergency aid, likely from the college and the Mining Company of Ireland.[134]

Despite appeals from the local relief committee based in Kilmacthomas, the College of Physicians refused to make a contribution to relief efforts arguing that its charter of foundation prohibited it from allocating funds other than for the purposes specified therein.[135] Despite this reluctance the committee, under the chairmanship of Rev. James Power, persevered in its work and was active in obtaining funds locally and from government, which it used to purchase Indian meal and to distribute it (largely gratuitously) and in payment for work in widening and repairing public roads. In the process, between April and August 1846, it catered for almost 800 applications weekly representing 3,520 individuals.[136] The recipients of relief were, as Rev. Power noted: "chiefly cottiers, farm labourers, who are paid for their work on the conacre system, and miners."[137] By the end of September, 1846 the relief committee had exhausted its funds for the purchase of meal, though this was relieved somewhat by the mining company making food available cheaply to its workforce.[138]

Advance

The food shortages and fever conditions of 1846 were repeated in 1847, causing a renewal in attempts by the local committee to obtain relief. The deluge of requests made to central government to provide relief, made the obtaining of local contributions all the more urgent and necessary. However, because these were not readily forthcoming, the local committee was forced to borrow £300 to buy wheat from local farmers to be ground into flour and sold to the poor at cost price.[139] This had a beneficial effect in that the committee was able to sell excellent food cheaper than was available in the local shops, thereby helping the poor and at the same time covering their own costs.[140] This practice which was in place for about three months in the spring of 1847—though lives continued to be lost around Bunmahon due to food shortages— assisted those in dire need and was achieved without selling food supplies under cost (a government requirement for obtaining continuing assistance from central funds).[141]

A report from the Quaker relief committee in Waterford in February, 1847 reported that "great misery prevails in the district around Bunmahon, where I fear not a few lives have been lost from the effects of an inadequate supply of food."[142] In response the Quakers set up soup kitchens at Bunmahon and Kilmacthomas in March 1847, a welcome initiative though it coincided with an increase in fever outbreaks.[143] The establishment and functioning of these soup outlets was supported by local contributions.[144] Contributions came from Ralph Osborne (£20), John Petherick, manager of the mines (£10), and the Rev. Thomas Power (£1), the local curate.[145] The sums raised became the basis upon which the local committee applied to government for a contribution.[146]

Other relief efforts were evident in the case of Bishop Robert Daly who spent his summers at the Uniacke estate at Woodhouse near Stradbally. During the time of distress there he employed many local poor people curing and salting hake (due to a particularly large catch) for their own use, he gave money to others for the purchase of pigs, and he provided clothing for poor children.[147] On a wider stage, in Waterford City Daly was proposed by Rev. John Sheehan, a Catholic priest, as chair of the city relief committee, a proposal which did not succeed, despite which Daly was made responsible for relief in one of the districts into which the city was divided, something which involved him going from house to house distributing vouchers for coal, meal, soup, and clothing.[148] He was also a contributor to other relief efforts in the city.[149] In addition, he was president of the Waterford Auxiliary Relief Association founded in December 1846 and was engaged in providing fuel, bread, and straw for bedding to the poor, imported meal and flour for distribution, and donated money to the fever hospital.[150] Daly was to the fore in actively participating in relief efforts during the famine period.

Among other relief initiatives evident in the first half of 1847, were those to keep the mines open in order to give employment to the miners so that they would thereby be kept out of the workhouse; miners and farm labourers receiving relief from Rev. William Elliott Shaw, minister at nearby Annestown; and a cargo of Indian meal being imported and sold to the miners at a low price.[151] Starvation in Bunmahon lingered into the middle of 1848, layoffs occurred in the mines, and 1849 saw a cholera outbreak locally and admissions from the Bunmahon area to the Dungarvan workhouse stood at 108.[152]

Aftermath and Impact

After the famine, crops still remained vulnerable to blight and weather fluctuations. Charles Farran, the agent on the College of Physicians estate, reported to his employers in April 1849 that "never did a property present such an appearance of decay as it [does] at this moment," while a year later his prognosis was no better for he reported that: "there are unmistakable appearances of the potato disease —if it progresses we will have anxious times about the tenantry."[153] In the summer of 1855, a decade after the blight first appeared, the potatoes continued to be subject to blight, the hay was only partially saved, and the grain crop was in danger of being lost because of heavy rains.[154] Fear of a recurrence of potato failure may have been an inducement to emigration locally.[155] As well, the price obtained locally for butter had dropped sharply in the post-famine years, Farran, reporting in March 1849 that prices had fallen from the usual 85s.–95s. range to 62s. per hundredweight and fell further the following year.[156]

With crops volatile, weather an unpredictable variable, prices for farm produce falling, and the mines dormant, it came as no surprise that many tenants were in arrears with their rent payments. Already the failure of the potato crop in 1846 impacted the solvency of tenants and their ability to meet rent obligations for many years after. The basis of arrears lay in the fact that there was a traditional dependence among smallholders on the fattening and sale of pigs as a means of attaining rent payments. Locally tenants on the College of Physicians lands, in order to continue to pay rents, tried to secure seed potatoes in order to use them to fatten their pigs.[157] In 1848 it was hoped that a better potato crop would help to restore the stock of pigs from becoming exhausted in the area.[158] In the summer of 1850 Farran, commenting on the fact that prospects for the harvest were satisfactory, noted that: "if the potatoes succeed I shall receive a large portion of the year's income, if they fail great distress mush follow… as the main dependence for the payment of rents rests on the fattening of pigs which the potato alone can do with profit."[159] It was some time before such hopes were realized and prospects for the local economy remained volatile.

Meantime arrears of rent for the entire college estate continued to be high into the 1850s, the figure for September, 1852 being over £1,700 with the rental at £2,616, or in excess of half.[160] At this date Bunmahon village itself with its 88 tenancies had an arrear of £145.4s., out of an annual rent of £246.15s. for that property, of which total only £191 was received.[161] In addition, there were arrears in the payment of poor rates on local estates.[162] In the aftermath of the famine, Farran was in favour of leveling the many vacant hovels on the college's property thus saving taxes paid as poor rates, and allowing the opportunity for better houses to be built in their place.[163] In this sense, Farran saw the opportunity the post-famine context offered to overhaul the tenancy arrangements on the estate.

Population Decline

The famine reduced the population of the Bunmahon area by about one-third. By 1851 the population of Bunmahon itself had fallen to 1,142 from 1,771 in 1841, while that of Knockmahon declined to 215; by 1861 the census figures were respectively 914 and 259. For the families that occupied the mass of one-roomed houses in Bunmahon only 18 of 129 such families had survived by 1851, and about one-quarter of the laboring class in the hinterland of the mines had disappeared.[164] Decline continued into the 1850s with the overall population of Bunmahon village itself falling by 8% in that decade, though this was a prelude to new growth evident in the number of new births locally by the early 1860s.[165] In Knockmahon, the stock of houses increased in the 1850s suggesting modest population increase (estimated at from 480 to 584 persons), and a core community of 54 houses with 259 people emerged consisting of the managerial staff of the mines and their families.[166]

The health needs of the population were attended to by the establishment of a dispensary. In early 1849 Doudney had pressed for the College of Physicians to contribute to the dispensary which was intended to serve the needs of the communities in Bunmahon, Annestown, and Kill, who were occupants of college property.[167] The dispensary had been established for about a year based on private subscriptions of £23, an amount doubled by the county grand jury as its contribution.[168] In addition, Dr. George Walker, the medical officer to the mines and one of the college tenants, was given funds necessary for the purchase of medicines and for payment of rent for the dispensary buildings.[169] Despite the pressing need and Doudney's representations, the college declined to allocate funds for the purpose.[170] Not deterred, Doudney went to Dublin to press his demands, but in a temporizing move the college requested printed reports for the dispensary and nothing appears to have materialized, despite the pressing need.[171] In 1850 in making an appeal for donations to the dispensary, it was commented that "the inhabitants are in deplorably destitute state, and but for the means which the dispensary affords, we should speedily be overrun with sickness and disease."[172] Clearly the dispensary was making a difference despite the college's lack of support.

In terms, of the impact of the famine on the religious denominational breakdown, the baseline proportion according to one observer's estimate was that about seven-eighths of the local population was comprised of Catholics.[173] As to the

Protestant population, it was said in 1845 that Monksland had "a large Protestant population brought together by extensive and profitable copper mines" many of whom were English families from Cornwall.[174] Doudney's congregation in Monksland seems not to have been less than 100 persons, and in 1845 before the famine hit it stood at 180 including children of whom there were about 70.[175] That population declined in the seven year period 1847–1854 by twenty-six Protestant families amounting to about 100 persons, a decline occasioned partly by death but mostly by emigration.[176] The Methodist component of the local Protestant population had declined to a mere nine by 1861.[177] Others who were skilled in their trade emigrated and found now hope in the copper mines of the American mid-west especially in Michigan, while others in Doudney's congregation went to Australia.[178] By 1855 emigration was said to have declined.[179]

The partial stemming of emigration was in part due to the recovery of the mining operations. The failure of the ore deposits in Knockmahon in the 1840s seemed to augur a dismal future. Employment declined from 1,200 before the famine to 800 in the early 1850s.[180] In the early 1850s, however, prospects for a recovery in the copper mining operations were more auspicious. More favourable prices for copper became evident from 1850, a new vein of copper ore was discovered in 1852, and new investment occurred in infrastructure (for example, a railway line to bring the ore from the newly discovered vein to the dressing floors, pumping engines, and water wheels).[181] By 1855 the mines were paying £350 in weekly wages to the locality.[182]

Another indicator of restored prosperity was the fact that the Mining Company of Ireland paid the costs of attendance for its employees at an evening school for young adult men which opened in September1861.[183] All these favourable conditions contributed to a restoration of profitability in the mines from 1852 to 1865, and this led to a general renewal of prosperity, though to a diminished workforce. This was apparent to visitors, such as W.H. Collingridge,

Doudney's London publisher, who when he arrived in Bunmahon in late May 1855 commented: "Though the land is barren and the constant drift of sand and sea spray renders farming difficult, all the elements of worldly prosperity are to be found here."[184] From the early 1850s, the worst of the famine conditions and decline in the mines had passed.

Cliffs at Bunmahon, c.1850. Source: *Memoir*, 120.

Doudney's Arrival and Early Phase

It was into an environment of declining population, impoverishment, emigration, educational conflict, and industrial decline that Doudney came in 1847. Given these circumstances it is not surprising that his first impressions of his new parish were not favourable, for he noted "the filth, the wretchedness, and the misery that presented itself on every hand."[185] Describing conditions on his arrival in Bunmahon, he relates that "one's heart perfectly sickened in walking through the village itself, and beholding the filth, the wretchedness and the misery that presented itself on every hand. It seemed unendurable. One felt as though one could never settle down in the midst of so much that was so exceedingly depressing."[186] However, he quickly became enamoured by the beach and the scenery of the cliffs. His period in the community up to 1858 was a time of adjustment and transition.

Apart from the famine-like conditions and economic depression which were off-putting to him, there was also the challenge of coming into an area where there appeared to be an inherent hostility to people of English or Protestant background, despite the fact that for almost twenty years a Cornish element had been present. Commenting on this he wrote: "Taught from very babyhood to believe that all their ailments arise, not from any radical defect in their own system, but solely as the result of English misrule and Protestant oppression, the difficulty of combating the deep-seated prejudices of the Roman Catholic peasantry in Ireland none can imagine but those who have tried the experiment." Such prejudice was only deepened when someone of English and Protestant background came to help them. "Introduced as their religion is into the every-day transactions of life, every effort for their mere temporal instruction and advantage awakens their suspicion; and, because such efforts may be those of a Protestant or of an Englishman, enmity is aroused and opposition offered."[187] Yet despite these perceptions of hostility towards him and despite offers of other positions in Sheffield in 1849 (where there was parish with 6,000 and a church to be built), Plymouth in 1850 and London in 1851, which he declined, Doudney did stay and tried by means of a number of educational projects to give the people, particularly the young people, a new sense of industry, worth, and achievement.[188]

His first and most immediate duty was to the local Protestant population in Monksland. Despite its smaller size compared to Inislounaght, the potential for Monksland to attract a sizeable Protestant population associated with the mines was sufficient enough for a new church to be built there by 1830 at a cost of £900 from public funds, with the site made available by the Osborne family.[189] This fits in with the broader pattern in Waterford as a whole where the majority of churches—functional and uninteresting architecturally as they were—were erected in the period 1811–1832.[190] As to the actual Protestant population, official figures indicate that Monksland had a population of 89 in 1834 (or 8% of the total), which had declined to 24 by 1871.[191] When Doudney arrived in 1847 his congregation numbered seventy-five persons, the majority of whom were Wesleyan Methodists who had emigrated from Cornwall to work in the copper mines.[192] Because there was no church nearby of their own denomination, the Church of Ireland church was their only option and thus, as recorded by Emily Doudney in her recollections, "everyone came to the little church as a matter of course."[193]

The early years of Doudney's ministry in this congregation (in 1851 consisting of 30 adults, irrespective of children) were a challenge. In a diary entry for February 1, 1851, Doudney recorded his frustrations: "I endeavor to preach the truth in the ful[l]ness of it, and in the preciousness of it; but with very few exceptions— some three of four— it is impugned. Most of my hearers are opposed to a full-grace gospel. They would amalgamate free will and free grace— a covenant of works and a covenant of grace. They resist the truth."[194] One of the two causes that contributed to Doudney feeling unsettled about being in ministry in Bunmahon, he frankly stated in 1851 was "the Methodism of the people."[195] In such a small congregation, a few individuals arose who challenged Doudney's ministry. They included a coast guard officer who was disliked by his own men and who was vocal in church in making his objections known, behaviour which continued for seven years when he suddenly left the village.[196] Overall the Cornish Methodists were a troublesome element in Doudney's congregation.

Conclusion

Bunmahon's remoteness was reduced during the course of the first half of the nineteenth century primarily because of the discovery and intensive exploitation of copper ore resources. The copper-mining industry drew disparate groups to the locality between experienced Cornish miners of Wesleyan Methodist background; company officials and mining administrators some of liberal English origin like John Petherick; Gaelic-speaking migrant workers from west Cork; the non-English speaking crews of vessels put aground in a storm who settled in the village and married local women; and local agricultural labourers from the hinterland attracted by the employment prospects the mines offered.[197] Together this disparate conglomeration (forming a workforce of 1,200 people by 1844) came to presage change, something that formed part of the vision of improvement that the Osborne family had for the area.

The mines brought prosperity and high wages to the area in the 1830s. However, sustained prosperity was subject to shifts in demand for copper. Thus the decline of the industry from 1843–4 had a ripple effect in terms of tenants' ability to meet rent obligations. Depression in the industry had begun before the arrival of the famine in the mid-1840s. Already at that point division had appeared in the area over the issue of education. This forms the background of circumstances into which the new curate of Monksland, Rev. David Alfred Doudney, arrived in late 1847.

CHAPTER 3

PIONEERS OF ANOTHER EXISTENCE TO THE BONMAHONITES

FROM THE TIME OF HIS arrival in Bunmahon in the latter half of 1847 Doudney felt that his ministry in the area would assume a different form than what was traditional in comparable rural areas of Ireland. Influenced in part by his overall sense of calling, in part by his experience in Templemore, partly by the particular circumstances he confronted and by a recognition of the particular gifts he brought to bear, Doudney felt that ministry in Monksland parish would involve promoting a variety of educational and industrial projects. Embarking on such a course of action, though not without its personal struggle, was consistent with what he had experienced earlier in life and, in his mind, was in obedience to divine direction.

On the one hand, he was cognizant of what the Bible said that might militate against such a variation in traditional ministry. There was, for instance, the verse in Acts 6:2 which said in part: "It would not be right for us to neglect the ministry of the Word of God in order to wait on tables" and another in 2 Timothy 2:4 which said: "No one serving as a soldier gets involved in civilian affairs—he wants to please his commanding officer." Both of these verses seemed to caution him not to abandon his primary calling as a minister, i.e. to preach the Word of God and thereby bring others to faith.

On the other hand, however, there were other verses that seemed to recommend a contrary course. Thus, there was the example of the apostle Paul who worked as a tentmaker (Acts 18: 3), and in 2 Thessalonians 3:8–10 it said: "nor did we eat anyone's food without paying for it. On the contrary, we worked night and day, labouring and toiling so that we would not be a burden to any of you. We did this, not because we do not have the right to such help, but in order to make ourselves a model for you to follow. For even when we were with you, we gave you this rule: 'If a man will not work, he shall not eat.'" All this seemed to suggest a different course of action in terms of ministry particularly in a location like Bunmahon where in Doudney's words "pauperism, and indolence, and wretchedness in the extreme prevailed to an almost incalculable extent."[1]

A Different Approach

More than many of the English clergy who came to Ireland in the mid-nineteenth century, Doudney was aware of the need to live and teach by example. In a later rejection of the charge of bribery and force to gain converts, he said that "We have lived among them, and by conduct and conversation—by precept and by example—have endeavoured to show what Christian Protestantism is, not in name only, but in word and in deed."[2]

In addition, Doudney came to recognize that there were particular challenges attached to ministry in the Church of Ireland, especially because of its minority status as a denomination in Irish society. He came to understand that the typical Irish clergyman ministered to a scattered Protestant population of 20 to 60 persons on average, but that their needs could not occupy all of his time.[3] This conclusion accords with the general evidence indicating underemployment among Church of Ireland clergy in the early nineteenth century.[4] Specifically in relation to Monksland Doudney noted his "small parish with less than a hundred Protestant souls [who] are not sufficient in themselves to engross the whole attention of an active mind."[5] Bishop Daly, however, in his charge to the clergy of the diocese in 1846, warned that paucity of numbers should not be an excuse for laziness and inactivity:

> "I feel it my duty to warn many of the clergy to guard against the natural tendency to sloth, engendered by the smallness of their flocks…it is discouraging to see a very small flock and find but very few valuing their ministrations. It requires more life and conscientious remembrance of our responsibility to the Good Shepherd to be faithful towards the few."[6]

As well as his congregation at Monksland (for whom he usually held Sunday services at 10 a.m. and 3 p.m.), Doudney on occasion would hold additional services for congregations at Annestown and Stradbally.[7] Despite such additional but occasional duties, his diary entry for February 1, 1851 recorded his realization that there were "So few claims upon one's time and teaching as far as the people are concerned."[8] Utilization of this surplus time could lead to two extremes in the minister's behaviour. On the one hand, if he spent too much time in his study then he would be less likely to be actively concerned about the needs of his neighbours in the wider community. On the other hand, it could dispose him to a life of compassion and service to the needs of the poor around him, but because he knew that he was likely to be an object of suspicion to his Catholic neighbours, he was constrained to act in this way.[9]

In the event, Doudney's solution to this quandary was to recommend that a clergyman in such circumstances should use whatever means God had put at his disposal and if he could not reach people through traditional ways, then he should try the means of service and compassion.[10] Implicit in the adoption of this approach was a recognition that the deep seeded antagonism of Irish Catholics towards Protestantism would not allow him to gain converts in the way commonly understood at the time. So he would instead demonstrate a practical Christianity. This shift he found easy to undertake because, as he noted, he had "very little sympathy with a lifeless, formal, merely nominal and political Protestantism. Too many are making it a passport to heaven, ignorant of the fact that they are as far from the kingdom, as their poor blinded Romanist neighbours."[11] It was on this basis that his wider ministry in the area was to proceed, and in time it led him to found educational and industrial establishments in Bunmahon that he thought would be beneficial to the area. In settling on this course of action, Doudney was in the tradition of English Anglican evangelicals who, influenced by the religious revival of the eighteenth-century, became involved in an array of social causes and movements. In following in this tradition, Doudney's approach was similar to that of his colleague, Rev. James Alcock, minister at Ring, Co. Waterford, who worked tirelessly to improve the lives of the fishing community there.[12]

Despite this background of evangelical activism, it is clear that Doudney felt a certain fear embarking upon this kind of work given the personal responsibility involved, the likely opposition, and the potential for failure.[13] Nevertheless he proceeded with his first initiative being a printing school started in October 1851 at a time when the local mines were at a standstill and wages stagnant.

Children of the parochial or scriptural school. Source: *PO*, 23.

The Printing School: Preliminaries

After four years residence (1847–51), Doudney decided that he wanted to set up a printing school based on a model he knew of in the east end of London.[14] Already as early as 1845 at his second meeting with Bishop Robert Daly, Doudney had broached the idea of an industrial printing school connected to a parochial school as a practical initiative.[15] The bishop was supportive at the time and subsequently of Doudney's efforts.[16] Yet Doudney hesitated implementing this plan for a long time in part because he felt the daunting nature of the undertaking, in part because he had the unsettledness about staying in Bunmahon (given the other offers he had for church positions in England), and in part because of his wife, Eliza's, unwillingness to remain in Ireland. However, by the summer of 1851 these hesitations and difficulties had been overcome and by October of that year the printing school was operational.[17]

As his first project for the printing school Doudney chose the reprinting of a commentary on the Bible by John Gill (1697–1771) entitled *Expositions of the Old and New Testaments*, a work long out of print and one he had a deep desire to see back in print. It had been originally published in the 1770s and had gone through a number of editions. Calvinist in its theological emphasis, Gill's work was, in the view of many, the best commentary in English on the Bible. Gill believed Scripture to be the inspired Word of God, consistent with itself, and needed to be interpreted from the perspective of faith. For the time, Gill's commentary was unique in that it was the only accessible work that treated the entirety of Scripture rather than individual books.[18] In addition what qualified Gill for such an undertaking was that he had a knowledge of biblical languages notably Hebrew, along with a familiarity with Jewish rabbinical writings (i.e. Jewish expositions of the Old Testament) which, in the view of some, he gave an undue prominence to in the commentary.[19] He also wrote concisely, condensing a great deal of ideas into a short space, with clarity and fairness of interpretation, and the work was admired for its comprehensiveness in that Gill did not avoid difficult passages as some other biblical commentators did.[20]

Works like that of Gill and others like Robert Hawker, another Calvinist author who upheld divine sovereignty to the degree of excluding virtually any role for human agency, were difficult to procure. In the opinion of one contributor to the *Gospel Magazine* in 1847: "In some cases the volumes are large, in many cases scarce, in almost all dear. The poor cannot purchase them, and being read by only a few, publishers have no inducement to print large and cheap editions, and no society exists to reprint and to distribute them at low prices."[21] Doudney hoped that his plan to bring out a new edition of Gill would help to overcome all these obstacles.

In addition, the republication of Gill had, in Doudney's estimation, some contemporary relevance. He deemed the commentary to be a necessary addition to any believer's home in order to "stem the progress of Romanism and infidelity" and as a means to fortify the mind from attacks from "the sophistry, the priestcraft, the Jesuitism with which your ears shall be assailed."[22] For all these reasons, therefore, the republication of Gill's commentary seemed like a timely undertaking as the first project of the new printing school.

Doudney's original plan, as outlined in the *Gospel Magazine* in March, 1851, was to publish an abridgement of the work and so he proposed that if 2,000 subscribers could be secured then the six volumes of Gill's commentary could be published for 3 guineas, an amount which he estimated could be attained by saving a penny a day over 25 months. He claimed that this amount represented more than one-fifth of the cost when the commentary was last published and about one-third of the average second-hand cost. He proposed to publish it in monthly parts or one volume every four months, and by such means the New Testament would be completed in eight months and the Old Testament in seventeen months, or two years and one month for the entire work by mid-1853.[23]

The initial response to this appeal for subscribers was not auspicious and by May 1851 their number had only reached 500, though by August, 1851 it had risen to about 700.[24] One reason for this sluggish response was that people were apparently waiting for the first part of the work to appear before they would commit their names as subscribers, whereas Doudney was hoping to have a sufficient number of committed subscribers at the outset in order to commence the work and cover costs.[25] Another reason for delay in the project proceeding was that one person who had promised to take a hundred copies at the proposed rate of three guineas, later relented feeling that the project should be undertaken by someone of larger capital and in London, not in a remote location in Ireland where it was likely to fail given the prejudice against such projects there.[26]

Further, Doudney implied that some of the slow response was due to some former Baptist and Independent friends in London feeling that his entering the ministry of the Church of Ireland in some way disqualified him from republishing the commentary because of Gill's revered status among them.[27] Doudney's disavowal of such criticism had the result of increasing the number of subscribers by the end of July 1851, but yet he called for an additional 300.[28] Another reason for the initial lack-lustre response to the appeal for subscribers was that second-hand booksellers, knowing the scarcity of copies of the commentary and seeking to maintain their own monopoly, sought to prejudice the public against the proposed project.[29] Despite these initial hurdles Doudney was eventually able to proceed.

In September 1851 he announced that he planned to have the first part of the commentary appear on January 1, 1852, though subscribers' names would continue to be received until October 10 after which subscriptions would close and the price of the work increase.[30] By the closing date for subscriptions he had a total of up to 1,100 names which he deemed sufficient to proceed because by doing without the process of stereotyping he was able to save £500 which covered the deficiency of subscribers.[31] At a later stage the number of subscribers declined to between 800 and 900.[32] The financial viability of the project was immeasurably assisted when one of the supporters of the *Gospel Magazine*, Mary Ann Way, left him £1,000 in her will, the advertisement of which fact in the public press served to increase publicity for the project and to elicit a large number of additional subscribers.[33] This Doudney interpreted as providential and a justification for proceeding with the project.

With the subscriber base secured, the issue then became the actual details of printing the work. To have it printed in England while Doudney was in Ireland would be impracticable. It was at that point that his desire to start a printing school in association with the parochial school based on a model he had observed in operation in the east end of London in 1836, came to the fore. He recognized that the older boys in the local parish or scriptural school were growing up without any prospect of attaining a useful occupation.[34] Already, given his thorough knowledge of the printing trade, he had introduced the preliminaries of the printing process to the boys attending his school; in September on a trip to London he engaged the firm of W.H. Collingridge to oversee the business matters; he purchased three new Columbian printing presses, new type, and other necessities for conducting a printing works, all at a cost of £400; and three London compositors and one pressman were engaged initially (later another compositor and pressman were added) to go to Ireland.[35] All then seemed in readiness for production to commence.

The Printing School: Production

Doudney's aim in establishing the printing works was to provide useful employment in a skilled trade initially for the elder boys in the parochial school adjoining his church, but also more broadly for the youth of the area the majority of whom were Catholic.[36]

The compositors and pressmen recruited in London agreed to come to Bunmahon to instruct the boys in the printing process. They included the editor of the *Leamington Chronicle*, a Mr. Burgess.[37] In time the staff of the printing works increased to 4 compositors (whose job it was to set up type for printing), 3 pressmen (who would operate the printing press), 3 labourers, 4 young women and 22 boys (initially there were only 15 boys, 10 of whom were Protestant, with 5 Catholics, all of whom required patient instruction in the printing craft), and there were daily applications on the part of other Catholics to be admitted.[38] Eventually there were, in addition to the assistants, between 20 and 30 boys employed in the composing room as well as half-dozen men and women.[39] Doudney's son, David junior, rendered significant help to his father in the entire enterprise.[40]

Printing School building at its first location.
Source: *Memoir*, 149.

The next requirement was some place to house the printing school. The landlady from whom he was renting a house in Annestown, refused to let him a barn for use as a printing school as she suspected he would use it for proselytizing purposes.[41] By October 1851, however, three locations had been offered to him and one of these, formerly a hotel leased by Timothy Connolly from the College of Physicians, measuring 57ft. in length by 18ft. with two storeys, he rented and adapted for use as a printing house.[42] The building had been offered to the parish priest of Ballylaneen for use as a chapel, but he wanted £20 per year more than the parishioners were prepared to donate.[43]

Once a premises had been secured then the printing equipment could be installed. Collingridge spent £800 on the purchase of material and paper, an enormous sum for the time, but providentially it was covered by a bequest of £1,000.[44] Two of the packages of materials were left behind on the docks at London, and this delayed the start-up of the project by two weeks while they waited for them to arrive in Waterford.[45] On September 13, 1851 Doudney moved the equipment into the former hotel. The premises was divided into press rooms, store, compositors' section, and binding shop.[46] Against considerable odds, therefore, he was able to acquire the necessary materials and equipment, find and equip suitable premises, and alter it for use as a printing works.

Within a week after the compositing room had been assembled (putting the frames together, laying the letters, and unpacking boxes) by the three compositors who had come over from England, twelve or fourteen boys were engaged in composing the type for the first sheet of Gill's *Exposition*. On the first day of actual work Doudney composed a few lines of type in order to get the project started, then he put the eight boys to work dividing the task so that each one would compose 12 to 20 lines during the day which was better than he expected, while an impression of the woodcut was taken at the small press in order to show the villagers what could be done.[47] The day the first sheet was run off a week later, coincided with a visit by Bishop Robert Daly to the facility.[48] In time, the two large presses that were to produce the work were made functional, a pressman arrived to take up his duties, and within a month of the arrival of the compositors the entire printing works were operational.[49]

Composing room of the Printing School. Source: *Memoir*, 153.

Immediately the works were giving employment to 20 boys, 4 journeymen, a labourer, and 4 girls, and this number soon expanded to 4 compositors, 3 pressmen, 3 labourers, 3 girls, and 22 boys.[50] By May of 1855, employment in the printing works consisted of 5 women in the binding department, 2 compositors, 5 pressmen, 15 boys, running three presses "full of bustling activity."[51] Within one year of operation their wages (earned on the basis of every thousand types) collectively served to put £1,000 into circulation in the area.[52] This amount has to be compared with an estimated £700 from wages which the mines dispensed locally in 1856.[53] By that date the mines had revived with mine workers earning three times what they did formerly as did those working in the printing school.[54] Such an infusion of cash into the local economy from the printing operation happened despite the fact that the early feeling was that the enterprise would not succeed because of the "depression of business in that town [Bunmahon] and the extreme destitution of the major part of the population."[55]

Gill's Commentary

The first pages of the massive work began to issue from the printing school on October 15, 1851, and despite the difficulties and delays (including a miscalculation of £400 in costs) and personal anguish on Doudney's part (in the early stages he worked on it from dawn to 9 or 10 p.m., even 3 a.m., and his wife was ill for long periods prior to Christmas in 1851), the initial supply of the first part or quarter volume of the commentary, the New Testament, consisting of up to 1,000 pages, was dispatched to London on November 23, 1851.[56]

Title page of John Gill, *An Exposition of the Old Testament*, volume 4 (London, 1854).

In terms of payment, the usual practice of requiring a deposit in advance (in this case a half-guinea or 10s. 6d.) was waived by Collingridge in order to accommodate those subscribers who could not afford this method and instead just to require pre-payment for each part or volume.[57] As to the cost of the individual parts (2s.6d.), Doudney felt that this would not justify allowing booksellers their usual commission of 25%. This amount, in addition to advertising, incidental expenses, and the London agency of Collingridge (to whom subscribers were expected to send their remittances ten days before the end of each month), would together not have given him a return of half of the retail price for his expenditure on the work.[58] Given that reality Doudney decided after the appearance of the first part that the trade would only receive 10% on subscribers copies and 20% on non-subscribers copies, while those who accepted the work in volumes the cost of binding would be included (binding with covers would normally incur an additional cost of 1s. per volume) which had not been planned originally.[59] Yet some subscribers were not merely satisfied with the quality of the work but were impressed with its relative cheapness.[60]

On March 16, 1852 the first supply of the complete volume 1 of the New Testament was dispatched for London, and all the remaining parts on March 23, and by mid-April was in readers' hands.[61] Once the first volume of the New Testament was completed, Doudney decided to commence with the Old Testament and in May, 1852 part 1 of the Old Testament was issued with the intention that when the first volume of the Old was completed (estimated to be September, 1852), he would then return to completing the New Testament whose completion he estimated as January 1853), and so on, every four months until the work was completed.[62] In response to queries as to why the New Testament was published before the Old Testament, Doudney defended the decision saying that it was normal procedure where commentaries were concerned and that it would be "more satisfactory" to have the New Testament completed punctually.[63]

By August 1852 two of the six volumes had been printed and issued, and work on the third volume which would complete the New Testament, was at an advanced stage.[64] A further volume was added by December 1852 when Doudney in a preface could report to subscribers: "The present volume completes the New Testament. We now resume the Old Testament, and trust by May 1 to issue the second volume in it; the third on the first of September and the fourth and concluding volume by Christmas 1853." By February, 1853 almost 3,000 pages had been composed, 15 tons of paper had been utilized, and about half a million sheets printed on both sides.[65] By April, 1853 Doudney was able to report that the fourth volume was nearly completed, the Psalms were being printed, and by early May it was hoped to have volume four with the binder.[66] In the event two further volumes appeared during 1853, but the final volume of six did not reach subscribers until February, 1854.

Thus it took Doudney, the printers, and their pupils less than two and a half years to complete the undertaking. This was no mean achievement when one considers that each volume of the work numbered over 900 or, in some cases, over 1,000 pages of text. This was a phenomenal achievement on the part of the boys who had not (with two exceptions) held a composing stick in their hands before. In the process 2,250 sets of the multi-volume work were printed, folded, stitched and covered In Bunmahon, giving a total of 13,500 volumes in all.[67] This involved the use of 25 tons of paper and the composing and arranging of nearly 47 million letters.

Boys in the composing room of the Printing School.
Source: *PO*, 14.

The additional difficulties of acquiring materials, refurbishing the premises, and establishing the printing works on a sufficiently large scale to conduct the work, all involving an expense of several thousand pounds, had been overcome. There were delays, frustrations, and disappointments around filling the multiple needs of the printing office in a punctual way. Production and distribution presented particular challenges. Among these was the fact that the 6,000 pages of text were printed on hand presses rather than the newer machines.[68] The nearness of the sea, humidity levels, and the exposed location of the building made the forms used in the production damp and hence unworkable, while the rollers had to be modified in order to make them functional.[69] At one point, the uninsured premises were apparently miraculously saved from going up in flames.[70]

On the supply and distribution side, there was the challenge of conducting the project in a remote village distant from London manifested in deficiencies in the steamboat and railway services which occasioned the loss or misplacement of goods and boxes, and even when service was reliable the cost of transportation was excessive.[71] On top of that was the cost. Already by August, 1852 Doudney estimated that he had spent almost £2,000 on the enterprise with, at that stage, only one-third of the whole work completed.[72] Yet despite all these challenges, the scale of the task, and local opposition by Catholic clergy, the mammoth project was completed.

In terms of the accuracy of the new edition of Gill to the original, Doudney made clear that he tried to adhere to the original text so far as possible. However, he did use contractions (e.g. "can't" for "cannot") and although he proofread each page, he admitted that inaccuracies in the Hebrew occurred in the first part to be published, and that there were mistakes overall in the Hebrew and Greek as well as misspellings of Latin words.[73] But overall, so far as the English text was concerned it was considered accurate and generally free of errors compared to more expensive editions.[74]

One source mentions that the first volume of Gill's work to be printed—*An Exposition of the New Testament* vol.1 (1852) —was put on show at the Cork Industrial Exhibition of 1852, and that those viewing it refused to credit the fact that the volume was printed in the County Waterford village of Bunmahon.[75] Doudney may have had the book on show at Cork but it is not mentioned in the official catalogue of the exhibition.[76] Nevertheless Gill's commentary had broad appeal for there where subscribers in Belgium, Holland, and Germany who were attracted by its cheapness.[77]

All in all the printing of Gill's *Exposition* was a notable achievement on the part of the Bunmahon boys and their instructors. It was therefore with a measure of pride that Doudney could preface the final volume (1854) with these notes to the subscribers: "Beloved friends: words will utterly fail in attempting to describe to you what are our feelings in announcing the close of this great and important undertaking. It seems verily like a dream. We ask ourselves again and again—Can it be true that Gill's Commentary is complete?—that the work upon which we entered somewhat less than two years and a half ago is brought to a close? that our hopes and fears—joys and sorrows—have subsided? To God—to God alone—be the glory."[78]

When the six volumes had been completed Doudney received 150 sovereigns and a silver tea and coffee set from his subscribers as a token of gratitude for his efforts.[79] The success of the project also brought him wider recognition for the lord lieutenant, the earl of Carlisle, presented him to the sinecure living (worth £50 yearly) of Kilcash near Clonmel in 1854, enabling Doudney to continue his active and highly individual work.[80] In April 1855 Doudney presented the lord lieutenant with a copy of Gill's commentary.[81] The boys in the printing school were made a gift of a pleasure boat which they sailed in to Tramore where they had a picnic, after which they proceeded by train to Waterford.[82]

Doudney's efforts also won the commendation of no less a person than the social reformer, Lord Shaftesbury.[83] The printing works were mentioned in the British House of Commons in June 1855 as an instance of the benefits of independent industrial education that emphasized an entrepreneurial self-reliance.[84] Such varied and widespread recognition was significant.

Gill's *Exposition* also allowed a surplus of £500 which Doudney used for the building of a glebe house, for the erection of which land (up to 7 acres at 30s. per acre) had already been secured from the College of Physicians.[85] Until it was erected the Doudneys lived in frugal circumstances. Doudney's daughter, Emily, later recorded of her time in Bunmahon that their house consisted of: "a long, low house of one stor[e]y, thatched and practically built of mud and stucco with long, low windows down to the ground and large rooms opening out of each other."[86] Such circumstances were now relieved because of the new glebe house made possible because of the recognition achieved through the publication of Gill's commentary.

Other Works

Encouraged by the success of Gill's *Exposition* Doudney was motivated to expand his printing activities. In the period 1852 to 1858 a large number of religious, evangelical books and tracts were printed at Bunmahon.[87]

Already, prior to the completion of Gill's commentary, Doudney had received requests to reprint Robert Hawker (1753–1827), *The poor man's morning and evening portions: being a selection of a verse of scripture, with short observations for every day in the year: intended for the use of the poor in spirit who are rich in faith and heirs of the Kingdom* (1829), Benjamin Keach (1640–1794), *Tropologia, or, A key to open Scripture metaphors* (1681), Samuel Rutherford (1600–1661), *Letters* (1664), John Gill, *An exposition of the book of Solomon's Song commonly called Canticles* (1776), and John Brown (1722–1787), *Sacred tropology, or, a brief view of the figures and explication of the metaphors contained in scripture* (1768), requests he acceded to.[88]

The first to appear was John Gill, *Canticles* which was issued soon after the completion of the *Exposition*.[89] By April 1854 Hawker's *Morning and Evening Portions* was in press, with 5,000 copies eventually printed.[90] The request to bring out a new edition of Samuel Rutherford's *Letters*, was apparently in response to the fact that editions available at the time were, in the view of at least one contributor to the *Gospel Magazine*, "considerably curtailed and altered in language to suit the taste of the professing public of the present day" and hence needed to be restored to the original.[91] In early 1855, Benjamin Keach's *Metaphors* reached subscribers after two or three months delay caused by inefficiencies in the steamship service through Waterford, although Doudney hoped that this was compensated for by its size and cheapness.[92] By the end of March, 1855 it was expected that every copy would be sold.[93] When W.H. Collingridge, the London publisher, visited Bunmahon at this time he was impressed by the reprint production of Keach's *Metaphors* given the paucity of errors it contained, and overall he believed that the typographical ability of the Bunmahon boys would not be unworthy of London printing establishments.[94] In late August 1856 another of Keach's works entitled *Gospel mysteries unveil'd, or, An exposition of all the parables and many express similitudes contained in the Four Evangelists spoken by our Lord and Saviour Jesus Christ: wherein also many things are doctrinally handled and practically improved by way of application* (1701), was issued at Bunmahon as a companion volume to the *Metaphors*.[95]

THE
GOSPEL MAGAZINE;
AND
Protestant Beacon.

"COMFORT YE, COMFORT YE, MY PEOPLE, SAITH YOUR GOD."
"ENDEAVOURING TO KEEP THE UNITY OF THE SPIRIT IN THE BOND OF PEACE."
"JESUS CHRIST, THE SAME YESTERDAY, AND TO-DAY, AND FOR EVER. WHOM TO KNOW IS LIFE ETERNAL."

FOR 1854.

IRELAND.
PRINTED AND PUBLISHED AT THE
BONMAHON INDUSTRIAL PRINTING SCHOOL, COUNTY OF WATERFORD, IRELAND.
(Established Oct 1851, by D. A. Doudney, Curate of Bonmahon.)

1854.

The *Gospel Magazine* for January, 1854.

As a means of making its production more cost effective and secondarily to increase the business of the printing school Doudney decided to print in Bunmahon the periodical *The Gospel Magazine and Protestant Beacon* which he had become editor and proprietor of in 1840. The *Gospel Magazine* was the oldest religious periodical in the English language, founded in 1766 with Augustus Toplady (author of the famous hymn, "Rock of Ages"), being an early editor in the years 1775–6. Contributors included John Newton and George Whitefield. It espoused the evangelical tradition in the Church of England, upholding the Thirty-Nine Articles and the King James Version of the Bible as standards.

Doudney first intimated his intention of printing the magazine in Bunmahon in the issue for November 1852 when he told readers:

> "We have made arrangements for henceforth printing and issuing the magazine at Bunmahon. God willing our next and future numbers will be printed at our Industrial Printing School. On, and after, January 1 (1853) the whole impression will be stamped. Each subscriber upon forwarding [his or her] name will receive the magazine direct through the post free of any additional charge. Each number will be published at sixpence stamped...A post office order upon Waterford for six shillings made payable to David Alfred Doudney, Bonmahon, ensures the regular receipt of the magazine for twelve months."[96]

The decision was made because for the previous two years at least, any profit from the magazine went towards expenses incurred from its printing and distribution. It was said that the magazine brought him an income of £200 to £300 annually.[97] It was not that circulation of the journal had decreased rather it was that the expenses had increased. In normal circumstances a discount of one-third on the cost of a book or journal was made to the bookseller and publisher, so that when advertising and other costs were taken in to account, only half the retail price was returned to the author or owner of the publication. To circumvent this and address the issue of costs, Doudney proposed that the magazine be issued direct to each subscriber.[98]

The magazine was issued on a monthly basis, twelve issues forming a yearly volume, and was published in Bunmahon for between four and five years (1853–1858). The subject matter of the magazine encompassed stories from the Bible, expositions, and correspondence with readers dealing with church matters and morals. The magazine also contained much valuable information on the finance and administration of Doudney's various schools at Bunmahon. In 1855 its monthly circulation was 2,000 copies, though in Doudney's estimation it was read by five times that number.[99] The magazine continued to publish even after his departure from Bunmahon, and he continued to edit it until shortly before his death, which constituted an amazing tenure of editorship of fifty-three years.

An associated periodical whose publication began in Bunmahon was *Old Jonathan or the District and Parish Helper*. Issued monthly, it first appeared in May, 1856, was printed in Bunmahon, and was published by Collingridge of London. It was described as "a fine broad sheet, handsomely illustrated with capital letter press, and matter selected and original in its columns well calculated to engage the attention, improve the mind, and lead to serious thinking." Cheaply priced (first issue 1d. normally 4d.), it aspired to a circulation of 10,000, although a readership of 50,000 was anticipated.[100]

The third and last example of a publication from the printing school illustrative of the range of titles produced is a work entitled *A Pictorial Outline of the Rise and Progress of the Bunmahon Industrial, Infant and Agricultural Schools Co. Waterford*, written by Doudney himself and published and printed in Bunmahon in 1855.[101] This work is of tremendous value, firstly, because it gives an account of Doudney's attempts to provide a useful education in both practical and mental skills for the deprived children of the area. Doudney in the work gives an informative report on the establishment and development of the printing, agricultural, junior and other schools. Secondly, the title page of the *Pictorial Outline* includes the phrase, "with Illustrations from Photographic Pictures" of Bunmahon and Knockmahon and of the various schools there. However, the photographs could not be reproduced in book format, thus necessitating their transposition into the *Pictorial Outline* in the form of etchings, though in this transposition there was some loss of accuracy and perspective.[102]

A

PICTORIAL OUTLINE

OF THE

RISE AND PROGRESS

OF THE

BONMAHON

INDUSTRIAL, INFANT, & AGRICULTURAL SCHOOLS,

County of Waterford.

WITH ILLUSTRATIONS FROM PHOTOGRAPHIC PICTURES.

ESTABLISHED
BY THE REV. DAVID A. DOUDNEY,
CURATE OF MONKSLAND.

IRELAND:
PRINTED AT THE BONMAHON INDUSTRIAL PRINTING SCHOOL,
ESTABLISHED OCT. MDCCCLI.

Title page of *A Pictorial Outline of the Rise and Progress of the Bonmahon Industrial, Infant, & Agricultural Schools, County of Waterford* ([Bunmahon: 1855]).

Distribution

Given the enormity and scale of the undertaking it is important to ask: How were the books printed at Bunmahon distributed, to where, and to whom? It seems that at that time mail from the Bunmahon area was brought to Kilmacthomas, then to Carrick-on-Suir, and then to Waterford. There was only one runner employed to convey post between Kilmacthomas, Bunmahon, and Stradbally. For Doudney this system meant considerable delay and inconvenience for distribution of the monthly journals. Because they were issued monthly, it was important that the two journals produced in Bunmahon, *The Gospel Magazine* and *Old Jonathan or the District and Parish Helper* (with a combined monthly circulation of 2,250), be delivered punctually.[103] The solution was that they be sent directly to Waterford.

In order that he might fulfill his commitment to his subscribers Doudney for two years, 1852–3, had the publications of the printing school sent directly from Bunmahon to Waterford at his own expense, which for the number of journal issues in excess of 2,000 per month at 1d. each amounted to £8. As he himself explained to a committee of enquiry into the postal services: "If we send them to Kilmacthomas there was frequently delay there; the driver of the Dungarvan car would say he had not room… therefore I generally send them into Waterford [a distance of 15 miles] direct in order to avoid those delays."[104] The issue of the Dungarvan car not having enough room to take on the journals was substantiated by W. H. Collingridge, the London publisher, who visited the Bunmahon schools in June 1858. Collingridge's account indicates that while Doudney paid for a lad to bring a donkey cart with the journals the four miles to Kilmacthomas, he was repeatedly unable to dispatch them because there was no room on the car coming from Dungarvan.[105] Collingridge interpreted this repeated unavailability of room as a prejudice against Protestant materials.

Because of these circumstances, the cost of carriage for the 13,500 volumes of Gill's *Exposition* amounted to more than £300.[106] Such heavy outlay on postage alone was clearly detrimental to the progress of the printing school, so Doudney petitioned the postal authorities to change their routes. In the event, a special arrangement was made in 1853 whereby the post office agreed to allow one car per month to go from Kilmacthomas to Bunmahon to collect the 2,250 copies of the journal issues.[107] That the postal authorities should adapt their services and routes to meet Doudney's needs is a good indicator of the importance of the Bunmahon printing works.

Readership

Through the pages of the *Gospel Magazine* Doudney established a collection and subscription system in England, both for the purchase of his publications, and for the support of his schools at Bunmahon.

Not surprisingly, therefore, most of the publications issuing from Bunmahon were distributed to and read by subscribers mainly in England. Attempts were made to advertise in the local press the availability of the *Gospel Magazine* and, later, *Old Jonathan*, for local subscribers.[108] However, it is apparent from a subscription list published in volume four of Gill's *Exposition* (1851) that the bulk of the readership was not local. In this list a total of 1,098 subscribers are given, but of these only about 20 have addresses in Ireland, the rest derive from England primarily.

From this list of subscribers it is also evident that Doudney received little support from his fellow clergymen in the diocese of Waterford and Lismore, at least in so far as the purchase of his publications is concerned. In 1852 there were 80 to 90 clergymen of the Church of Ireland in both dioceses but only a handful of these appear in the subscription list. It did not include Bishop Robert Daly. Among them, however, the following are worth mentioning: Rev. J. Burke, Kilmeaden, Rev. E. Dalton, Tramore, Rev. J.

Morgan, Waterford, Rev. J. Parker, Kilmacthomas, Rev. W.E. Shaw, Kinsalebeg, and Rev. N. Wilkinson, Kilrossanty.

What of other areas in the county? When asked, Doudney himself admitted that his journal did not have a large circulation in the locality, that for Dungarvan being "not half a dozen copies." The only subscriber on the list with an address at Dungarvan was O. Giles, and for Bunmahon itself the only one was a Mr. Attridge. Clergymen in the adjoining parishes to Monksland were apparently resentful of Doudney's presence in the area. When Doudney mentioned the *Gospel Magazine* to the curate of Stradbally, Rev. Richard H. Smith, who was friendly with Bishop Daly (and later became his chaplain), who had his summer residence in Stradbally, he responded: "That thing!"[109]

A meeting of clergy at the bishop's residence in Waterford, where the printing press was mentioned as an obstacle to mission work, further illustrates the reaction to Doudney's work. Although a minority expressed support for Doudney and while Daly was apologetic and dismissive of the charge, Doudney felt it as a personal attack on his efforts.[110] Doudney felt it was hypocritical that these very same critics of his work were the ones who readily accepted gift copies of Gill's commentary and other publications printed at his school. One fellow clergyman in particular, who was influential with Bishop Daly, was not averse to asking Doudney to stand in or substitute for him when he was absent from his parish.[111] Thus the subscription list indicates that Doudney's publications enjoyed their greatest circulation in England, while in his own diocese they were only of limited appeal to his fellow clergymen.

Printing School staff. Source: *PO*, 15.

How did those employed in the printing works benefit? At the point when there were 22 boys employed in the printing school and on the completion of Gill's *Exposition* Doudney claimed that each was paid from 3s. to 12s. per week according to ability, and based on every thousand types composed.[112] Speaking at a meeting in Nottingham in February 1853 Doudney said the boys in the printing works brought home from 2s.6d. to 7s.6d. per week, whereas he claimed many families of labourers had only a weekly income of 1s.[113] By 1858, Doudney noted with satisfaction that the head of each department in the printing establishment (compositing, pressman, and binding) had been trained in the establishment.[114] At that point employees of the printing school were earning three times the wages that obtained when the school first opened.[115]

Having completed their apprenticeship in the printing trade at Bunmahon many of the young people, Doudney says, took up positions of responsibility in printing houses in Ireland, England and America.[116] For example, by May 1853 a former assistant at the Bunmahon printing works had become editor of the *Clare Journal*; one boy progressed from Bunmahon to Liverpool where he gained a position; and a Bunmahon family—three of whose female members were engaged in the folding and stitching department of the printing school—emigrated to America to advance themselves in the printing trade there.[117]

Others of the printing trade remained in Bunmahon and married into local families. For instance on January 18, 1852 John Barret Chant aged 23, a printer at Bunmahon married Bithia aged 16, third daughter of John G. West, chief engineer with the Mining Company of Ireland. In 1852 also the marriage took place between J.J. Burgess, aged 26 years, a Bunmahon printer (whose father was also a printer) and M.G. Dunfoy, aged 21 years, whose father was a coast guard employee.[118] A third notable marriage took place in January 1855 when James Ryan, a printer at Doudney's works, married Mary only daughter of Capt. Lawrence Killeen of the copper mines.[119] These matrimonial links serve to indicate that the printers believed their trade to be on a sufficiently sound basis in Bunmahon to justify earning a living on.

In the summer of 1857 a donation of £150 was made to the printing school which Doudney decided to use to erect a suitable building adjacent to the glebe house, which made sense as he had been paying rent on the existing printing house.[120] By October 1857 this had been completed, and Doudney announced that "a large and airy building is now inseparably connected with the parish, and admirably adapted for printing, industrial, or any other school or benevolent purposes."[121]

With the new building he was desirous to have more work to do, given that the two journals they were producing (*The Gospel Magazine*, and *Old Jonathan: The District and Parish Helper*), were insufficient to keep the staff occupied. He proposed to reprint the entire works of Thomas Goodwin as a result of suggestions repeatedly made to him. The plan was to publish the set in six volumes, one volume to appear every four months, the entire to be completed in two years, as with the Gill commentary. However, despite the fact that one person had offered to take one hundred copies and although he was prepared to expend his energy in the task, Doudney was reluctant to proceed unless he had evidence of firm commitments from readers of the *Gospel Magazine*.¹²² By this stage, as we shall see below, other difficulties had arisen that were to make Doudney's tenure in Bunmahon uncertain, thus putting the long-term viability of the printing school under threat.

Conclusion

The industrial printing school was operational in Bunmahon for less than eight years from October 1851 to February 1858. Two factors characterize the experience of the printing works. Firstly, the business model begun with Gill whereby subscribers were secured in advance to cover the cost of printing and publishing was not maintained with the subsequent works that were produced. Secondly, in contrast to his other educational endeavours which we will examine in the next chapter and which depended on a public appeal for funds, the printing school was started and maintained at Doudney's own personal expense. The one donation (£150) that was designed by the donor for the printing school, Doudney applied to the cost of erecting a new building for that purpose.¹²³ Nevertheless, in the long term the responsibility of all aspects of the enterprise was to prove too much for Doudney.

After Gill's commentary was first produced and then sold, Doudney was put to great expense and he and Collingridge were left with a large stock of titles on hand, including Keach's, *Metaphors* an order for whose printing had been submitted by Collingridge himself. The strategy was to do reprints in order to ensure a continuance of employment for the schools, but the result was an accumulation of stock left unsold.¹²⁴ In the long term such a process of increasing the stock simply to maintain the schools would prove to be unviable. Yet the failure of the printing enterprise was not in Doudney's mind the primary reason why he ultimately departed from Bunmahon. There were other contributory factors. In the interim Doudney initiated a number of other educational projects in the locality.

Chapter 4

Industry and Self-Reliance

Chapter 2 identified the fact that there were three schools in the parish of Monksland: one, a scriptural or parochial school, under the auspices of the Church Education Society, the other two under the National Board. All three were intended to cater for children seven years and older. The parochial school, which was adjacent to the church, had by 1854 a good attendance, and provided a secular and scriptural education.[1] At one o'clock the pupils had a meal and at two o'clock the girls were instructed in needlework, while the boys were occupied with the tasks associated with the agricultural school, which will be treated below. A visit to the school by an inspector, J.E. Cuppaige, in December, 1855 found that the teacher was efficient and intelligent, and an examination of the 29 children present found them to be satisfactory in their secular and religious knowledge.[2]

The printing school catered for the older and more mature children, but Doudney also showed a concern for the welfare of the very young of Bunmahon. Specifically, there was nothing to meet the needs of the many poor children aged less than seven years who wandered the streets half-starved. In response to this need Doudney decided to establish an infant school where the children would be instructed, fed, and clothed.

The Infant School

In a letter of February 2, 1852 printed in the *Gospel Magazine* he addressed readers as follows:

> "Will you allow me to appeal to you on behalf of the inhabitants of this district? I have been in sole charge as curate of the parish of Monksland... for upwards of four years, during which the very neglected condition of the younger Roman Catholic children of the neighbourhood has made me most anxious to establish an Infant School, but hitherto I have been unable to do so for want of a suitable building. I am happy, however, to say that a house adapted for the purpose has just come into my possession and all I want now is—funds. Will you kindly help me?"[3]

One estimate put the cost of conducting the school at £50 annually made up of a teacher's salary (£30), and incidental expenses (£20); though Doudney's own estimate was £60 or £70.[4] However, soon after he had made known his intention to set up the school, funds began to arrive from people in England. Thus over the next few months funds arrived or were pledged with initial amounts of £3.3s. in February 1852, in March, £13.11s.6d., in April £28.10s., in May £15.17s.4d., in June and July £8.9s., and by October £38.12s.6d. and other amounts, much of these funds being obtained through the distribution of collection cards.[5] There was an appeal also from Doudney for cast off children's clothing which could be forwarded to Collingridge in London and from thence to Bunmahon.[6]

A building for a school such as the one envisaged by Doudney was difficult to secure as anything suitable was occupied by persons associated with the mines, the coast guard, or the police. A reflection of the lack of accommodation was the fact that at the time (1852) Doudney himself had no glebe house in the area to reside in, forcing him either to live initially in Annestown, four miles away, or to rent a cottage at a high rent in the area, which he did for four years.[7]

Eventually Doudney, as we have seen, erected a glebe house for which he entered into a lease with the College of Physicians for ten acres at 30s. per acre upon which property a house suitable for a clergyman was to be erected and paid for out of a government fund for the improvement of small livings.[8]

On this property stood a cottage which he thought suitable for conversion to a schoolhouse. The building, however, was in a very dilapidated state. He had resolved to reroof it with slate when the materials from another cottage about two miles distant became available necessitating their transportation to the school site such that it took a fortnight for all to be ready.[9] In fact, as matters transpired, the cottage had to be completely reconditioned for use as a schoolhouse. For instance, the roof which was of thatch was in a very defective state and it was resolved to completely reroof it with slates. Everything apart from the outer walls were knocked down, when it was discovered that water was seeping through the clay floor.[10] On May 22, 1852 Doudney reported to readers of the *Gospel Magazine*: "We hoped to have had it in full operation by this time; but, upon inspecting the roof, and the walls, and the drainage, we found it was necessary entirely to unroof the building, excavate here and there; so that, in fact, we have now, with the exception of a small portion of the outer walls, an entirely new and spacious house."[11]

Infant School building. Source: *GM* 52 (1852), 301 indicating its dimensions were 70 x 18½ ft.; while *Memoir* 155 says they were 70 x 20 ft. in the clear.).

By July 1852 the conversion of the building had been carried out, and on completion it measured 66 ft. by 21 ft. The schoolroom itself measured 39 ft. by 16 ft.9 ins., and in addition special accommodation for the mistress was provided; also a scullery, out-offices, and a gallery were constructed. By July 1852, a female teacher had been engaged for the school, and a set of prints for the walls donated and installed.[12]

Only verbal rather than public notice was given in advance of the school's opening. It was scheduled to open on August 2, 1852 and when it did so it had an eventful first month in operation.[13] On the first day, Monday August 2, three Protestant and sixteen Catholic children all under seven years of age attended. Through the generosity of subscribers to the *Gospel Magazine* a large quantity of clothing was sent and given to the children who needed it. Doudney decided to retain it as a reward for attendance.[14] The children also received a "plain and simple meal of 'stir-about' made from Indian meal and skim milk" which cost each child ½ d. per day. He saw the provision of a meal not as a bribe but as a vital necessity as otherwise the children could not learn on an empty stomach, a condition evidence of which he found at one of the local national schools.[15] His motives were recalled by his daughter Emily: "Father started the Infant School, but soon found it was necessary to feed the poor children if any good was to be done with them, so once a day a meal of good Indian meal stirabout was provided with milk."[16] Exemplary of how the meal made a material difference was the case of three small children who attended the school whose father was ill in hospital for weeks, whose brother was employed in the printing school he being the sole source of stable income for the support of the entire family, and whose mother was only able to secure a few days' work in the fields.[17]

On Wednesday four of the Catholic children were absent, three of whom belonged to a family suffering from fever, and they may have withdrawn either because of intimidation or because they were disappointed in not receiving clothing.[18] By Friday of the first week attendance rose to 3 Protestants and 22 Catholics.[19] Numbers continued to rise gradually until on Thursday, August 19, 35 children were present and attendance for a while remained at an average of 30, while on October 25 it was 43 (39 Catholics, 4 Protestants).[20] Despite an outbreak of sickness, probably fever, early in the year, by March 1853 Doudney could report that the average attendance for the month of February was 61. By Christmas attendance stood at between 50 and 60 pupils, most of them Catholics.[21] Clearly the infant school was filling a need in the community.

Infant School class. Source: *PO*, 18.

From his own resources Doudney could not afford to finance the infant school indefinitely simply because out of his curate's salary of £80 he had to deduct a third for rent, but even so he put forward £30 in advance of receiving donations.[22] In fact, the financial backing for the infant school and for Doudney's other educational projects at Bunmahon came from donations made by readers of the *Gospel Magazine*. Doudney apparently felt that the initial funds being donated through the *Magazine* were insufficient because in February 1853 he was in Nottingham at a meeting organized specifically to raise money for the infant school in Bunmahon.[23]

In September 1853 a reader made a proposal that treasurers be appointed for towns and villages in England who would be responsible for receiving contributions from subscribers of the *Gospel Magazine*, keeping receipt books, and forwarding the amounts for the use of the different educational initiatives in Bunmahon, including the infant school.[24] Doudney welcomed this suggestion and by 1855 treasurers for the Bunmahon schools were in existence in Astley, Birmingham, Bedfordshire, Bath, Dover, London (4), Lancashire, Manchester, Nottingham, Oakham, Plymouth, Portsmouth, Southampton, and Winsford.[25] The formation of this network is witness to how extensive a support system Doudney was able to draw on for the infant school.

Considerable funds must have been sent as a result for by December 1853 a total of £405.10s.4½d. was recorded as received in the *Gospel Magazine*. Upon his return from his fundraising tour, Doudney reported in February 1853, that there had been a great deal of sickness in the locality, many had succumbed including one of the infant school children, and though many of the other infants in the school were sick, the average monthly attendance stood at 61, although there were over 70 on the books.[26]

By January 1854 Doudney was in a position to publish an account of the various ways he had allocated the subscriptions sent to him for the infant school. Up to December 1853 a total of £405.10s.4½d. had been donated to the school, the vast majority of donors being from England, the exception where identities and locations are given being Rev. Thomas Power, Clashmore, Doudney's predecessor as curate.[27] What must be noted from this balance of accounts is that while most of the money went towards providing and equipping a suitable and commodious schoolhouse, a considerable sum was spent feeding and clothing the children. New clothes for each child accounted for part of £20, while the second largest item of expenditure of the entire operation —over £104—was spent on providing Indian meal, rice, and milk. Even this total for clothing and food by themselves (£124) was far in excess of Doudney's own estimate (£70) of the annual cost of running the infant school. As such it either reflects a gross miscalculation on his part or the phenomenal success of the school in meeting local needs.

As well as the daily ration a special feast was given every Christmas where, in addition to food and drink, new clothes were distributed. Thus the Christmas party held in December 1853 was attended by 70 children who feasted on a large dinner (consisting of soup, beef, bread, and plum pudding, a fare the majority of children would not have tasted before) under the gaze of the gentry and clergy of the area; while later 50 children of the parochial and printing schools had tea.[28] The annual Christmas feast reportedly received coverage in the *Illustrated London News* in February, 1855.[29] The provision of food and clothes then as well as the general education must have been important factors in inducing the children to attend the school. Doudney himself was convinced that such things contributed to "the improved health and appearance of the scholars."

Infant School Christmas feast.
Source: *Try and Try Again*, 177.

A visitor to the school in early October 1854 reported that the children, who numbered between 30 and 40 at the time of his visit, were engaged in singing hymns and being made acquainted with

Bible stories, as well as general instruction.[30] The average attendance for October, 1855 was 47, the same number when an inspector, J.E. Cuppaidge, visited in December of that year.[31] He was satisfied that the school was well conducted and the children well cared for in witness of which he noted that they received one meal a day and clothing occasionally.[32] Once they had completed their studies, children from the infant school proceeded to the parochial school and were placed in either the printing or agricultural schools (boys) or the embroidery school (girls).[33]

Doudney's founding of the infant school, likely prompted the establishment of the Bunmahon (Female) school in September, 1852 under the management of Rev. Michael Power. While Doudney was opposed to having his own schools under the National Board, he had no objection to Rev. Power's school doing so.[34] Yet despite such equanimity, as we shall see below, the infant school was to become the source of sectarian conflict.

The Agricultural School

The pupils proceeded from the infant to the parochial school and attached to the latter was an agricultural school in which the boys gained a practical knowledge of husbandry. When first established in 1854 the class consisted of 18 boys ranging in age between 10 and 15 years, though this number later declined to 12 boys.[35] The boys underwent regular instruction by an agricultural teacher who acquainted them with the various methods of farm practice such as crop rotation and soil preparation. The instructor was W.S. Moore who was also the teacher in the parochial school. In terms of instruction, he was primarily concerned to inculcate in the boys an understanding of crop rotation, ridging, furrowing, crop adaptability to the seasons, the effects of cropping on the soil, and the composition of different soils.[36] For instruction purposes,

Moore used various textbooks including agricultural class books published by the National Board.³⁷

The Agricultural School. Source: *Try and Try Again*, 179.

The main practical activity of the school was the growing of experimental crops on ground situated on the cliffs, specially laid out for the purpose. Attempts in 1854 to grow an acre and a half of oats and to save hay were a failure, likely because of this exposed situation. It was decided to concentrate on the growing of green crops and with these the school had relatively more success. The boys were very eager and they showed great energy in hoeing and preparing the ground with forks. For the year 1855 a number of vegetable crops including mangels, turnips, parsnips, carrots and potatoes were attempted. Of these the turnips, mangels, and parsnips turned out fairly well, though the carrots were a partial failure due to the badness of the seed but of those that came up, most were of good quality. More critically, the potato crop was not successful and had to be dug up, and the cleared area then sown with winter vetches, peas, and rye, using seeds supplied by Suttons of Reading.

In 1855 the agricultural school produced over 65 tons of vegetables from about 2 acres of land, with mangels being the best crop and potatoes and carrots turning out worst.[38] Lack of good crop yields was ascribed to bad soil, weeds, and the absence of good manure.[39]

Not only were crop yields generally depressing but the financial accounts of the agricultural school for 1855 show it to be running at a partial loss. Relatively large amounts were spent on labour, manure, and particularly the instructor's salary, while only a small sum was spent on seeds.

Despite the loss of £12.10s.10½d. in 1855 the farm school did continue. In his report Moore regretted that supervision of the farm took up so much of his time (by estimation from 2 p.m. to 6 p.m. daily) that he was not able to devote sufficient attention to the actual instruction of the boys in agriculture, an activity that was also curtailed by his duties in the parochial school. He tried to make up for this by imparting some agricultural knowledge while the boys were engaged in work on the farm, or when the weather prohibited work on the farm they stayed at school for instruction. Initially, the boys' lack of reading skills inhibited progress but when they gained a facility with reading, Moore was hoping to acquire some cheap books in agricultural science for them.[40]

Despite these worthy aspirations, during 1856 the number of boys attending the school declined. Two of the boys left the locality altogether and went to Portlaw, three more went to work in the mines and four more went as helpers on farms in the district. Moore did not object to the latter development because he saw it as one of the objects of the farm school that the boys would eventually find positions on farms. However he did regret the fact that these boys having left were denied the chance of further education.

During 1856 the fortunes of the agricultural school do not seem to have improved any great deal. Again the crops sown experienced only a partial success, but this may have been due to the adverse weather conditions in 1856 which were unfavourable to green crops. Mangels, which had been the most worthwhile crop in 1855, had to be sown twice and the second sowing was made in very dry weather. The result was that the mangel crop produced only 18 tons per acre. The other crops fared no better, with turnips realizing only 17 tons per acre, parsnips 6 tons, flax 12 cwt. of flax straw, and three-quarters of the carrot crop failed. When the flax crop was cut the ground was used to plant winter vetches and rye, which Moore said would be worth £2 or more if they turned out any way fair.

The greatest challenge, as identified by Moore, was that the farm could never be self-supporting given the limited scale of it operations.[41] Additional acres were needed for this purpose. To make it pay for itself there needed to be sufficient employment for the boys, or else they would have recourse to unproductive work.[42]

The financial accounts of the agricultural school for 1856 serve to enhance an already dismal picture. The institution seems to have operated at a continuing loss. Losses for 1856 had nearly trebled from the previous year to nearly £36. The reason for this loss must lie in the fact that so little was spent on seeds and supplies while an excessive amount went towards paying labour. This situation was certainly no help to the school maintaining itself.

Moore had reasons of his own to explain why his school was not progressing with the expected momentum. He explained in his report of January 1857 that "the farm as it stands as present is not, nor can never be self-supporting so long as we continue to work on such a limited scale.... there must be sufficient remunerative employment for the boys."[43] The under-employment of the boys, Moore claimed, was a hindrance to the expansion of the agricultural school and could only inevitably lead to stagnation. Continuing his report he stated that, "During the past year I had frequently to put boys to work that in itself was unproductive, though the wages paid were the same as usual... This would not have been the case had we more land to work....I feel warranted in asking for an addition of a few acres to the farm."⁴⁴ Moore, in addition, ascribed the lack of progress of the agricultural school to an insufficient acreage to grow the crops, resulting in the under-employment of the students. Nevertheless, there were at the outset of 1857, ten boys attending the agricultural school, with the prospect of more joining.⁴⁵

These reasons seem plausible enough, but in addition it is evident that the agricultural school did not receive as much financial support as the printing and infant schools did. Certainly appeals for funds for the agricultural school were not as frequent nor as insistent in the pages of the *Gospel Magazine*, as they were for Doudney's other educational efforts in Bunmahon. Nevertheless, some benefit locally was achieved from all this as boys from the agricultural school were placed with local farmers.⁴⁶

The Embroidery School

Following the foundation of the infant school, Doudney recognized a need to open a girls' industrial school, given the number of grown up girls and young women who were unemployed in the village. It was proposed that the work they would be engaged in would be that of embroidery for which a London firm had advanced an order for such work from the school.⁴⁷ As with Doudney's other schools the embroidery school maintained itself from donations made by readers of the *Gospel Magazine*. Doudney first asked for financial support for the embroidery school in July 1853 when he appealed to motivated readers to acquire collecting cards and have interested parties contribute 1d. or 2d. weekly. Soon the necessary funds began to accumulate and by January 1854, for instance, Doudney was able to acknowledge £25.12s.6d. donated for the support of the embroidery school.⁴⁸

Although Doudney made an initial appeal for funds from readers of the *Gospel Magazine* to set up the school, it was his hope that within a year the establishment would be self-supporting.⁴⁹

The appeal was a success for a house near the printing school was acquired and fitted out for the purpose. By December 1853 a visitor to Bunmahon could report that the school employed 28 girls who were instructed in the skills of sewing muslin and embroidery.[50] Doudney's daughter, Emily, later recalled the difference the school made in the lives of the girls:

> "The girls were wonderfully clever; a first-rate teacher was engaged for them, they learned to do the most exquisite open work and embroidery for which a ready sale was found in England. In six months girls who had been almost beggars were neatly clothed and looking so pretty…"[51]

The girls were taught by a mistress, supervised by Doudney's wife Eliza and by December 1853 their rate of pay was from 1s. to 2s.6d. and by 1855 from 4s. to 7s. (some 6s. to 7s.) each per week.[52] They were also provided with a free daily dinner. Attendance at the school was voluntary, and they also attended voluntarily the Thursday and Sunday evening lectures and Bible reading conducted in the infant school.[53] By the autumn of 1854, the twelve girls who attended the Sunday morning class were, with the exception of two, able to read the Bible for themselves.[54] Of those who attended the weekly evening class, six had by the same date made progress in learning to write, while their skills in mathematics were also improving, to the extent that they were able to calculate what they would have to pay for a certain number of yards of material, how long it would take for their earnings to be sufficient to purchase it, and then the cost of labour to make it before they could wear the result.[55]

The Embroidery School.
Source: *PO*, 22.

By 1855 the work of the embroidery school had expanded greatly. By that year interested ladies could purchase collars (from 2s. 9d.), sleeves (from 4s. 6d.), balloons (from 5s. 6d.), and cuffs. Those women who so wished could send their patterns and muslin to Mrs. Doudney at Bunmahon, and she would arrange to "have it embroidered neatly and expeditiously at the school." The work of the school was available for purchase at the Soho Bazaar, London, Mr. Wilkinson's, Chamber Street, Nottingham, Mrs. Luscombe's, High Street, Tunbridge Wells, and at Mrs. J. Doudney, Pelhari Place, Brixton, and Surrey.[56] During 1855 about £300 was paid in wages to the girls in the school, and many of them were able to appear in new clothing.[57] By December 1856 when an inspector came to visit, the school was accommodating between 20 and 30 girls who at that stage earned from 4s. to 7s. per week for the work they did.[58] Doudney was well pleased that by 1855 the girls in the embroidery school were earning an honest livelihood, were healthy and well clothed, and were gainfully employed.

Altogether, Doudney believed that the work of the embroidery school transformed the girls from "listlessness" and "slovenliness" to a situation where there was a "steady application, cleanliness of person, and altogether improved deportment." Such improvement was to the extent that "many that owe their habits of self-dependence to this school are now married."[59] The girls did well for themselves, many of them eventually emigrating to America.[60] The embroidery school was, compared to the agricultural school, one of the more successful of Doudney's initiatives in the educational and industrial realm.

With the development of the embroidery school, Doudney had evolved a complete educational provision for the children of the area. From the infant school the children proceeded to the parochial or scriptural school (where it was said they received "a good plain education"), with the girls taught needlework in the afternoon while the boys were occupied with the tasks of the agricultural school.[61] In time the older girls proceeded to the embroidery school, while some of the boys went on to the printing school. A final educational initiative was the Bible repository.

Bible Repository

The paucity of bibles available for distribution in Ireland was a concern to many who wished all Irish people to have access to the Word of God. As early as December 1848, Doudney was able to report that there were forty Catholics in groups in the immediate neighbourhood reading their "Irish Bibles" in their cabins until the early hours.[62] By "Irish Bibles" he meant not bibles in the Irish language, which as already noted above was in decline in the area, but likely the Douay Version of Scripture.

George Cowell of Birmingham, who had suggested to Doudney the idea of establishing a system of local treasurers to gather and convey funds for the Bunmahon schools, was also the one who in November, 1853 advocated the setting up of a Bible repository in the village.[63] It was eventually located in the same building as the embroidery school.[64] So far as funding this initiative, Cowell proposed the establishment of the Bunmahon Bible Fund to be overseen by Doudney and for interested supporters to send twelve postage stamps to him the equivalent price of three copies of the New Testament which could then be distributed locally.[65] At the end of 1853, £5.7s.2d., between January and May 1854, £20.0s.3d., and in November, 1855, £31.15s. 8d. had been donated for the purpose.[66] At a later date some of these funds were used to purchase supplies from the Waterford Auxiliary Bible Society.[67] The idea was to supply bibles and testaments at a reduced rate.

Doudney supported the initiative because it would fill a general need whereby bibles would circulate in the area, and a particular one given the level of emigration from the village and surrounding area. It was his hope that the bible depot would supply a bible to every emigrant leaving the area.

In support of the idea, Doudney cited the case of a poor farmer who in 1853 was preparing to depart for America, having to leave his wife and children behind. Doudney was able to empathize with him for, as we have seen, he had lost a wife and children to illness years before. At the time his comfort was the Bible and on that basis he offered the farmer a copy which he accepted. Doudney was later informed that the ship the farmer sailed on from Liverpool with 700 or 800 passengers experienced an outbreak of cholera (causing 60 bodies to be thrown overboard), the Bunmahon farmer assisted the reduced crew to work the ship, and the ship was eventually forced to dock at Cork; all this experience evoking in some of the passengers from Bunmahon a remembrance of some of the cautionary words Doudney had spoken.[68]

Conclusion

Doudney's purpose in all these educational initiatives can be summed up in his statement: "to give permanency to the system of industry and self-reliance."[69] The intention was not to create dependence but to encourage the development of skills and industriousness. It was clear to visitors to the area that the various educational and printing establishments inaugurated by Doudney were having a beneficial effect on the condition of the young people of the area. One such visitor was H. Whitney, who had lived in the area but had left before Doudney's arrival in 1847, returned for a visit to Bunmahon in 1857 while Doudney was absent in London. Whitney commented on the improvements he observed, particularly, the "cleanliness and comparative independence; the boys, many of whom I am sure, would not have known the luxury of shoes and stockings, are now well clad and industrious in earning their daily bread; and the girls had their work schools, also, with [a] town clock on their establishment."[70]

Clearly visitors were struck by the improvements. However, despite the tangible evidence of progress, the initiatives taken by Doudney met with local opposition, the theological basis for which we now turn to.

CHAPTER 5

THEOLOGICAL PRIMER

IT IS POSSIBLE TO EXPLAIN in a narrative way the religious controversies that emerged in Bunmahon in terms of processes, dynamics, and reactions in a given historical context. However, such an approach would be deficient if the essential theological points of difference are not elucidated and related to these controversies. Such an exercise is necessary in order to understand the nature of the religious conflict that took place. It will help us understand why people believed certain things so trenchantly, why the two worldviews collided, and what motivated and informed the opposing sides. This chapter, therefore, seeks to outline the basic theological positions as a prelude to understanding the conflict which is detailed in the next two chapters. The intention is not to simplify or summarize complex doctrines but to outline the essential background information so that the issues of religious difference are made comprehensible.

The church in which Rev. Doudney ministered, that is the Church of Ireland (or more accurately the United Church of England and Ireland as it was after the Act of Union (1801) until its disestablishment in 1869), in its theological identity saw the Bible, prayer, and the sacraments as foundational, for in each of these three areas the Christian believer encountered God and as such were essential sources for nurturing faith. For Roman Catholics there was less emphasis on the Bible and more on tradition, the sacraments, and allegiance to the institutional church generally and more particularly to the papacy, as sources of spiritual nurture and authority. In what follows, we will examine these features and the denominational emphases around them. The two basic areas of contention were over the Bible and the sacraments, with attendant issues around authority, freedom, and practice.[1]

The Bible

A modern Irish poet and academic of Catholic background has written candidly: "Very few Irish people know much about the Bible. It's a Protestant book. There is, mind you, a Catholic version called the Douai Bible, but it is rhetorical and sloppy and elaborately imprecise, a badly written thing. Good Irish Catholics know next to nothing about the Bible. That is a book for 'the other side.'"[2] The sentiments expressed in this quotation are reflective of a broader historical reality whose nature is pertinent to the present study. Its elucidation requires us to examine the essential beliefs of the Protestant Reformers of the sixteenth century and the Catholic response to the same.

The Reformers believed in the principle of *sola scriptura* (Scripture alone), i.e. that the Bible alone teaches what people need to know and is the single source of authority in matters of religion. Against such an authority, popes, councils and traditions were mere human inventions. For the Reformers and their successors, the Bible as the Word of God was foundational for from it was derived all Christian belief and practice. Because it was the Word of God the Bible had authority. Hence it was the standard and source from which belief was derived. It could be quoted in order to validate or refute points of view, decisions, or actions.

In addition, there was a belief in the sufficiency of Scripture by which was meant that only those doctrines deriving from Scripture were necessary for salvation. This doctrine was set out clearly in the Articles of Religion of the Church of England and Ireland (#6): "Holy Scripture containeth all things necessary to salvation: so that whatsoever is not read therein, nor may be proved thereby, is not to be required of any man, that it should be believed as an article of the Faith, or be thought requisite or necessary for salvation."[3]

Implicit in this were inter-related questions about the authenticity of the biblical text, its translation, and its interpretation. Illustrative of the issues here is an exchange regarding the Bible in 1853. In the midst of the controversy over the infant school, Doudney wrote an address dated June 17, 1853 directed to the inhabitants of Bunmahon.[4] In it he addressed the question of authority in the Roman Catholic Church and its relationship with the issue of access to the Bible. He pointed to the basis of papal and priestly claims to authority as deriving ultimately from the verse in Matthew 16:18 where Jesus is recorded as saying: "And I tell you, that you are Peter, and on this rock I will build my church, and the gates of Hades will not overcome it." If Scripture was to be resorted to in this way as the basis of papal and priestly authority, Doudney queried why in other respects its usefulness was dismissed and people denied access to it whereby they might benefit from its insights. This denial of access Doudney attributed to the action of the priests whose motivation, he claimed, was self-protective.

To prove his point Doudney engaged in a comparative exercise contrasting the behaviour of Jesus (as recounted in John 8: 3–11, Mark 8: 1–9, and Luke 7: 11–16) with priestly practice, noting the deviation of the latter from the former. The first of these (John 8: 3–11) recounted the forgiveness shown by Jesus to the adulterous woman, which Doudney contrasted with the treatment meted out by the priest towards the widowed mother following her refusal to withdraw her children from the infant school. The second (Mark 8: 1–9) recounted Jesus' performance of the miracle of the loaves and fishes whereby four thousand were fed; while the third (Luke 7: 11–16) recorded the raising from the dead of the widow's son of Nain. Doudney contrasted the action of Jesus in both these cases with the opportune moment chosen by the priests to implement the sanction of excommunication imposed on unfortunate people who had sent their children to the infant school where they had been educated, fed, and clothed.

Doudney's point in all this was to contrast the generous behaviour of Jesus as recorded in these New Testament passages (in reference to which Doudney quoted from the Catholic translation of the Bible) with the practices of the priests in the locality; and secondly, to point out by implication, that if the people themselves were allowed access to the Scriptures they could discern this contrast for themselves.

Ultimately the import of all this recalled a fundamental point of the Reformers of the sixteenth-century, i.e. allowing ordinary people access to the Word of God in the Bible was as much about power as it was about nurturing spiritual growth. For, placing the Bible in the hands of the people meant they were freed from the control of the clergy. Church authorities might fear such a development since it would allow common people to make an evaluation of how the Church and its clergy were performing on the issues of teaching and morality.

A fundamental principle of the Reformation was the right of all believers to read and interpret Scripture for themselves without fear that its essential message would be elusive, and without having to have an accompanying interpretation supplied by a pope or ecclesiastical bodies, as Catholics did. This principle was consistent with a broader Protestant emphasis on individual freedom and initiative. It was asserted that the plain sense or meaning of the Bible could be understood by ordinary believers. In the case of more difficult or more obscure parts, these could normally be understood through reference to other, clearer passages. In an instance of this and anticipating potential objections from his readers that the content of the Bible was too difficult for them, Doudney cited various passages (Hebrews 10:12, Matthew 11:28–30, 26:46, Ecclesiastes 12:14, Isaiah 55:1, Revelation 22:17) from the Douay Version of the Bible to illustrate that the plain sense of Scripture could be easily understood by all.[5]

The Catholic objection to this position was that allowing the ordinary person access to the Bible without the complementary interpretations supplied by the Church could only lead to a harmful diversity of opinions. The Catholic Church argued that the meaning of biblical passages was not always self-evident and that ordinary Christians needed help in uncovering and interpreting such passages. It was here that the teaching authority of the Church was instrumental in providing such interpretation in a standard way. On this point Catholic theologians argued that the Church had over the centuries accumulated a considerable scholarly tradition which could be deployed for understanding Scripture. So highly was the status of such tradition regarded that the Council of Trent (1546–64), which convened in the wake of the Reformation to reform the Catholic Church and respond to the Protestant challenge, advanced the notion that tradition and the Bible itself constituted equal sources for doctrine and morals, an equivalence Protestants were dismissive of. Thus Protestants did not place the same store on tradition as a source of authority as the Roman Catholic Church did.

What did the council mean by tradition? Why might it have an authority parallel to that of Scripture? And why might Protestants oppose it? In general tradition meant the Christian faith handed down over the centuries. However, in the middle ages the practice arose of using tradition to justify practices and beliefs not found in the Bible, for instance concerning the Virgin Mary. The Reformers, while they had a high regard for tradition represented by the writings of the early church fathers and the creeds, insisted that all tradition needed to be subject to or tested by the Bible. The Roman Catholic Church, however, continued to regard tradition handed down from the apostles as authoritative in its own right. The problem was that many such traditions were clearly later in origin than apostolic times. The result was to equate tradition with specific beliefs and practices separate from what was contained in the Bible. In the mind of someone like Doudney or Daly, this duality came to operate for

Catholics in such a way that tradition assumed a greater importance than the Word of God itself.

In response to Catholic charges that allowing individuals to study the Bible held out the danger of disseminating different meanings, Protestants, while maintaining that it was the right of the individual to read the Bible, stressed that interpretation was not just a matter for the individual only. It was an exercise conducted as part of the body of believers and drew on a rich heritage of interpretation down the centuries. While these elements together would assist in arriving at a clear understanding, in no way did this imply that such traditions of interpretation were equal or superior to Scripture itself.

Catholics argued against the pre-eminence given by the Reformers to the Bible on the grounds that since it was the Church that had determined the canon of Scripture (i.e. what books were included in it), it followed that the Church had authority over the Bible. The Protestant response to this was that it was neither the Church that had made the Bible, nor the Bible that had made the Church, but the gospel of Jesus Christ that had made both the Bible and the Church. Thus ultimate authority did not rest either in the Church or in the Bible but in the gospel, the message of Jesus Christ. However, since Scripture provided a more reliable witness to that gospel than the Church ruled by the papacy, or even Christian tradition, the Bible had authority over Church, pope, and tradition. These were fundamental differences.

Translation

One of the great legacies of the Reformation was to make the Bible available in vernacular languages. Up until that time it was only available in Latin for a select few who were the educated elite in the West. Beginning with John Wycliffe, then William Tyndale, and culminating with the Authorized Version published in 1611 under the aegis of King James I, Protestants responded to the need to have an accessible version in English. In Ireland, translations of the Bible into the Irish language date from the early 17th century onward. The Roman Catholic translation of the Bible came with the Douay-Rheims version, dating from 1582. One of the decrees of the Council of Trent stipulated that the Latin translation of the Bible (the Vulgate) was authoritative in matters of doctrine. This went against the preference of the Reformers who wanted to put God's Word into the hands of the people in a language they understood.

Illustrative of the dangers of utilizing tradition were the inaccuracies and hence misunderstandings that derived therefrom. Protestants since the Reformation were vigilant in pointing this out in Catholic translations of key verses. Local Waterford readership of the press would have been aware of this effort. In 1856, for instance, *The Waterford Mail* reproduced a letter from Rev. Thomas Mills, Blackrock, Dublin, to Rev. D. McCarthy, professor of sacred scripture, at Maynooth.[6] In it Mills communicated his understanding that the Roman Catholic Church wished to make the Douay Version of the Bible more widely available to the lower classes. While he commended this initiative, Mills was anxious to convey his concerns regarding the Douay translation which, in his opinion, was not "wholly free from error."

In proof of this assertion he cited the example of Matthew 3:2 which in the Authorized (King James) Version stated: "And saying, *repent ye* for the kingdom of heaven is at hand," but which in the Douay Version translated as: "And saying, *do penance* for the kingdom etc." To the latter a note was added in the Douay text explaining the phrase "do penance" which stated: "Do penance? *Poenitantem agite* —which word according to the use of the Scriptures and the Holy Fathers, does not only signify repentance and amendment of life, but also punishing past sins by fasting and such like penitential exercises." Querying which of the two was the most correct, Rev. Mills cited other passages (Mark 1: 15, Luke 17:4, Acts 3: 19, Revelation 2: 21) which in the Douay Version gave the translation exactly as in the Authorized Version, that is "Repent" only. Nor was the Roman Catholic translation of the term found in authoritative Greek lexicon sources notably that by Liddell and Scott which quoted the different meanings of words in the New Testament, nor did it include the idea presented in the additional note.

Why should all this matter? Was this just a difference of opinion among biblical scholars? Was it just an exercise in denominational rivalry and intransigence? For Rev. Mills the answer was clear: "it is of some consequence whether men are told, as on the authority of God, to repent, that is, to change their minds and opinions, or to lash, excoriate, or otherwise punish themselves for their past sins, by fasting and such like penitential exercises." Clearly inaccuracy in translation had serious implications for the correct understanding of the meaning and intent of Scripture, the exercise of priestly authority deriving therefrom, and for a whole range of religious practices among Catholics.

The status of the Bible as the authoritative Word of God was of vital concern for Doudney. That is why he was offended by a number of insensitive acts concerning it locally, which no doubt added to the emotional stress he felt in his final years in Bunmahon. In one such act of hostility towards him, pages from the Bible were ripped out and scattered along part of the road where it was known he would pass on his way to church.[7] He was particularly incensed in August 1852 when part of the New Testament was brought to him having been torn to pieces and cast on the seashore by a man whom Doudney categorized as "one of the more respectable neighbours."[8] When confronted by Doudney with this act, the man admitted it and declared that he felt it his duty to destroy a Bible or a Book of Common Prayer (the Church of Ireland prayer book) anytime either one came his way.[9] Such acts were clearly provocative and demeaning.

The experience caused Doudney to write an open letter to the Catholic inhabitants of the area in which he decried the act. Deploying his gift of communicating with ordinary people, he likened the Bible to a letter and expressed the view that had they received a letter from friends or relatives in America they would be unlikely to tear it up because of the value of the information it contained. On the basis of this analogy, Doudney queried: Why would we then want to tear up the Bible if we knew it was God's letter in love to us?[10] The incident bore witness to a lack of respect for the Bible as God's Word.

Justification By Faith

If the first great attribute of Reformation theology is the doctrine that the Bible is the final authority for Christians, then the second is that salvation is gained by faith alone (*sola fide*) and not by good works. Christian orthodoxy maintained that salvation is by faith alone, does not result from human effort, and as such is a free, unmerited gift of God. In contrast to the humanists of the day who asserted that human beings could exercise their will and thereby could choose to believe, sixteenth-century Reformers like Martin Luther maintained that humans were too corrupted by sin to make such a choice. For the Reformers like Luther good works on our part do not achieve salvation: they may result from it, but they cannot attain it. We cannot earn salvation from sin through our own performance of good works for these are the result not the basis of justification. Instead the believer is justified on the basis of faith alone.

Salvation depends on grace alone (*sola gratia*) which makes humans just in the eyes of God and is a free gift wholly independent of human actions. Grace was made available once and for all in the sacrificial death of Jesus Christ on the cross. God sent his only son, Jesus, through whose death and resurrection we are released from guilt and made children of God. God's grace is the basis of our justification. Salvation from sin is a gift because it is achieved at the price of Jesus' death. Faith is the means whereby justification becomes our own. It is our response to this great act of God.

Protestant theology maintained that the doctrine of justification by faith did not imply that God was indifferent to sin, or that he freely forgives us as if our sin was of no consequence. Since God is holy he is repelled by sin. We who sin are subject to God's judgment. Complementary to this, however, is the fact that God forgives, which is the good news of the gospel. What makes it good news is that it overpowers the gravity of our sin. The practical implication was that the believer at any one time was both sinful and justified. We do not cease to sin once we are justified rather a sense of justification highlights how sinful we are. We are sinners and justified believers. God declares us to be just even while we are still sinners. Developed by Luther, justification by faith was based on the consideration that the individual could have a direct relationship with God, that it was based on faith, and on a confidence in the salvation achieved by Christ's death and resurrection.

On this basis there was no longer any necessity for intermediaries (such as Mary or the saints) between human beings and God. The doctrine of justification undermined the entire cult of the saints so central to Catholic spirituality in the middle ages and later. As part of this cult, the saints were believed to play a part in one's salvation through their intervention and prayer. But the doctrine of justification held that Christ's death achieved everything in terms of salvation and the saints could add nothing to it. Similarly, in the belief of the Reformers, the intermediate state of purgatory and the sale of indulgences were unnecessary since salvation was a free gift of God in Jesus Christ, received by faith. However, at the Council of Trent the Catholic Church affirmed that justification was based on good works performed through collaboration between grace and the believer.

The Reformers claimed the focus on Mary as intercessor had developed in the middle ages and detracted from the centrality of Jesus as saviour and messiah. However, the Catholic Church continued its veneration of the Virgin Mary to the extent, during Doudney's time in Bunmahon, of issuing a decree making official the doctrine (and hence belief) of the immaculate conception (1854). This went beyond what the New Testament said or early Christian thought maintained, and hence the whole tendency of Catholics to go beyond what was in Scripture was again suspect to Protestants.

Consideration of justification and other matters devolved in large part on the nature of authority and the Church. The Roman Catholic view was that the "Church" is Christ's body on earth, based on Christ's giving of authority to the apostle Peter to build the Church. The successors of Peter, the bishops of Rome, were seen as sharing this authority. From this belief the pope formally proclaimed the doctrine of infallibility (1870), which held that since the pope is Christ's vicar (or representative) on earth God will not allow the Church to fall into error.

Protestants held that while individuals can be in relationship with God that also takes place corporately in the Church. The doctrine that every Christian is a member of the priesthood of believers meant that access to God was no longer controlled by a hierarchical priesthood. Thus in the community of believers, i.e. the Church or the body of Christ, each member is a priest for the rest. There was to be no basic distinction between clergy and laity. Both should receive communion in both kinds, while clergy should be allowed to marry. In addition, the Bible was important for the corporate life of Christians. When the Bible was read from at times of worship, this was a reminder that it was not merely intended for private instruction but was to be listened to communally.

Sacraments

For the Roman Catholic Church the sacraments were central to the Christian experience of God. A useful definition of a sacrament is "an outward and visible sign of an inward and spiritual grace, given to us by Christ himself, as a means whereby we receive this grace, and a pledge to assure us thereof."[11] The sacraments were viewed as the source of grace in special situations: for instance in baptism (for the removal of original sin), in confession (penance for forgiveness), and in the mass (for feeding on Christ).

The sixteenth century Reformers like Luther argued that for a rite to be a sacrament it must have been instituted by Christ and it must be a sign of, or specifically proclaim, the gospel. Based on such criteria, Luther concluded that there were only two sacraments: baptism and communion. While there might be other rites (confirmation, confession, matrimony, unction, and holy orders) that might be beneficial to believers in some way, they did not constitute sacraments in the true sense. The Catholic Church maintained that the rites rejected by Protestants were in fact sacraments also. It might be assumed that because baptism and communion were the two in common, there might be agreement as to their nature and import, but this was not the case.

Protestants and Catholics held the eucharist or holy communion with equal respect and devotion. They were central to the life of the Church. The issue of division from the time of the Reformation into modern times (and hence prevalent in the 1800s) related, firstly, to the character of the eucharistic elements (the consecrated bread and wine) in relation to the gathered congregation; and secondly, to the role of the priest in sacramental functions. The former we will now address, while the latter will be dealt with below.

Communion

Historically, while there has been an acknowledgement among Protestants and Roman Catholics of its centrality, there has been disagreement about the meaning and practice of communion. One difference is over terminology. Protestants use the terms holy communion, holy eucharist, the Lord's table, the breaking of bread, or the Lord's supper. Catholics speak of the altar, the eucharist, or the mass.

More specifically differences emerged over what happens to the bread and wine, and what happens to those present. Holy communion had its origins in the meal celebrated by Jesus on the night of his betrayal and arrest.[12] It was Jesus who instituted it and the New Testament understood it as a means of remembering his death on our behalf, as a way of drawing strength from our communion with him, and as an anticipation of the heavenly meal which will be inaugurated at his second coming.

When we say the eucharist was instituted by Jesus, what does this mean? It means that according to the New Testament accounts (Mark 14: 22–25, Matthew 26: 26–29, Luke 22: 15–20, 1 Cor. 11: 23–25) Jesus on the night before his crucifixion gathered with his disciples for the passover meal. At the meal Jesus took bread, gave thanks, broke it and distributed it with the words: "This is my body which is for you. Do this in remembrance of me." Then at the end of the meal, he continued with the cup, saying: "This cup is the new covenant in my blood. Do this, as often as you drink it, in remembrance of me." In total there were seven actions: he took the bread, he blessed it, he broke it, and he gave it. Then he took the cup, he blessed it, and he gave it. In the post-New Testament church believers accepted Jesus' words of institution: this is my body, this is my blood. As Christianity developed, these seven actions were reduced to four: taking the bread and cup, blessing the bread and wine, breaking the bread, and distributing the bread and cup. In liturgical terms these four actions are expressed as offertory, consecration, fraction, and communion.[13]

The eucharist was in the nature of a meal whereby the gathered community of baptized believers was fed spiritually, that is they ate and drank the spiritual body and blood of Christ, and were thereby nourished by divine life. The church fathers of the early church avoided trying to define what happened in the eucharist and the words of institution were accepted without much controversy.

However, during the middle ages the desire in the Church was for more concise teaching and doctrine. In the early thirteenth century, in a significant development the reforming pope, Innocent III, made the distinction between the form or appearance (bread and wine) and the real nature (body and blood of Christ) of the elements. From this developed the doctrine of transubstantiation, officially formulated at the Fourth Lateran Council in 1215 and later affirmed at the Council of Trent in the sixteenth century. It promulgated, and henceforth it was designated as the official doctrine of the Church, that when the priest pronounced the words of Christ, "This is my body" and "This is my blood", the elements of bread and wine were miraculously changed into the actual body and blood of Jesus. Following this they are then offered to God as a propitiatory sacrifice for sins and the gathered people worship them as the priest lifts them up. Then when the congregation partakes of the bread (though not the wine), they receive Jesus' body and blood.

The doctrine of transubstantiation was based on a philosophical supposition (proposed by Thomas Aquinas but derived from Aristotle) that all material things could be broken down into two parts: substance and accidents. Substance refers to the inner reality, that is, what makes a thing what it is. Accidents refer to the visible, external appearance of a thing. While such a distinction operates successfully at the level of logic, it does not in the measurable world. Thus it would be impossible to have substance in one hand and accidents in another. Nevertheless the logic had some validity when applied to the question of bread and wine, indeed in the hands of Aquinas it represented a synthesis between the philosophy of Aristotle and Christian thought. Thus the substance of the bread and wine changed to become the body and blood of Christ. The accident, however, does not change. Thus when the priest consecrated the bread and wine, these elements, though they retained their outward appearance (accidents), were changed in their essence (substance). So while the bread retained the attributes of taste, smell, and feel, its essence had changed into the body of Christ. Similarly with the wine which, while it retained its colour, taste and smell, was changed into the blood of Christ.

Thus the doctrine of transubstantiation held that there was no change in the external physical appearance, rather there was a real change at the level of the substance. This was what was adopted as the core of Roman Catholic doctrine and belief. But it raised many questions. For many, including Protestants, the difficulty was in accepting that reality can be divided into substance and accidents. Another was that the literal view lends itself to superstition and magic, for it suggested that the bread and wine were completely and actually changed into the body and blood of Christ, and hence are the same as the flesh of the person born of the Virgin Mary who lived in Palestine. How could it be exactly the same as such a body? Further, how could it be simultaneously present on so many altars or tables? The contrary Protestant view was that nothing actually happens to the bread and wine, and that if there is a transformation it is in the hearts of believers when they receive.

There were various Protestant views as to what was taking place at communion. The Lutheran position was that the glorified human nature of Jesus is really present in, with, and under the bread and wine (a doctrine known as consubstantiation). In other words what happened was that Christ's body and blood were received with the bread and wine. The position of the Swiss Reformer, Ulrich Zwingli, was that the bread and wine were symbols only, and that the stress should be placed on the remembrance aspect. The view adopted by the Anglican Reformers was that of John Calvin, who sought a middle way between the Lutheran and Zwinglian positions. Calvin maintained that Jesus is really present when the bread is eaten and wine is consumed, but present in a spiritual way. What made the position more complex was the variety of opinions in Anglicanism: mainstream Anglicans were Calvinist, some evangelical Anglicans (among whom we would include Doudney) veered towards the Zwinglian view (although some were Calvinist), while Anglo-Catholics (a group that had emerged in the Church of England by the time Doudney came to Ireland) veered towards a Roman Catholic and Lutheran view of communion. All would concur, however, in the statement that before the words of institution are said all there is, is bread; after the words of institution are said what there is, is the body of Christ. The bread and wine become the sacramental body and blood of Christ. Thus God is sacramentally present.

At the same time Luther did not regard communion as just a sign or symbol of a spiritual reality. For Luther when Jesus said: "This is my body" it meant that he was physically present at the sacrament. Other Reformers argued that when Jesus said these words he was pointing to himself. So at communion believers do literally receive the body of Christ. This did not mean (as the doctrine of transubstantiation held) that the bread becomes body and the wine becomes blood. The body and blood of Jesus are in them: the presence of the body of Christ is in, with, under, around, and behind the bread and wine. The believer is nourished spiritually by partaking of both elements. (The Catholic Church decreed at the Council of Trent that reception by the laity of communion in both kinds (bread and wine) was not necessary.)

The communion service was also a visible preaching of the gospel because it pointed to Jesus' sacrificial death as the focus of salvation. When the faithful meet and celebrate the eucharist, Jesus is present and is received by faith. The sacrifice of Christ is remembered and in the consumption of the bread and wine is acted out by our receiving of him who made that sacrifice.

How does it happen that we are sharing in a meal with Christ? The Christian answer is this happens by God's grace. What is grace? In general it is what God gives us and does for us freely as a gift. More specifically in the context of communion it is sacramental grace. As we have seen a sacrament is an outward and visible sign of an inward spiritual grace. So the eucharist was given by Christ as a means of receiving divine grace, the outward and visible sign being the bread and wine.

A sacrament has a physical, material, and spiritual dimension. Holy communion for this reason is a sensual experience, since it involves seeing, touching, smelling and tasting. In essence a sensual experience has a spiritual purpose. The outward part of communion is bread and wine, while the inward part is the body and blood of Christ. By the action of the Holy Spirit the bread and wine become the body and blood of Christ.

There were other aspects of the Catholic mass that the Reformers challenged. In particular, they opposed the notion that it was somehow a repetition of Jesus' sacrifice on the cross. This was in contrast to the doctrine of the Catholic Church which maintained that the mass was a true sacrifice that can be offered for the benefit of the dead. Secondly, Luther challenged the Catholic notion that the mass conveyed merits and objected to the way in which the doctrine of transubstantiation was linked to the idea that the mass was a meritorious sacrifice, because this was contrary to justification by faith. Thirdly, Protestants opposed the concept of reservation, i.e. that the body of Christ remains present in the bread after the celebration of communion ends.

Priestly Role

The issue of what actually happened in the communion service or mass in many respects converged on the role of the priest. Protestants were concerned that making the eucharistic act solely dependent upon the priestly prayers both focused the sacrament unduly on specific persons and things as to invest them through popular habit and repetition with quasi-magical powers. The result, Protestants maintained, was that priests and church authorities became manipulators of power over people and that the latter lost their basic engagement in faith with the reality of the eucharistic act, which should entail a sharing of God's life in Christ with them.

The Roman Catholic Church laid great emphasis on priestly authority. It was based on the action of Christ who conveyed on the apostle Peter the power to forgive (the so-called power of the keys), and thus only those ordained by the successor of Peter (or his designate, i.e. bishops) can administer the divine graces of the sacraments. For the Catholic Church there was a concentration on the priestly and sacramental ministry whereby the priest is set apart to represent the people. In contrast, for the Reformers there was only one priesthood, that of the priesthood of all believers. There was no need for a special priesthood since the eucharist is not a sacrifice because Jesus's death cannot be repeated. Instead, for Protestants, there was an emphasis on the ministry of the word.

Given their sacerdotal functions, priests were credited by the populace with possessing magical powers and with the ability to perform miracles. This was specifically evident in the action priests performed at the consecration of the elements of bread and wine whereby, it was believed, they were transformed into the body and blood of Christ. Belief in this ability extended itself in the popular mind to other areas such as priestly ability to ensure the success of crops, to heal people from sickness, and even to bring people back to life. Such popular confidence in clerical ability added to the power and authority of individual priests in their communities. However, this perceived magical ability did not give priests immunity from criticism or attack for there was a long tradition of anti-clericalism in Ireland over matters such as arbitrary demands and excessive dues. Additionally, the famine itself demonstrated the limits of priestly magical ability, for if such powers were so real then why was it so ineffective in preventing such a large loss of life through crop failure and starvation?

In the mid-nineteenth century a renewed vigour in papal power emanated in greater supervision by Rome of the activities of bishops, priests, and churches. Clergy became more professional, more disciplined, and more committed to the implementation of Tridentine formulations of Catholicism. The intent was to inculcate greater personal devotion among the laity. The champion of this ultramontane approach was Paul Cullen, archbishop of Armagh (1849) and archbishop of Dublin (1852). Combined with his desire to implement Roman policy in Ireland, was his belief that being Irish and Catholic was synonymous. As part of his policy of bringing the Irish church more firmly in line with Rome, Cullen convened a special synod of Irish bishops which opened at Thurles in August 1850. Indicative of the wide interest taken in the Thurles gathering is the fact that its proceedings were even reported on by the conservative, *Waterford Mail* in September 1850.[14]

The most important provisions of the synod so far as practice and doctrine are concerned, pertained to eliminating the celebration of sacraments in homes and instead transferring them to the church building. Thus it stipulated that henceforth baptisms, confessions, and marriages were to be conducted in a church, the only exceptions were to be those approved by the bishop, and if they were to be held in the home then a collection for the priest was to be banned entirely or severely restricted.[15] Priests were not to withhold the administration of the sacraments on the pretext that offerings had not been made for their celebration. Significantly for the context of the conflict that took place in Bunmahon, priests were forbidden to denounce people from the altar.[16]

The decrees passed at Thurles were approved by the Vatican and published in Dublin in 1851 and as of May 23, 1851 they came into force in Ireland. However, as previous experience in Ireland over the centuries showed, it was one thing to approve such ecclesiastical legislation, it was quite another to have it implemented in practice. One impediment to its implementation was that the decrees were clearly unpopular with the clergy. Even three years after the synod, Archbishop Cullen was complaining that the decrees were not being observed even around Thurles itself where the synod had been held.[17] It was in the area of implementation that the role of the local bishop and the diocesan clergy under him was critical.

The diocese of Waterford and Lismore had been the location of some of the abuses such as clerical cliques and squabbles over appointments, that the new centralizing policy sought to neutralize.[18] But it was also the region that had a significantly strong and articulate Catholic political and educational culture, exemplified in the opening of a new cathedral in Waterford City in 1793 (the oldest Roman Catholic cathedral in Ireland), followed soon after by the foundation of the Christian Brothers order in the city in 1802, the re-establishment of the Cistercian monastic tradition with the foundation of Mount Melleray in 1832, coupled with the 1826 victory of Villiers-Stuart over the Beresford interest that was so formative in the achievement of Catholic emancipation in 1829.

This newly assertive context was also productive of a new calibre of priest. Although a diocesan college had existed in Waterford since 1807, increasingly the training of priests was centralized in Maynooth. Despite the comments of its detractors who maintained that those coming out of Maynooth were from the lower orders in society, graduates were in origin mainly from the farmer class.[19] It was this new class of priest who was delegated with imposing a greater discipline on the Catholic population through the control or elimination of such practices as wakes and patterns, agrarian unrest, sexual deviance, and clandestine marriage. In tandem with this task there was the Church's battle to suppress its adherents' belief in the non-Christian realm manifested in belief in the otherworld, popular magic, and other superstitions associated with banshees, fairies, patterns, and holy wells. Together these represented an alternative system of belief to the official institutional church and its doctrines, which on occasion provided the apparatus for interpreting phenomena and events in a way the Catholic Church could not, or they served to supplement its doctrines.

As matters stood Catholic laity had no apparent conflict in aligning popular belief in a supernatural otherworld with subscription to official church doctrine. For many, elements of the Christian and non-Christian worlds could subsist side by side, the entire emanating in particular popular devotional practices. It was among the poorer classes particularly that a preference for the folk custom and belief over official Catholic doctrine was apparent, and the institutional church was more intent on weeding out such allegiance.

Although popular beliefs and traditions were on the wane in the early nineteenth century, they continued to be prevalent until at least mid-century. The event that dealt a devastating blow to their existence was the famine itself in the 1840s, for at one stroke the segment in society among whom such traditions were most prevalent (the labourers, and cottiers, and the landless) were severely diminished and with them a whole tradition of belief in the pagan supernatural and defiance of official church policy. While such popular beliefs lingered on even into the twentieth century, the fact was they held less of a hold on the population that survived the famine. This was the context into which the decrees of the synod of Thurles were addressed and the local context into which Doudney came.

On the one hand, the new post-famine context was one in which the Catholic Church availed of the opportunity to impose its authority more fully on its flock, something that was timely given that the social groups most loyal to the superstitions was now severely decimated due to the famine. The new clerical attitude was characterized by an informed Catholic in 1849 in the following terms: "The tone of society in Ireland is becoming more and more *'Protestant'* every year; the literature is a Protestant one, and even the priests are becoming more Protestant in their conversation and manners. They have condemned all the holy wells and resorts of pilgrims..."[20] Already in 1837 a similar trend among the priests was discerned by another observer who commented: "The priests, I am sorry to see and to say, inclining very much to Protestant notions, are putting an end to all those venerable old customs."[21] Interestingly, in both these comments the term "Protestant" is utilized to describe the shift away from traditional folk beliefs and practices, to a more serious adherence to orthodox Christian practice. A variant in all this was that the particular commitment of local Catholic clergy to official church policy and doctrine, and their tolerance of and participation in popular customs, depended on local circumstances, particular clerical personalities, and family background and loyalties.

On the other hand, old ways died hard. Therefore, in mid-nineteenth century Bunmahon, as in many other places, we can discern two parallel systems existing concurrently: the one epitomized by Paul Cullen and the Thurles agenda; the other, the lingering of traditional beliefs. This duality is exemplified in the case of Bunmahon which was, as we have seen, regarded as a remote location as a result of which traditional customs and folk beliefs are likely to have survived. In tandem with this, however, was the element of change. The provision of chapel facilities in Bunmahon itself in 1854 can be seen as inaugurating the new order. Thus Doudney's period in Bunmahon was at a time when transition in the Catholic ecclesiastical order was occurring. His presence along with that of the Methodist miners from Cornwall, meant that mid-nineteenth century Bunmahon was in transition and flux in a religious sense.

Conclusion

Some essential points of difference between Protestant and Catholic around such central matters as the Bible and the sacraments have been outlined in the foregoing. We cannot be certain as to the extent to which these theological differences were understood by the respective groups in Bunmahon. More likely they constituted points of difference appreciated only by their respective church leaders. The religious conflict that occurred in Bunmahon in the mid-1850s was not about the details of theological difference, but as we shall see in the next two chapters centred on its derivatives and expressions.

CHAPTER 6

THE STIRABOUT CREED
1847-1855

JUST AS WE MUST UNDERSTAND the theological differences that contributed to the religious conflict in Bunmahon as it unfolded, so also must we view it against the wider movements in Irish denominational and religious history in the period. This chapter outlines the general political developments in Ireland in the first half of the nineteenth century as a formational backdrop, the significance of Robert Daly's appointment as bishop in 1843, and the issues that occasioned conflict in Bunmahon in the first eight years of Doudney's curacy there.

Churches and Issues

The privileged position of the Church of Ireland was under attack in the first half of the century. The first significant dent came with the Catholic Emancipation Act (1829) which allowed Catholics to enter parliament, to belong to corporations, and attain higher civil and military offices. This was followed in 1831 by the creation of a non-denominational system of elementary education, a development viewed by Church of Ireland adherents as an undermining of their prerogative in the area of education. Following this, in 1833 the Church Temporalities Act reduced the number of archbishoprics from four to two and of bishops by ten, and appointed ecclesiastical commissioners with broad powers over the church's income. The

1830s saw an intensified attack on the main source of that income, i.e. tithe, with a compromise act ensuing in 1838 which subsumed the tithe into the rent charge and reduced the amount payable. All these reforms cumulatively served to undermine the privileged position of the Church of Ireland in Irish society.

In contrast, the Catholic Church witnessed an upsurge in its fortunes at this time. The struggles for Catholic emancipation, the campaign against tithes, and the agitation for the repeal of the act of union, saw priests involved in popular causes as local agents and organizers to a degree never witnessed before. If the early decades of the nineteenth century were ones of decline in the privileged status for the Church of Ireland, they were ones of political attainment and concession for Catholics.

As to the local disposition of denominational developments in their cultural and political manifestations, one can point to certain key events and indicators. One of the central works that defined Protestant interpretations of the 1798 rebellion was entitled *Memoirs of the different Rebellions in Ireland* (1801), authored by the west Waterford landlord Sir Richard Musgrave. In it Musgrave depicted the rebellion as led and encouraged by Catholic clergy, and the publication strongly influenced local and national views of Protestants subsequently.[1]

Secondly, evidence of cooperation among the denominations locally and nationally can be seen with the Society for Education of the Poor in Ireland (commonly known as the Kildare Place Society, from the location of its offices in Dublin) established in 1811. The society's management was denominationally mixed. Locally in Waterford there were up to 30 schools supported by the society in the period 1817–1840.[2] Ultimately the society came under suspicion because of allegations regarding the reading of Scripture without note or comment, and that proselytizing had occurred in the society's schools. As a result in the 1820s Catholic opposition to the society's activities tended in time to restrict its effectiveness, particularly after 1831 with the establishment of the National

Board of Education. Already by this stage a teaching order, the Christian Brothers, had been established in Waterford in 1802 and was expanding nation-wide. Education was to be one of the key areas that determined the tenor of denominational relationships, nationally and locally.

Thirdly, the political campaign of the 1820s in pursuit of Catholic emancipation inaugurated a new style of popular politics (epitomized by O'Connell's ability to mobilize clerical support) that emanated in success for Catholics, but these methods were deeply divisive denominationally. In particular, the 1826 general election contest in Waterford which saw the defeat by the liberal candidate, Henry Villiers Stuart (supported by Daniel O'Connell) of the conservative and powerful representative of the Beresford family, Lord George Beresford, was the turning point in Catholic fortunes.[3] In the wake of the emancipation achievement, the leadership of the priests in galvanizing local Catholic support continued, with Rev. John Sheehan (d. 1854), parish priest of St. Patrick's, Waterford City (1828–1854), having a national profile.[4] On the political scene, Thomas Wyse (1791–1862) of Waterford was prominent as an advocate of Catholic claims and as an educational reformer.

Success with emancipation was followed by Catholic demands for the abolition of tithes. The issue of tithes, which were essentially a tax on agricultural produce intended for the support of Church of Ireland clergy, was largely resolved by the act of 1838.[5] There followed demands for a repeal of the act of union, a demand advanced primarily by Catholics. In all these campaigns, Catholic clergy played a prominent role in organizing popular agitation.

By the time Doudney arrived in Bunmahon these various issues and campaigns—though the agitation around them had passed—had left a legacy of deep division among people in Ireland. One movement that contributed to this particularly, we will now turn to in more detail.

Second Reformation

From the early the nineteenth century there was renewed interest among Protestants in conducting missionary activity among Catholics. This was part of a broader evangelical revival taking place in Britain and North America, a movement dating from the 1730s. Termed the "Second Reformation," in the Irish context this movement dated between about 1820 and 1870.[6]

After 1822 there were various attempts by the evangelical wing of the Church of Ireland to initiate a movement of conversion among Catholics. This developed into a struggle waged at various levels of society—religious, political and social. By the late 1840s, it had assumed the character of a cultural conflict between the two denominations. One estimate in 1853 put the number of conversions at 40,000 since 1848.[7] The high point of the Protestant movement was reached in the early 1850s, when the Irish Church Missions, a body financed and supported from England, had a number of proselytizing projects underway in Ireland. After the mid-1850s, attempts at missionary conversion activity by Protestants in Ireland declined sharply.

The areas of greatest missionary activity were in the west of Ireland, notably Kerry (especially at Dingle and Ventry), Connemara, and Mayo (notably Achill Island), rather than in the relatively more affluent areas of the east. The exception was the mission around Doon, Co. Limerick, a location explicable because of the interest Bishop Robert Daly took in it as it was located in one of his dioceses.

The evangelical cause made notable advances in Waterford in the 1820s, though this was a passing phenomenon brought on as a reaction to the advances made by Daniel O'Connell's Catholic emancipation campaign in the county at the time.[8] Expressions of evangelicalism in the county were counterbalanced by the existence of a strong liberal Protestant tradition, one with which the Osbornes of Newtown Anner identified. Thus by the time Daly arrived in the diocese in 1843, evangelicalism was at a nadir despite the trends nationally and in the west in particular.

When we talk of proselytism and its related attribute in an Irish context, souperism, it is important to clarify what is meant by these terms. Souperism is a term used to describe how ultra-Protestant missionaries supposedly took advantage of the plight of vulnerable Irish Catholics primarily during the famine, whereby they gave them much needed food in exchange for a change in religion by the recipient. The charge of souperism was reinforced by folk memory and passed down the generations to modern times. One casualty of this has been the lack of due acknowledgement of the sincere exertions— often to the point of death—made by Church of Ireland clergy to dispense relief to those in need during the famine untrammeled by religious considerations.[9]

On the legitimacy of the charge of souperism, modern scholarship has concluded that much of the charge is misplaced in that it did not apply generally, that such methods were not supported by the majority of Church of Ireland members, that where it did occur it was conducted and supported by external groups and individuals, and that on the whole charges of souperism are difficult to substantiate.[10] In local terms, while the effects of the famine in Waterford were serious and cannot be minimized, they were not of a scale comparable to the west of Ireland, notably Mayo, Sligo, and Galway, where the indiscriminate souper and those who distributed relief were most active. In Waterford, while there were reports and charges of souperism from different parts of the county, these were not sufficiently numerous to suggest that incidence was organized, concerted, or widespread.[11] However, an emotional familiarity with the terms "souper" or "souperism" evolved sufficient for them to be deployed by Catholic opponents in the armoury of charges levelled against Doudney as a means of indicating disavowal or discrediting of his activities.

Often accompanying the charge of souperism in popular perceptions of the famine was that of proselytism. From its inception

Christianity contained a message whose intrinsic content meant that it was intended to be shared. Verses in Scripture, particularly ones like Matthew 28:19 ("Go and make disciples of all nations"), had since the early centuries of Christianity provided believers with a mandate to spread the Christian faith. Down the centuries this included the active preaching of the gospel, the publishing of pamphlets outlining the essentials of the Christian faith, the defence of orthodox beliefs based on interpretation of Scripture, and, for instance, engaging in debates whereby differences were elucidated. Much of these activities had been normative over time, however from the early nineteenth century there was a new animation and purposefulness among a minority in the Church of Ireland (supplemented by a committed group of English evangelicals) to bring the missionary mandate to a new level through a more committed endeavour to convert Irish Catholics to the reformed faith. This endeavour was central to the movement known as the "Second Reformation."

The tragedy of the famine caused many to respond through providing relief not just in a humanitarian way through food, but also spiritually when people were dying and were without hope. In doing so Irish clergy, Catholic and Protestant, were simply doing their pastoral duty when people needed spiritual comfort. We have seen how Doudney ministered in this way multiple times while he was in Templemore. Even if such activity and similar expressions of it by Church of Ireland clergy all over Ireland constituted the dispensing of spiritual comfort to people which some interpreted as proselytism, this was not equivalent to souperism. Yet at the time (by an understandably defensive Catholic Church) and since (in the popular imagination), the two were conflated. Except in the hands of the unscrupulous, the two were in fact separate. Modern scholarship has concluded that intentional and programmatic proselytism was not a feature of the Waterford area during the famine or its aftermath, even at the high-point of missionary activity in the early 1850s.[12] Yet charges of proselytism or souperism remained as a tool to be utilized when demanded by particular contexts.

Situation in Bunmahon

In Doudney's case, the situation as regards proselytism and souperism is best understood by reference to the reply he gave to the charge as part of the controversy over the case of the workhouse (the details of which will be examined below.) In a printed address to the inhabitants of Bunmahon, dated August 6, 1855, in a clear denial of the charge, Doudney stated:

> "From the way in which the term [proselytizing] is used against me, you are to understand it to mean, an influencing or compelling persons under threats or promises, to go contrary or in opposition to their own opinions of faith. Now I deny this. I have never used for any such purposes either threat or promise. I have lived nearly eight years among you, and I defy any man, woman, or child, to come forward and say, that in a *single instance* I have made threats or promises. Ask for yourselves those whom I have employed, or whom I *now* employ, whether any such influence has been used. Ask whether there has been the slightest difference made between Protestants and Roman Catholics?"[13]

He made clear that he could have filled a church with people who had come to him wishing to convert, but he had declined such advances because he had detected an insincere motive in their approaches. On this point, he continued his address: "I would not give a straw for a score of converts who became such for the sake of what they could gain by it." Yet, he made it clear, "If an individual change his opinions from a conscientious conviction that I was right, and he was wrong, I should not be worthy of the name of a Protestant—to say nothing of being a Christian Minister—if I did not cheerfully receive such."[14]

These were important distinctions and clarifications for him to publicize.

Rather than having as his purpose the obtaining of nominal converts (which was largely the result achieved by missionary activity in the west of Ireland), Doudney sought to act out the gospel since he did not have the chance to preach it directly on a continuing basis to Catholics. In this he sought to exemplify what the gospel was "in its working and effects; that it cares for the bodies, as for the souls of men; that it seeks to raise them in the scale of being; that it feeds the hungry, clothes the naked, instructs the ignorant, [and] finds occupation for the idle." He asked his audience to judge if in this he had had any measure of success. He pointed to the children taken from the streets, clothed, fed and taught; the £100 per month additional funds earned in his schools contributed to the local economy; and the general improvement evident among the children he gave education and employment to.

Given Doudney's disavowal of involuntary conversion, how then does Bunmahon fit into this wider pattern of missionary endeavour? Are there other points of differentiation? In a spatial and temporal sense Doudney's activity in Bunmahon in the 1850s certainly coincided with the high point of missionary activity in Ireland as a whole, but this did not mean that he was officially part of the missionary societies and groups that were active at the time.[15]

Secondly, as Doudney asserted on occasion, he did not receive financial support in his efforts from any of the larger missionary organizations, such as the Society for Irish Church Missions (founded 1849).[16] This meant that he did not participate in the wider missionary endeavour in an organized way, and that he very much operated out of his own agenda within the diocesan context relying on his network of support in England through the readership of the *Gospel Magazine*. In other centres such as Doon, Co. Limerick, it was the coalescence of local efforts by the rector that led to the introduction of the Irish Society into the area and that was critical in obtaining converts and the encouragement of scripture readers.[17] Reports of the level of conversions in such centres ran into the hundreds, and though this may have been inflated the numbers were still likely to have been significant.

Even if in reality converts in places like Doon, Cappamore, and Pallasgreen numbered in the tens rather than in the hundreds or thousands, there was nothing comparable in Bunmahon. While conversions elsewhere may have been largely temporary and hence insincere, Doudney eschewed such an approach and was more concerned to gain converts out of conviction, though in the event these turned out to be few.

Doudney did not have the support of any missionary society, conversions were not numerous, there were no colonies of converts like elsewhere, and charges of souperism lack substantiation given his refutation of the charge. In addition, conserted efforts by Catholic clergy to counter ostensible proselytism in the area are absent which is indicative of the fact it was not extensive. Indeed overt Catholic offensive action only took place after Doudney's departure from the locality.

Thirdly, there were particular circumstances, ecclesiastical and personal, that brought Doudney to Bunmahon and this gave the choice of location its exceptionality in relation to the wider pattern. Finally, however, some local iteration of the wider pattern of missionary activity can be seen in the fact while locations such Kerry and Connemara were remote on the national level, Bunmahon was considered remote and inaccessible at the level of County Waterford, though increasingly less so.

Despite the foregoing evidence differentiating the context of Bunmahon with the pattern elsewhere, nevertheless Doudney kept informed of the happenings at the main missionary centres in other parts of the country. For instance, he kept current about the missions at Cappamore and Doon, Co. Limerick through letters from Edward Ellis, an advocate of missionary activity in these locations.[18] Both locations were within Bishop Daly's jurisdiction and he took a keen interest in promoting conversion efforts in them.[19] Also as a result of a tour of such missionary centres in the west of Ireland,

Doudney published, *A Run Through Connemara: by the editor of the "Gospel Magazine"* (Dublin, 1856). Earlier in 1850, as editor of the *Gospel Magazine*, he published updates from correspondents, notably Herbert I. Clifford of Tramore, who was in close touch with developments in Dingle, Co. Kerry, where he had resided for eight years between 1838 and 1846, such reports giving information about happenings in the mission centre there.[20] The latter reports brought accounts of persecution induced by four Catholic priests against the Protestant missionaries active in the area and against those who converted (including ostracism and boycott of the 350–400 converts from purchasing food); of the need for employment for those who had converted so that they could be sustained; and of the provision of education. These elements of persecution, employment, and education, were to characterize the experience Doudney was to have while in Bunmahon in subsequent years.

Robert Daly and Societies

The Church of Ireland clergy and laity as a whole were unsupportive of the open, militant proselytising activity carried on by missionaries from England at such places as Dingle and Connemara. However, the two most notable exceptions to this rule among leading Irish churchmen, were the Archbishop of Tuam, Power le Poer Trench, and Robert Daly, whose family was of Catholic background but a member of whom had converted in the eighteenth-century. After 1839, with the death of Trench, Daly assumed the leadership of Church of Ireland evangelicals. This position was strengthened when Daly was created bishop of Cashel, Emly, Waterford and Lismore in 1843, an office he held until his death in 1872. During his long episcopal reign, Daly openly supported Protestant missionary activity and vigorously encouraged the clergy of his four dioceses, Cashel, Emly, Lismore and Waterford, in the religious conversion of Catholics.[21] Daly was initially reluctant to come to live in Waterford, but according to one of his former parishioners, he grew "very fond of Waterford and of the people there."[22] It was to be the centre of his activities in promoting a vision of evangelical Christianity for almost thirty years, and as part of this it was he who was responsible for introducing Doudney to Ireland and to Bunmahon.

Daly was particularly prominent in the Irish Society for Promoting the Education of the Native Irish through the Medium of their own Language (or the Irish Society for short) which he helped found in 1818, and he reportedly never missed one of its committee meetings.[23] The society was dedicated to the conversion of Irish Catholics who were speakers of the Irish language. To what extent were such bodies active in Waterford generally and in the Bunmahon district particularly?

The Irish Society, given its focus on Irish speakers, was less likely to be directly active in the east Waterford area where the native language was in decline, and in Bunmahon we have noted evidence of the increasing prevalence of English. The society tended, therefore, to concentrate its efforts in the Gaelic-speaking areas of the west of Ireland like Dingle and Bandon. As to other societies, we know that the London Hibernian Society which had been founded in 1806 for the purpose of establishing schools and disseminating the Bible among Irish Catholics, had three day schools with 77 pupils (14 Catholics, 63 Protestants) in operation in Waterford in 1835, and among its supporters were Lady Osborne of Newtown Anner and Mrs. Uniacke of Woodhouse.[24] In 1836, the society had five day schools (150 pupils: 31 Catholics, 119 Protestants) in Waterford, with Lady Osborne and Mrs. Uniacke again among its prime supporters.[25] Unfortunately, the annual reports of the society do not specify where in the county or city these schools were located, so we cannot be sure if the Bunmahon area was one, but as we have seen the school established in Monksland by Lady Osborne had an early association with the society, though this association was later severed.

Another society that had some presence in the county was the Church Missionary Society, originally founded in England in 1799 by Church of England adherents who sought to spread the gospel. Its Irish branch had a Waterford auxiliary by at least 1844, probably prompted by the arrival of Robert Daly as bishop in the city, for in that year he was its branch president. In that year alone the local branch raised over £115. There were sub-branches in Dunmore, Lismore, Tramore, Stradbally (where the Uniacke family were again prominent supporters), Dungarvan, and Ardmore.[26] By 1852 there was a new branch established at Monksland, for in that year it is recorded that £2.11s. was collected at a meeting there organized by Doudney.[27] Amounts continued to be collected locally in the 1850s by Doudney and his successor, Rev. P.J. Lee (or Leo).[28] These local branches appear to have been merely for fundraising purposes, the amount raised being forwarded to the Waterford City auxiliary and then to the CMS headquarters for its work overseas. Hence Doudney's involvement was merely as a fund-raising convenor. He always claimed that he never received support from any of the official missionary agencies active in Ireland at the time, and this is certainly true of the Irish Church Missions, for a survey of January 1852 indicates that in the distribution of the mission stations none are shown for Waterford.[29]

In the mid-nineteenth century Waterford had an Auxiliary Bible Society, devoted to the raising of funds locally to support the production and distribution of bibles.[30] Bishop Daly was among its supporters and in addition to the city there were branches in Portlaw, Stradbally, Tramore, and Lismore.[31] Sales for 1854 were in excess of 1,100 copies, and in 1858 it is recorded that the society sold books to the Bunmahon branch.[32] Bishop Daly presided over meetings of the Waterford auxiliary of the Hibernian Bible Society.[33]

Another society that had a local presence was the Sunday School Society for Ireland, founded in 1809 for the purpose of supplying bibles at a reduced price for use in schools. In 1846 local schools applying for such supplies included Stradbally and in 1853 applicants included Kilmacthomas, Comeragh, and Stradbally (Woodhouse), indicating that no specific application was received from Bunmahon or Monksland schools.[34] Robert Jocelyn, earl of Roden, a prominent Irish evangelical, whom Doudney had met in London and visited at his Tollymore estate in Co. Down, was president of the society in 1849.[35]

Daly's Leadership

Leadership of evangelical endeavours locally was provided by Bishop Daly. He laid particular stress on the fact that the clergy under his aegis were of a similar outlook as himself. One of his first acts as bishop was to initiate monthly meetings of the clergy of his dioceses at the Bishop's Palace in Waterford City. These meetings were attended on average by about 40 clergy with whom he became personally acquainted, and they continued for almost his entire occupancy of the see.[36] These monthly gatherings entailed filling the Bishop's Palace and nearby hotels with guests, all at the bishop's expense and in time the practice assumed the status, it was said, of a "salutary custom."[37] For one such meeting, Daly requested that each clergyman supply him with a list of his favourite hymns which Daly then incorporated into a new hymn book for use in the diocese, a volume that was favourably adopted since each clergyman felt he had a part in its compilation.[38]

Daly's period as bishop was a time of growth and renewal in the Church of Ireland locally. There are a number of indices of this. As well as the support given to the various societies, the religious tenor of Church of Ireland adherents seems to have risen. For instance, the numbers being confirmed annually were impressive, with 110 for the diocese in 1851 alone.[39] Daly promoted sermon series in Waterford City churches on controversial topics in which local clergy preached in refutation of key Catholic doctrines relating to, for instance, infallibility, priestly power, the confessional, the mass, transubstantiation, invocation of saints, and access to God's Word.[40]

Not only did Daly's period as bishop witness a new spiritual liveliness among local Church of Ireland members, but it was also a time when there was a deliberate and conscious effort on the bishop's part to marshal his clergy in active engagement with Catholics. In the aftermath of the famine, Daly addressed the clergy of his dioceses in 1849 in the following terms:

> "The aspect of the time is very peculiar, full of especial solemn awfulness... May we not hope that the present judgements... may soften many hard hearts and dispose them to receive the Gospel of Christ. We should surely be ready to take advantage of every soft moment, of every favourable impression made upon men's minds... ready to press the saving truth upon all... upon those who profess to belong to our communion, that we may build up those that are in the faith, and that we may lead to Christ those who, though they have a name to live, are yet dead before God... and ready to offer the truth to those who are not of our communion, if God's dealings with the world should open any door for the entrance of the truth."[41]

From the tone of this address we can discern that Bishop Daly was a prelate whom we would expect to find encouraging clergymen in projects of a missionary nature in the dioceses under his control. Clearly he perceived the times to be opportune for such an endeavour. By 1851, when evangelical activity by English missionaries among Irish Catholics was about to assume a high level of intensity, Bishop Daly could address the clergy of his dioceses and claim that:

> "We have reason to be thankful that the great body of our clergy are sound....whilst among the population of our country there is a great spirit of enquiry, and many

thousands are giving up the errors of Rome and joining our Scriptural Church."

In this matter the clergy must be prepared to assume the duty laid upon them: "you should be prepared to set before your Roman Catholic neighbours that there is 'boldness to enter into the holiest' allowed to every sinner through the blood of Jesus."[42] Given the tone and content of both these addresses of 1849 and 1851, one can safely assume that Bishop Daly supported Doudney's various educational initiatives at Bunmahon.

It has already been noted how Daly's involvement with educational controversy in Bunmahon pre-dated Doudney's arrival there. There were, in addition, other prior manifestations of sectarian tension in the area. For example, there was a decided local reaction to the conversion of Laurence Lynch of Bunmahon in the mid-1830s for he and his family became the objects of hostility, ostracism, and arson.[43] The arrival from Cornwall of miners of a Methodist persuasion to work in the mines occasioned tension with local Catholics. Simmering sectarian resentments lingered into the early 1840s, to the extent that John Petherick, the mine manager, had in 1842 to warn Protestant miners who spoke disrespectfully of the Catholic Church or its priests that they were in danger of dismissal.[44] In 1845 the controversy between Bishop Daly and Ralph Osborne over the location of the scriptural school in the grounds of Knockmahon church contributed to the nascent sectarianism. All this is to indicate that tension on religious matters was not something whose advent can be dated solely to Doudney's arrival in the community in 1847.

Upon his arrival there was speculation among Catholics that he was a Protestant evangelical attempting to gain new converts to his faith. Thus the *Waterford News* of October 17, 1851, having reported on the arrival of the printers Doudney had recruited in London, asserted that "the general opinion is that they are a gang of soupers who came over for the purpose of proselytizing." Further, once the first sheets of Gill's commentary began to appear, Doudney reported that "the ire of the priests [has] been excited by this simple endeavour to do good to this poor half-starving population" and that he had been "harangued" from the altar of a neighbouring chapel which he says was "a matter of course."[45] The opinion of the *Waterford News* was that Doudney's intention was to set up an outlet in Bunmahon for the publishing of tracts for proselytizing purposes, and it was the opinion of one correspondent writing from Kilmacthomas that the arrival of the printers was opportune for it was likely to prove a "bad business" given the "depression of business in that town [Bunmahon] and the extreme destitution of the major part of the population."[46]

For Doudney, such a reaction was no surprise. Already the first impressions he had upon arriving in Bunmahon were not auspicious. He immediately discerned a hostility to everything English and Protestant, something that, in his view, had been bred into Irish Catholics from birth and that they were conditioned to believe that all the country's troubles were to be ascribed to English misgovernment and Protestant oppression.[47] In his view this mindset made Irish Catholics inherently suspicious of any attempts by English people or Protestants generally to contribute to an improvement in their condition.[48] In this regard, Doudney like others saw the famine as a timely occurrence, despite the ravages it wrought, which in his tenure in Templemore he tried to relieve as his situation allowed. In his opinion the famine was:

> "among the greatest benefits that could have befallen Ireland. It was attended with a twofold good. It drew off the cotter from his hereditary and indolent dependence upon the potato crop, and it placed Protestantism before him in a light in which he was never wont to regard it. He saw the earnest, active, self-denying efforts of its ministers in relation to the poor and the perishing. By their instrumentality they were snatched, as it were, from the brink of the grave, and brought back again into

life; and, in due time, their energies were directed into a new and prosperous channel."[49]

Such a realization of opportunity encouraged Doudney to promote various projects that would inculcate education, initiative, industry, and self-reliance. But there were to be many hindrances to the realization of these objectives, the first coming within a year of his arrival in Bunmahon.

Rebellion 1848

In the early 1840s rumours were circulating locally as to a planned uprising but these proved to be groundless.[50] There was heightened political tension in Waterford as a result of a local election in the city in February1848. It witnessed the defeat of local Young Irelander, Thomas Francis Meagher, and the victory of the Sir Henry Winston Barron who had the support of a majority of the landowners, forty shilling freeholders, and the clergy.[51] In the ensuing months, evidence of drilling and pike-making caused apprehensions among the local population resulting in an increase in policing. However, evidence of early confederate clubs being established comes from south Tipperary rather than Waterford. The month of July 1848 was decisive for on the twelfth of that month Meagher was arrested in Waterford City, but this did not precipitate any general outbreak.

Evidence that Waterford remained placid in the summer months of 1848, is seen in the fact that rebel activity was on Waterford's periphery in south Tipperary; an attempt to establish a confederate club in Dungarvan was resisted by local merchants, shopkeepers, and traders; a high level of registration of arms locally by those who might be called on by government in the event of an insurrection; a heightened police presence resulting in the dissolution of clubs; and, critically, a shift away in support by Catholic priests for Young Ireland.[52] All this was illustrative of the fact that Waterford remained a residual centre of O'Connellite support, not one that supported the more radical politics of the Young Ireland movement, despite the presence locally of Meagher. By the end of the summer the leaders, including Meagher, had been arrested, with their trials scheduled for Clonmel in September and October, 1848. The planned insurrection had been a fiasco.

Despite this eventual outcome, rumours as to the prospect of rebellion caused a stir locally in Bunmahon in the spring of 1848. In April, 1848, after arriving back from a visit to England, Doudney had reports of an intended uprising confirmed by Captain Clifford of the coast guard, and in his preaching on the ensuing Sunday, he chose as his text 2 Chronicles 20: 12 ("O our God, will you not judge them? For we have no power to face this vast army that is attacking us. We do not know what to do, but our eyes are upon you"), as well as taking succour from verses in Psalm 91.[53] In the evening, people were seen assembling on the nearby hills, the coast guard remained in the village (Annestown where he was then living), and by arrangement on the first alarm all Protestants (30 in number including women and children) were to take refuge in Doudney's cottage.[54] A group advancing on the cottage was presumed to be rebels but were in fact police who scoured the area for two hours, and eventually Doudney and his group felt secure.[55]

In April also William James, a church warden and Cornish miner, who had been working in the area for ten years, reported to the Dublin administration a rumour that the intended massacre of Protestants in the locality was immanent, a charge that was summarily dismissed as alarmist by twenty-seven other local Protestants whose signatures had been obtained by Petherick.[56] However, James' representations to Dublin were taken sufficiently seriously to cause the dispatch by the local sub-inspector of twenty police to patrol the area on Palm Sunday.[57] However, rather than serving to quell tension the presence of the police only exacerbated it to the extent that mine employees declared their intention to strike if William James was not dismissed, which Petherick eventually did with the cost of transportation back to Cornwall for James and his family being paid.[58]

Earlier in July a visitor to his house had warned Doudney to make plans for an escape should the rising happen. With an invalided wife and four children, the fact that the extent of the conspiracy was unknown, and with two of the most disturbed districts only ten or twelve miles distant, this advice seemed compelling.[59] This was more the case since shortly after the rebellion had broken out, 2,000 or 3,000 of the rebels reportedly sent Doudney a message that they planned to burn down his thatched dwelling house in Annestown; the rebels attacked a police station in a village eight miles distant possibly Kill with the loss of life; and a bonfire was lit close to his dwelling by the rebels.[60] These and other incidents brought to recollection earlier rebellions when Protestants were massacred, particularly in adjacent Wexford in 1798.[61]

Rumours persisted even after it was evident that the rebellion was a clear failure. In August 1848 Doudney reported on such rumours of a general rising after the harvest had been gathered, in which the massacre of Protestants was intended, stirred up by the power and influence of the priests over a poverty-stricken peasantry, who themselves had no disposition to rebel but had been urged on by the priests.[62] Doudney, despite all the wild reports of rebellion, coupled with a reminder from a friend of his responsibilities as a husband and a father of four children, and though he witnessed first-hand crowded steamers of Protestants leaving through the port of Waterford, rejected advice that he should make arrangements to leave Ireland.[63] In fact he stayed and over the next ten years was to experience opposition to the various initiatives he made to improve the conditions and prospects of the people, particularly the children. The first instance of opposition concerned the printing works.

Initial Conflict: Printing Works

Early indications of the sectarian animus that was to pervade local responses to Doudney's various educational initiatives occurred when two of the compositors from England came to Bunmahon in October, 1851. Having arrived in the village when it was dark, they found that no house could be found to accommodate them despite the fact that several of these houses had sufficient space and despite the fact that the compositors indicated that they were willing to pay for accommodation.[64] They were joined by another compositor on October 13, 1851, and were soon successful in securing premises though they had to pay double the normal rent.[65] Even by this stage *The Waterford News*, without any supporting evidence, had labeled the compositors as "soupers."[66] In addition, Doudney had initial difficulty securing premises for the printing school, for first a house and then a barn next to the cottage he was occupying, was refused upon suspicion that he was going to use it for proselytizing purposes.[67]

The reporter who had made the initial accusation concerning the proselytizing intent of the printing school, visited the establishment on October 24, 1851, was shown around, and, as recorded by Doudney, "in the most flattering terms, eulogized the undertaking."[68] The parish priest, Rev. Michael Power, also visited in October in the company of the local doctor, George Walker (whose family was to remain well disposed to the Doudneys throughout their time in Bunmahon), and was anxious to discount a report that he had gone from house to house in the village denouncing the printing school and discouraging boys from attending. Power then made clear "in very measured terms" that if the printing school was not put to a proselytizing purpose then it would be a benefit to the area but if it was then he would be called upon to intervene.[69]

In response to Rev. Power's declaration, Doudney made it clear that he had originally intended the printing school to act as an extension to the work of his own parochial school, but that so many applications for admission had been received from Catholics that he felt he had to allow them access to it also. Further, he clarified that, in his own words, "I had not intended, nor did I intend, to usurp any authority over the minds and consciences of the youth thus employed."[70] Nevertheless, Doudney made clear that he longed for the day when a Bible should be in the hands of all people as their right. On that point of significance, the priest queried as to which Bible he was alluding to, to which Doudney replied that he would not mind if it was the Catholic [i.e. Douay] version as long as it was without note or comment. The priest made it clear that the notes were necessary in order to make some difficult words clear to people who were ignorant. This latter remark proved to be an opening for Doudney, who queried why the priest considered his people to be ignorant:

> "And why are they so ignorant? …Such is continually the answer, if I talk with a Roman Catholic—and I don't hesitate to tell you that, during my four years' residence here, I have talked with many—but they tell me directly, if urged to think or to read for themselves, that they are so poor, so ignorant … they say, 'It is the priest's business.' I should be very sorry to take such a responsibility upon myself; because, undoubtedly, it is the nature of their system which leads to such a conclusion."[71]

Wishing to avoid controversy, the priest made a concluding remark that "I don't expect you will be accountable for my flock, nor shall I be accountable for yours. And if you remain peaceable, I shall not be the aggressor," upon which he left.[72] Thus they parted company, seemingly amicably.

Doudney later attributed this lack of hostility towards the printing school on the part of the priests to the fact that they were aware of the high estimation in which was held by the people of the area because of the contribution it was making. The instruction and employment it provided, the valuable skills acquired, along with the money put into circulation, were tangible benefits appreciated by the community.[73] So far as wages from the printing works are concerned, individually the weekly total amount of £12-£15 translated into 2s.6d. to 7s.6d. per week as earnings for each boy, an amount which exceeded the weekly amount paid to labourers in the area, i.e. 1s.[74] Together these benefits of skills and wages served to neutralize the effect of the altar threats so far as the printing school is concerned. It is clear that the boys themselves appreciated the opportunity to learn and be productive for they would often make their way to the printing school even before daylight and would often stay until late at night.[75]

Surprisingly, the arrival of additional English artisans in the area did not provoke any hostile reaction, perhaps because they were aware that those who had preceded them had settled in successfully. One reporter commented on:

> "The urbane deportment of the English artists, and their willingness to explain the details of the curious processes then going on, created a degree of satisfaction in my mind, which feeling is universal in the neighbourhood, for these intelligent workmen have even the good opinion of their newly-adopted neighbours, and the conciliating deportment has removed prejudices to a lengthened distance."[76]

At least one of these artisans, who had the initials W.H., came to Ireland with a similar desire to serve in the way Doudney had. Describing a visit to the library of the British Museum in London in the autumn of 1851, he tells of coming across volumes and papers in a glass case which included items from some of the Protestant martyrs—in particular that of Nicholas Ridley—who gave their lives because of their faith in Christ. This experience and a perusal of other works by eminent divines prompted him to think about whether he could do the same for his beliefs if called upon. He mused:

> "I could not help pondering over in the mind the varied condition and circumstances of those former fellow-labourers, most of them the occupants of obscure places of the world, and the subjects of poverty, persecution, and opposition; and yet God was pleased to bless their labours abundantly to succeeding generations."[77]

On this basis, a couple of months later he found himself being part of the group of initial staff of the printing school in Bunmahon.

If hostility to the printing school was not overt because of a recognition of the direct benefits the community had therefrom, the same was not true of the other schools.

Infant School

When Doudney resolved to open the infant school in 1852 he encountered much opposition from the Catholic clergy, who claimed he would use the school to gain converts to Protestantism. Altar denunciations, some of them in Irish, and contrary to the directives of the Thurles synod, were forthcoming.[78] In one such denouncement the priest cautioned his hearers that it would be better for them to endure their poverty than to accept employment in any of Doudney's various enterprises.[79] At both masses on Sunday, February 15, 1852 at the chapel (likely Ballylaneen) the infant school proposal was condemned from the altar by two priests, one of whom, Rev. Michael Power, was the one who had visited the printing works the previous October. The focus of the condemnation was a circular letter Doudney had written in order to raise funds for the infant school.

In an address to the people of Bunmahon on February 16, 1852, in response to the condemnation on the Sunday before,

Doudney defended himself against the charge of proselytizing.[80] He stated that he intended to set up an infant school to relieve the children from their poverty and misery and to provide them with an elementary education, food and clothing. In doing so, he said: "I am asking English friends to help me...I want to see them taught; and as your priests have not got up a school for them, I will try." Further, he claimed that no compulsion would be used either for Catholic parents to send their infants to the school or to force the children to adopt the Protestant religion: "And though I will not ask the children to become Protestants, nor will I ask them to attend our church... yet this I will tell you plainly, all that come to our Infant School will be taught to read, and taught to read the Bible too."[81] There was nothing in the Bible, whether the Catholic or Protestant versions, Doudney maintained, that prohibited its use by poor or rich alike.

Doudney's address was the focus of a further denunciation from the altar at the masses on the ensuing Sunday, February 22, 1852. As part of his response the priest encouraged the people to read the passages from the Bible referred to in Doudney's address, something Doudney was pleased with.[82]

At this point it is worth noting that public denunciations including curses by priests from the altar was not normal practice. In certain Irish dioceses they were only to be used with the permission of the bishop or his designate, though disregard of indiscriminate use of denunciations was within the purview of parish priests and curates.[83] One visitor to the area in May 1855 reported that the "priests terrify the parishioners by cursing him [Doudney] from the altar."[84] The use of denunciations in Bunmahon in the 1850s illustrates the seriousness with which the local clergy regarded the threat from Doudney.

On March 14, 1852 there was a further denunciation in Irish from the altar.[85] The proposed infant school continued to be a source of controversy even before it opened in August 1852. But despite the rising tension, as things happened, the opening of the infant school was delayed because of the ferment locally over the general election, which had a particularly sectarian dimension. In the Waterford county constituency, the Catholic liberal candidates, Nicholas Mahon Power and John Esmonde, were successful over the Protestant tory candidate Richard Hely-Hutchinson.[86] Locally in Bunmahon Protestants became the objects of hostility because of the election hysteria. A fellow clergyman on his way to one of Doudney's weekly evening lectures was, he reported, "hooted and pelted at with stones" to the extent that he had to turn back.[87] In another instance, a Catholic father who with his two children had been attending Doudney's church, was, after morning service, "hunted like a dog."[88] Further evidence of what Doudney termed "riot and dissipation" occurred when one man fled past his dwelling pursued by 200 or 300 people simply because his father had voted for the conservative candidate.[89] In the election itself priests used their influence to sway voters.[90] What further exacerbated the situation was that it was not a particularly good summer for crops locally what with blight hitting the potatoes and the wheat crop was also unsatisfactory.[91]

At any rate, as we have observed already, the infant school opened in August, 1852. During its first month in operation Doudney, in a series of progress reports to readers of the *Gospel Magazine*, conveyed news of attacks made on it by the local Catholic clergy. For Monday August 9, he reported that the "priest denounced our proceedings from the altar yesterday," and if any parents continued to send their children there, they would hear about it the following Sunday.[92]

On one occasion, the priest gave notice that on a forthcoming Sunday, there would only be one mass instead of the usual two, and that on that occasion he would demonstrate what he could do with the Protestant minister who had intruded on his flock. In response to this notice a huge crowd gathered in anticipation at the one location (likely Ballylaneen), to the extent that other chapels were abandoned and the village was deserted. As the crowds passed by the newly built glebe house on their way to the assembly, Doudney gathered from their conversation that their expectation was that the priest was going to perform a magical act such that Doudney would be transformed into an ass or a goat.[93]

For Doudney this and other similar incidents exemplified the power the priests had over the people and their propensity to superstition. It was an opinion also expressed earlier by Lady Catherine Osborne, one of the landowners of the area, when she commented: "Nothing but living in Ireland could enable anyone to understand the power of the priests, for once people invest human beings with infallibility there must be an end to all liberty and certain rectitude."[94] Coming from Lady Osborne who in other respects was liberal in her stance towards Catholics this observation was insightful.

In addition, the priest's attack implied an accusation that Doudney was well paid for his work from England.[95] Doudney firmly denied this particular charge, asserting that he was not in the pay of any society, nor did he receive a continuous supply of funds from England and America for proselytizing purposes, nor was he personally benefiting from the printing works, the contrary being the case for it was more costly to conduct the printing works in Bunmahon than in London.[96] In particular, he disavowed the rumour that he was receiving £100 for every convert he made.[97] Evidence from the repeated appeals in the columns of the *Gospel Magazine* clearly demonstrates that funds were not easily acquired. Indeed, as we shall see, one of the reasons why Doudney eventually had to leave Ireland was that he could not justify the continuance of his ministry there given how regularly he was absent in England trying to raise funds for his various educational projects. Nevertheless, in the short term the false rumour that Doudney was a well-paid agent of various proselytizing societies was sufficient to turn people's minds against him.[98] The charge provided fodder for his enemies. The experience of the famine and the work of the Irish Church Missions—then reaching the height of its intensity—made people suspicious of his presence and motives.

Opposition to the infant school continued. On the Monday following the priest's warning, the Catholic Bishop of Waterford, Nicholas Foran, at a confirmation ceremony in a neighbouring parish, ordered the parish priest, Rev. Michael Power, to excommunicate those children who went to the infant school.[99] This threat apparently had no effect as applications for admission to the school continued unabated, including one from two widows who lived in the cliffs and who sought admission for their seven or eight children.[100] One of these widows is likely the same one whose husband worked in the mines and who had recently died of fever.[101] The following Monday August 16, the news was that "The altar harangue was in Irish yesterday."[102] The substance of this attack was the charge that since Doudney had failed to convince older people, he had now targeted the young. Despite the accusations, attendance at the school seems to have held up at the 30 mark.[103]

The infant school attracted an array of enquiring visitors. In its first week of operation, a "respectable-looking" young woman visited who had at one point worked for a Protestant family who had given her a Bible but her father and brother had taken it from her. She declared her willingness to attend Protestant services but that it might put her life in danger, and so she requested that Doudney secure a position for her at a distance from her family and friends.[104] From another spectrum, Bishop Robert Daly, was a visitor in the first couple of weeks of the infant school's operation, though his presence was the occasion for some disruptive behavior on the part of a crowd who shouted that they "wished all the Protestants at the devil."[105] Some of those who formed part of this crowd were apparently sent a few days later by the priest and positioned themselves outside the entrance to the school in order to record the names of those children entering.[106]

The altar threats continued against those parents sending their children to the infant school.[107] That these attempts increased is evident for on Friday August 20, Doudney told readers that "Four priests have been in the village again today and have been busily engaged in each cabin whence the children came."[108] In one case the priest spent two to three hours trying to persuade one woman to take her children out of the school. She pleaded poverty, claiming that at least at the school her children would get a meal. As an alternative, the priest reportedly suggested that she beg from her neighbours, which she refused to do, a reply similar to his suggestion that she go to the workhouse. With all these alternatives refused, in the end she was threatened with excommunication.[109] One Catholic parent was refused absolution by the priest and was forced to have resort to Bishop Foran, all because he had sent his son to the printing school.[110] Another father, recognizing the value of the printing school for his two sons, reportedly declared that "If the Pope himself were to order me to take my boys away, I would not do it."[111] Finally, according to Doudney, two mothers were turned out of their lodgings and those who had taken them in were threatened; while another poor woman was told to desist sending her children to the infant school else her cabin would be demolished.[112] Clearly concerted pressure was brought to bear on parents to withdraw their children from attending the infant school.

That this effort proved ineffective is evident from the comments of the mistress of the school. When she compared her experience elsewhere (where in similar circumstances the children would be withdrawn from the school for a lengthy period), she was in no doubt that the altar denunciations issued against the infant school in Bunmahon were ineffective.[113]

All the denunciations happened in the first three weeks of the infant school's operation. Eventually, attendance at the school leveled out after a month to about 30 pupils.[114] About a month after the infant school opened, further controversy arose because Doudney, while repairs were being carried out on his church building, made use of the infant school to conduct the services. A number of Catholics wished to attend, but were afraid if they went inside word would get back to the priest, and so they hovered outside the windows and doors hoping to hear what was being said inside.[115] One individual ventured inside, returned for a Wednesday evening lecture, and later listened in while a fellow worker, a Protestant, read aloud from the Bible.[116] Less than a year was to elapse before there were more developments with the school.

Excommunication

In the early summer of 1853 the priests, having found that their denunciations of the previous autumn, winter, and spring were ineffective, extended their threats into actual excommunication of those who did not comply with their strictures with regard to attendance at the infant school. While not exceptional, the trend in Ireland as a whole by the 1850s was for the Catholic Church authorities to be more discriminating and cautious in the use of this penalty of excommunication than had obtained previously. Thus its deployment in Bunmahon in 1853 was a serious step for the priests to take and it reflected the gravity with which they regarded the threat posed by the infant school and the intransigence of those Catholic parents whose children attended it.

While the use of excommunication as a penalty of last resort was a serious step on the part of the Catholic clergy, it was seemingly out of proportion to the gravity of the offence. This is because of the fact that the minor form of excommunication, whereby the offenders were excluded from participation in the sacraments of the church, which would have been commensurate with the infraction, was not apparently considered or imposed. Rather it was the more serious form of major excommunication that was resorted to, whereby the offenders were completely excluded from entire membership of the Catholic Church. In this case, not only were the parties concerned denied the benefits of the sacraments but they were in addition denied participation in any other church activities and particularly they were ostracized from society, for henceforth no one was to speak to them, eat with them, pray with them, or in any other way have society with them. If another Catholic did not obey this prescription of excluding the offenders from social intercourse, then such a person would himself or herself become liable to minor excommunication.[117]

It was rare for the major form of excommunication to be imposed, recourse to it being more common, for instance in cases of clandestine marriage or membership of an agrarian secret society for which the penalty was automatic. However, in cases where the penalty was pronounced by name against the offending parties and when this was done publically, then the full version of the excommunication held force.[118] This last, when carried out in public, had the intent of excluding the person from the sacraments of the Church and of ostracizing the guilty party from local society. In effect the person no longer had membership of the Catholic Church, was denied access to its sacraments, and in effect faced eternal damnation unless he or she repented.

The public ceremony attendant upon full excommunication was intended to reinforce the full impact of this traumatic judgment in a dramatic way.[119] The constituent elements centred on the bell, book, and candle. The ringing of the bell denoted that the excommunication was published; the closing of the book (likely the mass-book rather than the Bible) signified that the promises of Christ contained therein were denied to the offender unless he or she repented; and the extinguishing of the candles demonstrated that the offender, if unrepentant, would be denied the light of heaven and consigned to the darkness and the flames of hell. In conclusion, the shutting of the church doors symbolized the exclusion of the offender from the services of the church and membership of the body of the faithful.[120]

Accordingly, in mid-June 1853 sixteen children were withdrawn from the infant school, their names having been obtained in advance. These children belonged to the nine families implicated. Of these, three families complied with the threat beforehand, while the six others including Larry and Biddy Veale were excommunicated by bell, book, and candle at a Sunday mass.[121] There was a crowded attendance for the awesome ceremony of excommunication which involved six large lit candles (one for each family) placed on the altar in front of which was the priest, Rev. Michael Power, parish priest of Stradbally and Ballylaneen (1834–60) who read the service of excommunication after which he closed the mass book with a thud, the candles were extinguished, and sighs of despair emanated from the friends of those who had been expunged from belonging to the church body.[122] An eye witness, reporting to Doudney on the excommunication, dwelt on the finality of that event, "its terror," and how "a thrill of horror, it is said, passed through that crowded assembly as the candles were extinguished."[123] Another person who was present reportedly commented: "I would sooner see a man hanging than witness that scene again."[124]

At the second mass following the excommunication, the assistant priest issued a warning to his listeners not to have any dealings or conversation with those who had been excommunicated.[125] The offending parents in Bunmahon were, in their act of sending children to a Protestant infant school, deemed equivalent in this act to rural criminals such as the Whiteboys, adulterers, and those who contracted unlawful marriages, misdemeanours which also incurred the sanction of excommunication. The experience of the excommunicated person in many ways paralleled the rejection and ostracism that the convert Laurence Lynch experienced in the 1830s.

There can be no doubt as to the sense of drama, finality, and exclusion incumbent on the event and its impact on the community. The people affected were essentially given the ecclesiastical equivalent of a curse (whose folkloric version would have been familiar to people in general), and debarred from the church, its sacraments (and hence from heaven), unless they became reconciled before death. Excommunication meant for those who believed in its power, that heaven was barred indefinitely. By such means were the recalcitrant among the Catholic population brought into compliance and quietude.

In addition, the excommunicated persons were ostracized by other members of the community. Thus, for example, one excommunicated member owed another person 15d. but the person to whom it was owed could not request it or else she would have had to account to Bishop Foran who lived at a distance of 15 miles in Waterford whence she would have to go in her bare feet. In another case, one of the excommunicated boys owed a woman a penny but when he offered to repay her she turned away without responding.[126] Another was a poor widow with an aging mother to maintain along with four children and another on the way.[127]

There were instances where the penalty of social ostracism of the offenders might not be applied to its full extent. Its full application depended on the perceived gravity of the offence, the sway of local circumstances, and the disposition of the particular priest. And although priests in general might deny that the intent of the punishment was to prevent all interaction with the excommunicated and that it was only unnecessary communication that was intended, it is clear that in a tightly-knit community such a fine distinction was not self-apparent and hence social relationships in Bunmahon were impacted significantly by the excommunication. To many it must have appeared that the punishment was disproportionate to the crime.

Aftermath: Priestly Authority Undermined

Critically, to be effective excommunication had to have the cooperation of the community. But since excommunication was the penultimate sanction, with its implementation priestly power reached its limit. That this was the case became evident, for, while in the aftermath of the excommunications attendance at the infant school fell in the short term, it is clear that there was a change in attitude between priest and people. Doudney reported that many parents, who recognized the advantage the school had to the village, were "disgusted" at the action of the priests and thought less of them and the system they supported. Some of them were now less deferential to the power of the priests, while others were more open to what the Bible said.[128]

People in need, who saw the advantage of the schools for their children, were not pleased with the action of the priests and became more critical of them. In particular, those who previously believed in the power of the priests were now less assured, and there was a greater openness to what the Bible had to say.[129] All this was emblematic of a strong anti-clerical element in Irish society that traditionally came to the fore on such occasions.[130]

In Doudney's mind the entire episode seemed severe, reactionary, and a blatant exercise of clerical power with a handful of parents being targeted just for sending children to a Protestant infant school for their betterment. In addition, he contended that the priests' timing of this action was not accidental, for they chose to implement it at a time when the people were availing of an improvement in their circumstances what with the vegetable crop promising, the gathering of sea weed proceeding (it was much in demand as manure for potatoes), and the potato crop auspicious.[131] Such activities would entail in normal circumstances a degree of social interaction and cooperation. But the policy of social ostracism incumbent on the penalty of excommunication—well chosen by the priests in terms of timing, in Doudney's mind—likely disrupted these activities involving communal labour. The policy of social exclusion could, therefore, have detrimental economic consequences for those affected. Yet, while there is evidence from elsewhere in Ireland that parties successfully sued the Catholic clergy because of such consequences, there is no evidence that the Bunmahon parents did so.[132] There was still a modicum of fear and deference towards the clergy, though this was to change as a result of the issues raised by Doudney's initiatives in the area.

A week after the excommunications, in a letter to the inhabitants of Bunmahon dated June 17, 1853 Doudney identified the entire issue as centring on the question of authority. Catholics, he maintained, would identify the pope as Christ's representative on earth and priests as the successors of Christ's apostles. Such claims were based on the authority of the Church whose authority in turn was based on the Bible. To Doudney there appeared to be an inconsistency in this; for how could the pope and priests have recourse to scriptural authority (exemplified in the exercise of excommunication) on the one hand, while on the hand disparaging the Bible as a work not worthy to be read independently by people.[133]

Secondly, accepting for the purposes of argument that the pope was the vicar of Christ and the priests the successors of the apostles, there was a clear discrepancy between the example set by Christ and the behavior of the Catholic clergy which in effect in Doudney's mind made them unfit successors.[134] Coupled with this was the insensitivity around the timing of the excommunication and the social exclusion incumbent upon it.

Thirdly, while the Bible was rejected, on the other hand the priests proclaimed to the people that they were the only ones who could interpret it for them. In the tradition of the Reformation, Doudney questioned why this was so: why should not people have access to the Bible in order to read it for themselves and so test the things they were taught to believe? He believed that it was every person's right to have such access. Why was it that Catholic clergy discouraged people having such access, whereas the Protestant clergy encouraged enquiry? He concluded: "The one keeps you in darkness, ignorance, and superstition; the other endeavours to lead you to light, and knowledge, and peace, and prosperity."[135]

Subsequent to addressing this letter to the inhabitants, Doudney learned that the priests had no objection to people reading Scripture for themselves but only if it was in the Douay Version. Picking up on this invitation, Doudney proposed that if the priests made a public declaration to that effect, then he would make 100 copies of the Douay Version available for free for those who wanted a copy.[136]

This development is significant for two reasons. Firstly, it demonstrated the willingness of the priests to allow people to read the Bible in response to the arguments Doudney had made publicly. Had he not articulated this, it is unlikely that the priests would have responded in the way they did. Secondly, Doudney's offer to make copies of Scripture available in the Catholic version (the accuracy of which he might normally have had reservations about) indicated his basic concern that people have unencumbered access to God's Word. On the issue of version and interpretation, Doudney was charitable and inclusive, in that he encouraged Catholics to read the Douay Version: he was more concerned that they read something than that they read nothing at all. This demonstrated his flexibility and broader purpose. This liberal gesture showed his confidence that that God's Word would potentially have its impact irrespective of the particular translation or denominational preference. In this he was likely more liberal than other Church of Ireland clergy in the diocese, for many of whom the accuracy of biblical translation was paramount and a matter of denominational self-definition.

Doudney's exercise in inclusiveness so far as versions of the Bible is concerned, was already paralleled by activities on the part of the local Catholic community. In November 1849, for instance, when a member of his congregation died of fever, hundreds of people mostly Catholics joined the funeral procession to the church, where Doudney records, "many, very many entered and listened attentively to the service" and later gathered around the grave for the burial service.[137] Similarly, in May 1852 one of the young people from the printing school died, an interment was held in the graveyard adjoining the church which was full of Catholics for the funeral service with around 500 attending the graveside. As part of the service Doudney read from the Bible, first in the Protestant version, then the same passage in the Douay Version "in order to meet scruples" the effect being that they were "riveted."[138]

These instances demonstrated Doudney's desire to have people become familiar with God's Word irrespective of the version they read, even to the extent of foregoing his own preference in that regard. However, such accommodation was not universally welcomed by the local Catholic clergy. Further priestly activity was intent on demonstrating that Bible reading was unnecessary and redundant.[139] On a Sunday following the funeral service at which so many of his parishioners attended, the event was the subject of an attack from the altar by the priest at the chapel in Ballylaneen, the substance of which was that Doudney had no right to preach to Catholics and they had no right to listen to him.[140] However, in an instance of lay defiance, it was made clear to Doudney subsequently by some Catholics who visited him that such denunciations were not going to deter them from attending Protestant funerals.[141] They continued to do so. For instance, the burial service for Lieutenant Charles Shaw, who was in charge of the coast guard service, was reportedly attended by a "most attentive group of Roman Catholics, as well as Protestants."[142]

In an attempt to restrict attendance by Catholics at Protestant services, Bishop Foran on January 27, 1852 issued instructions to the clergy in his diocese containing a list of reserved sins, one of which concerned communication with heretics, specifically attendance at their services and sermons.[143] Its inclusion in the list reflected concern about situations such as that in Bunmahon, but the evidence indicates that the Catholics of Bunmahon continued to attend Protestant funerals despite episcopal proscriptions that such a practice was grievously sinful.

Continued Defiance of Priestly Authority

While the act of excommunication represented the exceptional exercise of priestly authority and power, the more normal and recurring exercise of the latter was most obviously seen in the celebration of the mass. However for Doudney and Protestants as a whole the mass, as we have noted in Chapter 5, contained various anomalies. Some specific features can be noted again here in the context of challenges to priestly authority. For one thing, the fact that it was celebrated in Latin meant that it was not understood by people and this was a departure from the practice of Jesus who at the Last Supper (which the mass claimed to re-enact) spoke in a language understood by his hearers. Doudney had in his employment a young Catholic man (who had worked for his predecessor and whom Doudney kept on) whom he led to recognize that because the mass was said in Latin people did not know whether the priest was blessing or cursing them in what he said. On this basis the man ceased to attend mass and later emigrated to America.[144] Another person who had been among the mourners at Shaw's funeral having heard Doudney's graveside address was so stuck by it that he shortly after emigrated to Australia.[145] It was Doudney's conviction that he and the many others who emigrated had left Ireland with a different view of religion, but while they were in Ireland they did not have "sufficient light, strength, or moral courage to come boldly out, and brave the bitter persecution of relatives and the diabolical conspiring of enemies."[146] The use of the Latin language bolstered priestly authority.

Secondly, only the priest was allowed to partake of the cup, something that was contrary to what Christ commanded at the Last Supper. Thirdly, people were required to fast before receiving the wafer in communion, in contrast to what Christ had done at the Last Supper when he administered the sacrament while the disciples were still eating. Fourthly, in the mass the priest offered the body and blood as a perpetual sacrifice for the sins of the living and the dead, whereas the Bible showed that it was done once and once only. Finally, in the mass the priest instructed people to worship the consecrated wafer, which in Protestant eyes was idolatry.[147] An offshoot of the entire authoritarian system in Doudney's eyes was the character of the relationship between priest and people, i.e. that it was "not from love, but from dread; not from approval, but from apprehension."[148]

An additional objection Doudney had was how, in his eyes, the priests on many occasions withheld celebrating the mass for people in dire need because no fee for doing so was forthcoming.[149] In April 1852 a poor miner, Michael Veale, was accidentally killed in the copper mines leaving a sick wife and four young children. A local subscription to provide for them raised 15s. which was given to the mother by the manager of the mine, likely Petherick. But she gave 10s. out of the 15s. for the priest to say mass for her deceased husband.[150]

There were other cases of apparent extortion communicated to Doudney, one involving the priest's refusal to bless a candle for less than the sum of 1s.8d needed by a woman emigrating to America.[151] In another case, while the fee for the mass was paid, it did not produce the desired result immediately. The case concerned a man, who used to repair the roads, being drowned because of his drunkenness while trying to get to his boat off Annestown, resulting in a three-day search for his body without success. This failure occasioned a request for the priest to say mass on the strand and even those searching were told to desist so confident were others that the presence of the priest would make it unnecessary. But despite the mass no body was located or emerged until days later when it was found in the sea twenty miles away.[152]

The issue of observance of a fast day was another area where the authority of the priest was exercised. There was the case reported where a group of guests at a local wedding reception danced away oblivious of the time, and when it came time to eat the feast they realized that they had danced too long into the next day which was a fast day. The result was that the two Protestants present at the reception could indulge themselves, while the Catholics had to look on because they had neglected to ask the priest for an exemption from the fast requirement because of the wedding.[153]

There was also a strong belief in the healing or magical powers of the priest. In one case, a farmer paid for masses to be said by the priest to halt a mysterious disease which had decimated nine cows on a farm near the glebe house where Doudney lived but this was to no avail, such that resort to the bishop, Nicholas Foran, was contemplated, though cow mortality continued.[154]

There was also the case of the Catholic Church's refusal to bury people suspected of or having committed suicide. In June 1848, a man named Sullivan was gathering seaweed when he was washed over and drowned. His recovered body was brought successively to be buried at Ballylaneen, Kill, and finally to Stradbally, but at each of them burial was refused because a report had circulated that he had committed suicide and so could not be buried in consecrated ground. After two days he was buried in the graveyard at Monksland church.[155]

In another case the recovered body of a man who supposedly threw himself over a cliff was refused burial, the body was brought back to the village and left on the side of the roadway in his coffin, leaving the man's widow distraught. The man's former employer hearing of the situation had the coffin stored in a stable and sought permission for the body to be buried in the Protestant graveyard, likely in Stradbally. Such permission having been obtained, the next day a grave was dug but before the body could be interred, a group of Catholic villagers with "the most determined effrontery" secured the body and brought it back to their own village (likely Bunmahon) for burial apparently in the Monksland graveyard. A complaint was brought to Bishop Daly against Doudney for allowing this, but the bishop was supportive of Doudney's action.[156]

In these cases of suicide, it appears that the community, knowing that Catholic clergy would not allow burial within the confines of consecrated ground, would take matters into its own hands with respect to the disposal of the body, such as throwing it over a cliff or bringing it out to sea and tossing it overboard. In the latter case, often the body washed to shore, and if this repeated itself the body was buried in unconsecrated ground, or as we have seen in a Protestant graveyard. [157]

There were other cases of conflict around burials. In early May 1852, an eighteen-month old girl, the daughter of a Protestant father and a Catholic mother, died. The mother was anxious that the child be buried alongside its grandfather in the graveyard of the Catholic church in Stradbally. To accommodate the wishes of both parents a service in the Protestant tradition was held first, then the body was brought to Stradbally for burial. No sooner had the latter been done than the priests came to the grave, one of whom declared that the girl was "a little whelp" and that the ground was desecrated by her presence. When this was brought to the attention of the mother, she with her husband proceeded to have the body of their daughter disinterred and buried in the Protestant graveyard instead.[158]

All this was happening at a time in the early 1850s when there was an increasing policy on the part of the Catholic Church to have the body of the dead person brought to the church for the funeral mass, rather than having it said in the deceased house as had been the common practice.[159] This is indicative of the fact that conflict over burials was occurring at a time of change or transition. These multiple instances of collective defiance of priestly authority align with the response of parents following the excommunications of June 1853.

Further Division

It is apparent that the excommunications and their aftermath caused division in the community. As expressed by a letter to the editor of a local newspaper, "the quiet of Bonmahon and its neighbourhood has again been disturbed by the powerless struggles of the Church of Rome…The good feelings which were beginning to subsist between Protestants and Papists are swept away by the anathemas of the altar."[160]

Articulating the concerns of the community in the wake of the excommunications, Doudney composed a stylized dialogue between

John and Paddy in which the action of the priests was criticized, the excesses of the excommunications were decried, and their uncharitableness highlighted.[161] Provocatively, Doudney forwarded a copy to the priest, Rev. Michael Power, with the request that if he or his assistant would answer the charges implicit in the dialogue, he would have one thousand copies of the reply printed free of charge in his printing school and would send the copies to Power for distribution in Bunmahon, at the chapel gates or elsewhere.[162] However, there is no evidence that Power took him up on this offer.

Soon controversy over voluntary attendance at Bible classes became apparent in the autumn of 1853. These classes were conducted by Doudney's wife, Eliza, and were intended for girls who attended the new embroidery school. She told the girls under her charge in the school that she, out of concern for their spiritual as well as their physical nurture, would attend at the infant school to allow such girls as wished to come voluntarily to hear the Bible read. She made it clear that they would not be paid for doing so, no extra material benefit would accrue, and whether they came or not all would be treated equally so far as attendance at the embroidery school was concerned.[163] Initially, only two girls came but in successive weeks 9, 13, and eventually by the third week, 16 out of the 25 girls who attended the embroidery school came.[164]

In addition, twenty of these girls of their own accord and without any invitation chose to attend the Sunday and Thursday evening lectures hosted by Doudney, and they participated in singing lessons.[165] They expressed a wish to acquire the ability to read and for that purpose an evening school was proposed in 1854. This might seem a surprise given the age and maturity of the girls, however, apparently while they had been taught to read in the national school, they had no textbooks to maintain their reading habits and hence had lost the facility to do so.[166] Though these lectures were not compulsory and though Catholics were known to attend, attendance declined for several weeks in early 1855, a development Doudney was at a loss to explain.[167] Perhaps it was connected with the response of the Catholic authorities in early 1855.

Catholic Response

The early part of 1855 was marked by two developments. The first of these was the intervention of the Catholic bishop, Nicholas Foran, who reportedly instructed his flock in Bunmahon: "Avoid that Doudney; it is the greatest trap God Almighty ever suffered to exist."[168] The bishop's intervention demonstrates the seriousness with which he regarded the local situation, points to the ineffectiveness of the excommunications, and shows the breakdown in deference between local priests and people not merely over infant school attendance but over a range of issues.

The second development of this period was that by the time Doudney had returned from a visit to England in early 1855 a new Catholic chapel had opened. Prior to this development local Catholics had to walk the two miles to Ballylaneen (erected in 1824), or go further to Kill village for mass. However, in October 1854 the building formerly used as a temperance hall and hospital, was purchased for the purpose of converting it into a chapel.[169]

Because the new chapel was more convenient than the church at Ballylaneen attendance at the latter (and hence people's financial contributions) was considerably reduced. This development was blamed on Doudney, the more so as the building which became the printing school had originally been offered to the priest of Ballylaneen, the Rev. Michael Power (who was also responsible for Stradbally and with whom Doudney already had dealings) for use as a new chapel but because the £20 needed to pay for it would be an additional cost to the parishioners, the offer passed.[170]

The Rev. Roger Power, parish priest of Kill and Newtown (until 1871), assumed responsibility for the former temperance building and converted it into an auxiliary chapel.[171] Instead of attacking

Doudney's schools and activities, Power preached from the Bible on topics like Jesus Christ (instead of the saints which would have been typical) and predestination.[172] Apparently the congregation was struck with the contrast, and to Doudney's mind Power was not the typical "dogmatical, overbearing, unapproachable man (as very many of the priests are) [but rather] a gentle, affable, comely-looking man."[173] In fact, Doudney declared himself contented that while all the other efforts made to counteract his projects had failed, Roger Power's arrival as priest was a welcome development.[174]

If Doudney's presence in the area achieved nothing else it at least forced the Catholic Church to invest greater effort into pastoral provision of its flock in Bunmahon. Until the new chapel opened, the diocese had nothing in terms of church buildings conveniently located for the Catholic population of the mining centre, despite the fact that intense exploitation of the mines had been current for over twenty years and the population of the area had grown to over 2,000 by 1841. The opening of the refurbished chapel in 1854 thus represents a more direct engagement with pastoral provision for Bunmahon that can in part be ascribed to Doudney's presence.

Other Controversies

Another educational initiative, the evening school for boys who were in the printing school during the day, also became the subject of controversy. Sometime in October 1852, Doudney decided to start an evening school for the boys in the printing school because he was concerned that their general education would be neglected because they were occupied during the day and he wanted to give them something to do during the winter evenings. He arranged for a teacher to provide instruction between 7 p.m. and 9 p.m., parents were happy with the arrangement, and there was almost full attendance the first couple of evenings.[175] However, on the third day of its operation, a so-called "station" was held in the village whereby the priest would visit some house for the hearing of confessions and the granting of absolution, after which he dined with the host family.

Traditionally, this form of hospitality occurred once or twice a year when the priest would visit selected private houses in the parish for the purpose of hearing confessions and giving communion. The practice was an important source of income in kind for the priest that helped to supplement the other income he had from fees for baptisms, marriages, and funerals.[176] The fact that confessions and stations were still being held in private houses in the Bunmahon area instead of a church building, shows the survival of more archaic practices that the Catholic Church was attempting to change in the 1850s following the synod of Thurles. On this score, resistance to change appears to have been acute in Munster.[177]

At any rate on the occasion in question, one of the boys from the printing school was present at the station and made known his intention of attending the evening school, to which the priest responded by forbidding the boy not only from attending the school but even from entering the building.[178] It was later communicated to Doudney that the boy received a spanking from his father for agreeing to stay from the school and insisted that he attend in future.[179] In response, the priest charged the people not to communicate with the Protestants but rather to ostracize and avoid them.[180]

Relations between Doudney and the priests continued to remain tense during 1852 and 1853. The suspicion lingered that Doudney was using the schools for the purposes of converting vulnerable Catholics. This charge was exacerbated when reports circulated that when speaking in Birkenhead in October 1853 on the subject of Protestant conversions, the militant Catholic preacher, Rev. Daniel William Cahill (1796–1864), declared that the conversions were obtained by bribing the poor starving Irish with soup, clothes and employment, that the price of a convert was 10s. per week, and that the converts so obtained were no more than "liars, hypocrites, and perjurers."[181] Such an accusation flew in the face of those English people who were genuinely moved to provide some relief to needy people in Ireland.

Further, there were additional charges that Doudney was an agent of an English secret society, that he received £100 for every convert he made, that he gave every convert a leg of mutton and half-a-crown or 5s. per week for their maintenance, and that he had received £2,000 to make converts in the village.[182] Doudney firmly denied these charges of bribery which had been made many times against him, basing his position on the fact that they could not be substantiated.

In his defence, Doudney conceded that while in the past two years he had the opportunity on many occasions to place biblical truth before the many who were in his employment, yet on no occasion did he use threats or inducements to make them change their opinions.[183] Rather by living among the people he tried to demonstrate what Protestantism was in word and deed.[184] He asserted that there were no material gains to be obtained for those who wished to convert. This explains why he had so few converts, and hence there was nothing in Bunmahon or Knockmahon comparable to the extensive and elaborate colonies established in Dingle, Achill, or Connemara for the protection of converts.

It is important to remember that Doudney opposed nominalism of any kind, whether it was found in the Church of Ireland or the Catholic Church communities. What was an additional barrier in communicating this distinction was traditional Irish hostility to anything English, especially anything associated with Protestantism. Anticipating the latter, at the outset of his time in Bunmahon, Doudney resolved as follows:

> "that instead of endeavouring to make converts in the common acceptation of the term, he would try to let his neighbours—almost exclusively Roman Catholic—see what Christian Protestantism was in operation. He uses the term *Christian* Protestantism, because he has very

little sympathy with a lifeless, formal, merely nominal and political Protestantism. Too many are making *it* a passport to heaven, ignorant of the fact that they are as far from the kingdom as their poor blinded Romanist neighbours."[185]

Elaborating on this further, he made it clear that he was more interested in sincerity of conviction as the prime motive for conversion: "He had no wish to make converts (so-called) in name. He would prefer one leaving Romanism from thorough principle and sound conviction (and he believes he has at least one such) to a hundred from a half-heartedness, or selfish, or impure motive."[186] This stance would differentiate him from the majority of those like Edward Nangle, and Alexander Dallas who were active in Connemara, west Kerry, and Mayo who it would appear were more concerned with numbers than depth of conviction.[187]

Indicative of what Doudney sought was the situation described by outsiders who visited his schools. Such visitors observed that the children attending the schools brought the scriptural knowledge they acquired into their homes where the parents were impacted in varying degrees but were constrained from advancing in knowledge because of fear of persecution.[188] That such a latter occurrence could materialize is evident from a case in 1853. On September 29, 1853, *The Waterford News* reported that at Ballylaneen four girls from Bunmahon, Mary Fry, Mary Fitzgerald, Kitty Lane and Catherine Cahill, renounced the Protestant creed which they had adopted, and returned to Catholicism.[189] Thus the paucity of converts, sincere or otherwise, can in part be explained by the potential presence of persecution.

On the other hand, the fact that not many converts were made in Bunmahon reflected well on Doundey's insistence on sincerity not material gain as the prime motive. For this reason the evidently insignificant number of converts is witness to the fact that local Catholics were unwilling to entertain conversion either because they were constrained by the prospect of persecution at the hands of their Catholic families, neighbours, and clergy, or because they were aware that Doudney discouraged them from proceeding out of an insincere motive. These considerations should inform any assessment of the veracity of the charges of proselytism that were levelled against Doudney.

Conclusion

Waterford was a highly politicized county by the time Doudney came there in 1847. There was the legacy of ultra-protestantism epitomized by Sir Richard Musgrave; the highly contentious political campaigns of the 1820s in which the Beresford monolith was undermined; and there was the arrival on the scene of Robert Daly as bishop in 1843. In all this religion and politics were intermixed.

On the one hand, Doudney was typical of his clerical class in that he ministered to a small congregation in the midst of a majority Catholic population. He was atypical, however, in how he viewed the parameters of that ministry. He sought to implement a series of educational and entrepreneurial projects to help the children of the Bunmahon area. This won him the support of parents, but the ire of the Catholic clergy who viewed Doudney as a real threat.

The authority exercised by priest over people in pre-famine Ireland was limited. The presence of Doudney in the community gave Catholic clergy the opportunity to show leadership and assert authority over people in a mining community. However, the methods used notably excommunication were archaic and extreme. The experience demonstrated the reactionary nature and ultimate ineffectiveness of that instrument, as lay Catholics defied their priests in a clear undermining of their authority. While such a development might augur well for lay independence of action, ultimately it did not help to halt the campaign against Doudney in the next three years.

Chapter 7

Burned In Effigy
1855-1858

After the failure of the excommunications to curb lay Catholic participation in Doudney's schools, the authority of the priests was undermined and discredited. In the second phase of tension covering the years from 1855 to 1858, the vacuum of authority was filled by extremists reflected in the issuing of a series of threatening letters. Contributory to this development was the semi-permanent departure of John Petherick, the manager of the mines between 1832 and 1852. Petherick was well regarded in the community for his fairness with the workers on the issues that arose.[1] He was a local correspondent for the National Board schools in Knockmahon. Although he returned intermittently, Petherick left the area permanently for London by the end of 1859.[2] His departure, initially in 1852, likely contributed to the sharpness of the religious division, as he had been a mediating figure in the community for twenty years.

For the new year of 1855, the motto Doudney and his congregation adopted was: "And the God of peace shall be with you."[3] However, this was to prove difficult to attain in practice given the events and controversies that were to transpire in the ensuing year. The first conflict to surface in 1855 was over the sensitive issue of workhouse admission; it was followed by an apparent suicide, death threats, and an effigy burning; and it culminated with Doudney's abrupt decision to depart from Bunmahon in early 1858.

Workhouse Tensions

Tensions in the New Year began with the matter of workhouse admissions. The workhouse in nearby Kilmacthomas had only recently opened in 1851, the other three at Lismore, Dungarvan, and Waterford City had come into operation a decade earlier in the early 1840s. Ironically the Kilmacthomas workhouse opened at a time when the worst of the famine conditions in Waterford had subsided, though disease, death, and emigration lingered, and it did not admit paupers until 1853.[4] This fluid arrangement meant that the poor and destitute moved in and out of the workhouse in Kilmacthomas as their needs dictated. Specifically, demand peaked in the May to July period when the old crop of potatoes had been used up and the new crop had not yet become available. This was a situation that affected women and children particularly and there was a strong desire to alleviate their circumstances by assisting them to emigrate.[5]

This situation had a two-fold impact. Firstly, after the famine the role of the workhouse changed from that of a centre of poor relief to the destitute, to being one that dispensed medical aid, being in effect a community hospital for non-contagious diseases. Secondly, this altered role was underlined because after 1850 there was in general a declining incidence of potato blight. These considerations provide the context within which the controversies concerning workhouse admissions that emerged in 1855 in Bunmahon should be considered.

In the first case, Anne Condon, a mother from Bunmahon, along with four or five of her daughters (aged between 10 and 15 years) and a little boy, arrived at the Kilmacthomas workhouse in March 1855 seeking admission. However, this request was challenged by the workhouse staff on the basis that the girls were employed in Doudney's embroidery school and hence were not entitled to receive assistance. The mother, however, challenged this refusal by claiming that she had withdrawn two of her girls (likely

Bridget and Catherine Condon) from the embroidery school, where they were earning "comfortable" wages (7s.6d. weekly between the two), because reportedly they "used to be asking them to read the Bible and go to the prayers."[6] Given the new service orientation of the workhouses post-1850, on the face of it a purportedly sectarian charge such as this was an unlikely reason to seek assistance, apart altogether as a consideration for admission.

Nevertheless, one of the guardians, William Power, who represented Stradbally on the board though his address was given as Bunmahon, believed the veracity of Condon's story as to the force being used. However, another board member, Joseph N. Power of Rockview who represented the Ballylaneen area on the board, was dubious of this as a reason to seek assistance at the workhouse. Investigating the case further Power was able to inform other board members that a small sum was deducted weekly from the wages of everyone employed by Doudney, which sum could accumulate to a large amount, or could be used for the purchase of clothing or goods, as the girls chose. In this way, Condon's two girls had saved 7s. a sum their mother withdrew and spent, leaving the girls without a job, since it was a condition that if the saving fund was used up then employees could not continue to work.

Obviously well informed about the context, Power then asserted that the real reason the girls had been withdrawn from the school was that the mother wished to appropriate the few shillings the girls were entitled to from the clothes club, a fund operated by the embroidery school. Only then when that amount of money was exhausted, was the mother driven to seek assistance from or admission to the workhouse, for as by the rules of the school the girls could not be re-admitted.[7]

On interviewing the elder of the girls, Power found that she flatly contradicted her mother's statement on both counts. She admitted that she was not forced to read the tracts and books, and while they were asked to attend Doudney's talks outside formal school hours, they were not forced to do so. Both girls on a later visit to the village retracted the statements attributed to them by their mother.[8]

The background to this situation was that Doudney normally held a weekly lecture on Thursdays in the building used for the infant school. All the children attending his schools were free to attend this as well as the Sunday services. It was a rule that they could not be forced to attend, but equally, attendance was never made a condition of employment nor was non-attendance a cause for making an employee unemployed. In the case of the elder Condon girl, she decided not to go, but this refusal did not interfere with her continued employment in the embroidery school. Despite this, the girls' mother, Anne Condon, went to the priest and informed him that Doudney was forcing them to attend his talks. The priest then assumed this to be fact.

As a resolution to the case, William Power suggested the Condons return to Bunmahon and if coercion occurred, then they should come back to the workhouse to which they would then be admitted. However, the mother was reluctant to return to Bunmahon. The second daughter suggested going to Portlaw where they could get good employment and conditions in the factory there (likely the cotton factory operated by the Malcomsons), however, her mother declared that she "would leave Mr. and Mrs. Doudney her blessing before she'd go to Portlaw." In the end, not wishing to either return to Bunmahon or go to Portlaw, they were all admitted to the workhouse.[9]

All this was preliminary to a similar but more serious case, that of Catherine Coughlan. Her story was first made public on June 8, 1855 by the *Waterford News* in which it was claimed that she had been expelled from the school in Bunmahon for refusing to read the Bible and say prayers resulting in the denial of work and food for her.[10] In response, Doudney whom the *News* charged with being "silent as the grave" on the charge, forwarded to the newspaper copies of an exchange of correspondence between him and the Kilmacthomas board of guardians on the Coughlan case, sufficient to indicate that he was far from silent. Doudney claimed that his denial of the charge was brought before the guardians three days before the *News* made the original charge public.[11]

From the exchange of correspondence it appears that although the guardians had discussed the issue at their meeting of May 29, the day on which Catherine Coughlan applied for admission to the workhouse, they did not communicate their concern to Doudney until June 4. In their letter of that date the guardians sought clarification of the charge made by Catherine that Mrs. Doudney said that she (Catherine) would not be given work in the school unless she and all the girls in the school attended prayers.[12] In his reply, given by return messenger and read by the guardians at their meeting on June 5, Doudney maintained that the charge was false, that Catherine who had paid 4s. or 5s. into the clothes club withdrew the money, left the school on the pretext of going to Dungarvan to stay with her aunt, and that when the money was gone, knowing she would not be re-admitted to the school, sought admission to the workhouse.[13] Additionally, he challenged anyone to prove that either he or his wife had coerced or even asked the children under their charge to attend his church or lectures.[14]

The guardians, in their reply to Doudney dated June 11, clarified that they never inferred from Catherine's statement that she was coerced to attend church, but rather that the prayers she referred to were conducted in the school room, sought his response to this point, and solicited his view as to whether if Catherine was discharged from the workhouse he would accept her back into the school again.[15] In supportive evidence the guardians cited a former case (likely that of the Condons above) of a mother who sought admission for herself and her daughters who had been given a Bible and who had been asked to attend prayers in the school.[16]

In his reply of the same date, June 11, Doudney made it clear that if Catherine Coghlan in referring to prayers in the school room meant the embroidery school, then the accusation was false as no form of prayer was used there. Even if the charge referred to the infant school, where Sunday and Thursday evening lectures were held and where she may have attended occasionally, then the charge was equally false because attendance there was voluntary.[17] In support of his position as to the lack of coercion, Doudney stated that when William Power, one of the guardians, visited the embroidery school on June 6, all the girls in attendance declared to him that they were neither asked or compelled to attend church or lectures.[18]

As to the other point, Doudney thought it likely that a Bible was given to the family concerned with the natural expectation that it might be read, and he was confident that in all cases where he had given out bibles this was only at the desire of the person concerned. Further, rather than confining himself to the specifically Protestant version of the Bible, it was a matter of public record that he was willing to give out the Catholic Douay Version if needed, in acknowledgment of the fact that it was the duty and privilege of Catholics to read that version, however much he might question the accuracy of its translation.[19] Answering the final query from the guardians, Doudney declined taking Catherine back into the school as it would be against the rules which she was well aware of and despite which she chose to withdraw from the school.[20]

In conclusion, Doudney pointed out that the first of his schools had been in operation for almost four years, that in all his operations he had been open and transparent, that he received no local or government support, that attendance at the schools was voluntary and for the benefit of those who chose to attend and for the area generally, and yet he was subjected to continuous enquiry and vilification in the press "because every now and then, a disaffected pupil chooses to withdraw from the schools, their attendance upon which is altogether unsolicited, and for their own profit alone."[21] To Doudney it all seemed patently unjust and ungrateful when he was doing so much to try and improve the condition of the children and contribute to the well-being of the local community.

The Coughlan case was not an end to the matter over workhouse admissions. In early August, 1855 a statement purportedly by Bridget and Catherine Condon and Mary Brien was read out in the chapel at a Sunday mass. The statement contradicted what had been said to the board of guardians previously when one of the Condon girls admitted that no effort had been made to coerce them to read the Bible or attend prayer services or lectures.[22]

In response to this public declaration Doudney reiterated his previously stated view that the real reason the girls were withdrawn from the school was not coercion or fear of losing their faith, but rather because their mother wanted access to the money in the clothes club. He challenged the community to ask the other girls in the school as to whether they advised the mother, the Widow Condon, that it was foolish to withdraw her daughters from the school merely to appropriate the clothes club money. These same daughters since their admission to the workhouse (suggesting that this latter was at their mother's insistence, and not their personal preference) had begged Mrs. Doudney to take them back into the school. Reverend Doudney was also dismissive of the authenticity of the declaration made by Julia Tobin to the same effect, given that its details were three years old, that she never attended the embroidery school but rather as an eight- or ten-year old she had attended the infant school where the Bible was read.

Monksland Church built 1830. Source: *PO*, 11.

Conversion Again

The case of the girls brought to the fore, again, the issue of whether Doudney was proselytizing or not. In the mind of the *Waterford News* there was no doubt that he was and in its columns urged him to come clean on his motives. It charged him that because he had found no converts among the rich or among the farming class, he had instead targeted the poor and starving who were vulnerable.[23] Responding to the charge, Doudney firmly denied it by stating that if he had wanted multiple converts he would have had no problem filling his church many times over. Indeed in the time since he had come to the area "multitudes" had approached him wishing to convert, but he had given them no encouragement.[24] He was not concerned with external alteration or a change in name from Catholic to Protestant, rather "We place Romanism and Christian Protestantism side by side; let them work together; and the observer shall judge by their relative fruits."[25] It was his purpose to present this model of Christianity before people and allow them to judge for themselves. He had no interest in making converts just in name only or in using force or inducement.

Doudney elaborated on this point again on August 6, 1855 in the context of charges made by the priests and declarations read in the chapels the previous Sunday (which resulted in a riot), that he was instigating "revolution". He challenged the community of Bunmahon to show in any instance whether in the case of current or former attendees of the schools threats or inducements were used to gain converts. He was adamant in declaring that he never encouraged the many that came to him seeking conversion for what they would get out of it materially. However, if there was an individual who sincerely desired to convert out of genuine conviction, he would not be true to his calling as a minister if he rejected an approach from such a person. He was very clear in his own mind about the distinction between nominal and sincere conversion.[26] He wanted this distinction to be more broadly understood, if not appreciated.

As events were to demonstrate, the context of Bunmahon in the 1850s made such a hope elusive.

Doudney had expressed his opinion about nominal and sincere conversions from early on in his time in Bunmahon. Following a service in June, 1852, he commented on:

> "the indifference of the people here [which] chills my already cold heart. For the most part—that is as far as I have been able to judge—the nominal Protestants of Ireland are, in common with the Romanists, satisfied with once attending their church on the Sabbath. If, as I have been telling them tonight, some great person were announced as about to hold a levee in the neighbourhood, what interest would be excited—how many would flock to it—what difficulties would be overcome—what dangers encountered; but when the King of kings and Lord of lords invites [them] to his banquet—the gospel feast—how indifferent then."[27]

To Doudney indifference to true Christianity was not confined to any one denomination for it was present among Protestants and Catholics alike.

Even in the midst of giving notice of his resignation when the girls of the embroidery school all offered to become Protestants if he would stay, Doudney resolutely declined, declaring that it was a voluntary commitment based on principle he sought.[28] If he had chosen the approach of proselytism and bribery, he would have gained converts by the score but such a path was disdainful to him. However, rumours circulated that he received funds in order to induce people to convert, allegations he trenchantly denied.[29] He challenged his Catholic opponents to cite one instance where force or bribery had been used in such cases.[30] Rather his approach was open and fair through training and teaching, without threat or promise of reward to those in his employment.

He recognized early on that there was no point in trying to make converts in the traditional way, given the deeply ingrained antagonism between Catholics and Protestants. Instead his approach was to demonstrate to his neighbours what true "Christian Protestantism" looked like, something that was different than a "lifeless, formal, merely nominal and political Protestantism" something that in his view characterized the Church of Ireland in general.[31] It was this aim of inculcating a more vital Christianity that motivated him to start the different educational enterprises in his parish. It was sincerity based on principle that he sought evidence of, not a desire merely for a denominational switch, given which he refuted any insinuation or charge of bribery.[32] However, he was equally clear that even nominal conversions had some value, "because by them men renounce positive error, and are brought, more or less, under the sound of the truth."[33] It was perhaps a fine distinction that, again, the community of Bunmahon did not appreciate.

As well as indifference, there was also the element of fear. Doudney from the outset made it clear that he was not interested in converts from Catholicism in a way commonly achieved at the time by organizations such as the Irish Society. Not being interested merely in nominal converts, Doudney sought, as he said himself, "one leaving Romanism from thorough principle and sound conviction... to a hundred from a half-heartedness or selfish, impure motive."[34] While he declared that he was only interested in sincere converts, he was convinced that many wanted to enquire into the Protestant faith further but were constrained by fear. He felt that among Catholics there was "an inward consciousness that there is something wrong in their system, but where there is not, as yet, fortitude to encounter the persecution which would necessarily follow an abandonment of it."[35]

The likelihood of conversions on a significant scale was minimal given the fear and intimidation current. On this point, he commented: "The hope of converts from the Church of Rome was doomed to meet with disappointment, for the number was small indeed who, whatever the convictions of right and wrong, were prepared to combat the persecution that must necessarily follow the throwing off of Popery, and the open espousal of Protestantism."[36] As we shall see below, it was the experience of Edward Kelly converting that led to so much persecution and contributed to Doudney realizing that his work in Bunmahon had come to an end.

We can learn of the process of conversion from the story of one young woman, Norah Veale, who was the daughter of Larry and Biddy Veale, the couple who had been excommunicated in June, 1853.[37] When Norah first attended one of Doudney's evening lectures in the infant school, she firmly believed that in holding the Bible in his hand, Doudney was holding the devil. Yet in time she came to revere the Bible, to the extent of saving up to buy a candle in order to read it in the evenings unbeknown to her family, and at church she followed the passages being preached upon. Her family tried to prohibit her from going to the Protestant service, but she escaped, and because of her steadfastness Catholics themselves came to recognize the sincerity of her conversion. In order to make her recant her attachment to biblical faith, her friends sent her to relatives in Liverpool where she was forced to attend mass. She soon after returned to Bunmahon and was among five or six young persons whom Doudney sent out to Canada at the time he left the area.

General apathy and indifference, the fear of intimidation, and Doudney's insistence on sincerity of motive, meant that conversions were not numerous for the duration of his ministry in Bunmahon.

Rising Tensions

Clerical attacks on the schools in general continued through the summer of 1855 and assumed a more threatening tone. On one particular occasion the priests declared at Sunday mass in the two chapels (Ballylaneen and Saleen, the location of the new one in

Bunmahon) that Doudney was receiving £100 per week in support of the schools.[38] Further, one priest is said to have declared that he would demonstrate the power of the Church and rid the village of Doudney (whom he equated with the devil) once and for all.[39] In another declaration from the altar, the priest is reported to have advised the girls to do anything rather than attend the embroidery school and informed a mother that it would be better for her to throw her children over the cliff than send them to the infant school, all of which left the girls in apprehension that the schools would close causing them to return to their idleness.[40]

The most ominous development was the announcement that instead of the normal two masses, there would be only one mass held on Sunday, August 29 at which the attendance of everyone was required as there would be some miracle or extraordinary demonstration of priestly power.[41] The prospect of a high attendance (which the teacher at the national school, Michael Kelly, went around the village to enforce) was made all the more certain when it was reported that the Catholic bishop, Dr. Foran, and eight priests were to attend, thus accentuating the prospect of something eventful happening.[42]

In the two weeks preceding the special Sunday mass, a directive was sent out that everyone within an eight-mile radius was to attend, something Kelly went around a second time to promote and canvass, particularly among the recalcitrant. Though significant numbers attended, many whom Doudney never saw at his church or his lectures refused to comply with the order to attend.[43]

On the Sunday in question the village was deserted as crowds made their way to the chapel which, by report, was "crammed to suffocation" what with not only local people (including many who had not attended mass for several years) but also those from Waterford City and Carrick-on-Suir who were drawn by the prospect of the miracle that might occur.[44] Other "multitudes" could not get into the chapel, while neighbouring chapels were deserted. Many had been on the move since six o'clock in the morning and all arrived in the chapel precincts having fasted all the way.[45]

Matters appeared to be ominous when on the preceding Friday two priests visited the printing school and on Saturday two copies of the *Gospel Magazine* were purchased there for the purpose of being placed on either side of the priest at the altar where it was predicted they would catch fire.[46] As well it was said that part of the miraculous happening would be that Doudney himself would feel the exercise of priestly power to the extent that he would experience transformation into a rabbit, a sheep, a donkey, or a goat, or whatever the priest chose. The drama was heightened when the priest dressed differently for the occasion, causing the people to remark as they entered the church: "Spare him! Spare him!" in reference to Doudney.[47]

Despite all the preparations, the heightened expectations, and the multitudes assembled, nothing miraculous happened. The journals did not catch fire, Doudney was not transformed, and the consensus was that it was all an elaborate hoax.[48]

This failure aside, the incident highlighted two important considerations. Firstly, the fact that the priests would create popular expectation around the use of a semi-magical act as a means of countering Doudney's influence in the area, was archaic and out of step with the reforming agenda as outlined in the decrees of the synod of Thurles. Much of the authority and status of the priest centred on the popular belief in the extraordinary, semi-magical powers he possessed including his ability to curse with effect and cause a change in appearance. Possession of such powers evoked a sense of respect in parishioners, but also a sense of fear. Doudney's daughter, Emily, records with reference to the threat that the priests could turn her father into a goat: "the people pitied us as they passed along to the service to see it done."[49] Expressions of pity bespoke a belief in the ability of the priests to perform the proposed act of transformation.

This point is illustrated in a supposed dialogue, supplied by Doudney, between two local people, wherein one party says: "There was a time when I used to hear such stories, about the priests, that I thought they could do anything. I was told when I was a boy that they could turn a man into a dog, or a hare, or a rabbit, or anything they choose." His conversant queried whether he still believed they could do such, the reply being: "I am sure they can't."[50] While this dialogue is contrived, it nevertheless is indicative of how attitudes were changing towards the priests locally. The conseuqunece of the failure to perform the predicted transformation of Doudney was a diminution in the power, status, and credibility of the priest in the eyes of the community.

Secondly and relatedly, the fall-out from the failure of the magical act to transpire was that the gulf between priest and people widened. During the proceedings at the mass in question a "Roman Catholic gentleman" who was seated in the gallery, stood up and in the midst of the large assembly publicly reprimanded the priest that he was going too far and that but for Doudney's effort and his schools many in the area would have starved or gone to the workhouse.[51] Doudney's daughter, Emily, recalled that the gentleman in question condemned the proceedings in the chapel as "a piece of hypocrisy."[52] The person concerned was John Petherick, the mine manager, who was of Protestant background but likely only nominal (said by Emily Doudney to be "practically an atheist"), liberal in his politics, an O'Connellite supporter, one who had married a Catholic, and who by virtue of that alliance was in attendance at the special mass.[53] For someone of Petherick's background and politics, this action of challenging the priest so publicly was unprecedented, but the effect was that the priest ceased his diatribe against Doudney.[54] It was also a moment of conviction for Petherick himself as he recognized how people could so easily be led on. In the words of Doudney's daughter: "It opened his [Petherick] eyes as to what lengths the poor people might be led in their ignorance and superstitious belief."[55]

Changes in Catholicism

Petherick's action in confronting the priest publicly during mass—the more pointed as it was in the space where clerical authority held sway—represented a challenge to the priest's traditional role as a social and moral leader in the community.

Traditional Irish Catholic society was stratified and marked by clear divisions between the different ranks. At times of economic difficulty those at the bottom of the social rung, i.e. labourers and cottiers, directed their ire at landlord, tithe proctor, tenant farmer, or priest, depending on the issue of grievance. At such times the voluntary offerings for christenings, marriages, and burials (which by tradition were more important in Waterford parishes), and dues (usually a shilling at Christmas and Easter) demanded by Catholic clergy, were resented and often priests became the target of popular ire.[56] Even priests themselves occasionally acknowledged the expropriating nature of such demands. Thus Francis O'Neill, a Waterford priest, said that the priests in Ireland were accused of demanding money for celebrating the sacraments and conceded that "this is no false charge against them for all whoever had any experience even in our own Diocese...will acknowledge that too much cannot be said against it."[57] Although the Catholic bishops as a body forbade priests to receive dues during the hearing of confessions, which was a common occurrence when stations in houses were held, the practice continued since fees and dues particularly were the main source of support for clergy. Such demands could, therefore, be a source of conflict between priests and people, especially during times of economic downturn as was the case in Bunmahon in the 1840s. Its legacy may have lingered into the early 1850s.

As the decades progressed while there was less and less deference to the priest as the person of authority in the locality as Petherick's action epitomized, this cannot be taken too far. For, as the events in Bunmahon indicate, the local clergy still possessed sufficient influence over the people for them to take the initiative in efforts to counter Doudney. Yet the relationship between priest and people was shifting in the post-famine decades. Nationally the popular anti-clericalism of the first half of the nineteenth century gave way to a greater degree of deference, the post-famine decades witnessed improvements in ecclesiastical discipline, and deficiencies in manpower and resources were less problematic than what had obtained in the pre-famine decades.[58]

While there was a fall in population due to famine and emigration, there was a concomitant rise in prosperity for those who remained, circumstances that coalesced in what has been labeled a "devotional revolution." The Catholic Church gained in influence over people's lives, the range of folk customs and beliefs with which it had to contend in the pre-famine period were no longer a threat as the social group (labourers, cottiers) among whom they were most prevalent was decimated by the famine, leaving more affluent sectors to be more compliant to Catholic teaching. But this was not necessarily universal compliance as the experience at Bunmahon illustrated.

Doudney and his educational initiatives were initially controversial in their own right, but in due time they became the cause of division between priest and people. A minority of the latter came to recognize the worth of the educational services introduced and were prepared to defy their priests in order to benefit from them, even to the extent of an accommodation to the Protestant ethos that permeated their operation. From religious considerations and a desire to protect their flock, the priests felt they needed to resist the operation of the schools. The result of Doudney's presence, therefore, was to free segments of the Catholic laity locally from compliance with a narrow clerical authority in order that their families might benefit from the general educational provision. In their over-reaction to members of their flock sending children to the infant school, it was the priests who, in part, contributed to conflict in the community. Doudney arrived and stayed at a time of transition in Irish Catholicism from the older traditional folk religion to one of more doctrinal and administrative discipline. So there were tension points within the Catholic Church to which his presence added an extraneous and ultimately divisive dimension.

Prior to this development, the seeds of division between priest and people were evident already in deficiencies in pastoral provision. In terms of weekly mass attendance (rarely greater than 40% in the pre-famine period), historians have shown that in the pre-famine decades it was highest in the south-east of Ireland which included Waterford.[59] Bunmahon and Knockmahon were likely the exception to this pattern. Given its remoteness, the rise of the mining industry, and the influx of workers, the church was slow to respond to the spiritual needs of the new mining centre with its burgeoning population. The nearest churches were in Ballylaneen (built 1842) and Kill (built 1800) each an uncomfortable distance for miners and their families to get to in a punctual way.[60]

In the absence of a church or chapel in the immediate area until 1854, Catholics are likely to have depended in part on the traditional stations when the sacraments (including mass) would be celebrated in different houses around the parish. On such occasions, hospitality was dispensed (with the attendant expense) to the visiting priest by the host family, as well as at such times as christenings, weddings, and funerals. Only with the change in function of the building in Knockmahon from temperance hall to chapel in 1854, was dependence on the stations eliminated with the provision of a chapel building in the immediate locality. Even then, however, the converted chapel at Saleen was an addional responsibility for the parish priest of Kill and Newtown, Roger Power, and not a single parish responsibility in its own right despite the large population locally.

As well as the availability of a physical building there is the complementary consideration of actual practice. On this issue it has been demonstrated that nationally mass attendance was well below half prior to the famine, while the annual obligation of confession and communion were also typically neglected rather than adhered to as was confirmation, though baptism and extreme unction were received.[61]

The changes enacted at the synod of Thurles (1850) took some time to filter down to the individual dioceses and their constituent parishes. A report of 1853 indicated that attempts to do away with the traditional stations were abandoned because in their absence numbers fulfilling the annual confession obligation had declined so markedly, and the ban on holding baptisms in private houses proved difficult to enforce.[62] While it may be asserted that devotional changes in Irish Catholicism may have been selectively occurring in southeastern counties (including Waterford) even before the famine, these may not have applied to remote locations like Bunmahon and the novel circumstances prevailing there. Because of the rapid growth in settlement from the 1830s, there was no tradition of pastoral provision (as in adjacent centres like Ballylaneen, Kill, and Dunhill, for instance) that could accommodate to new circumstances. Direct pastoral care for Catholics in terms of new institutional provision came late to the mining community of Bunmahon.

Orphan House

The incidents over the workhouse admission and the failure of the proceedings in August, show that there was a feeling of entrenchment on both sides, with Doudney justifying his attempts to give the youth of the locality, Catholic and Protestant, a useful education along with a biblically based faith, and the Catholic clergy resisting any attempts to induce their parishioners to avail of these opportunities on the basis that they were an attempt to convert their flock to Protestantism.

As a result, as one might expect, conditions for those Catholics attending Doudney's schools became very difficult. They were ostracized from houses and cabins where they were formerly welcomed. Doudney observed that the effect of this opposition had been carried to the extent that "the doors of many a cabin (comfortless as those cabins are) have been closed against those who sought to earn an honest livelihood by means of these schools."[63] He resolved to establish a location for their protection, so in 1854 he opened an institution known as the "Refuge" where five children received protection. They were typically engaged in learning the habits of cleanliness and reading (normally the Bible).[64] By 1855, he proposed to expand this into an orphanage or sanctuary for those children who had been turned out or ostracized from the community because of their attendance at his schools.[65]

Doudney felt that his efforts were only half achieving their potential, because whatever was learned was effaced in the homes of the children. He wanted more control over those he employed so that this would not happen.[66] He envisaged the establishment of refuges for those who experienced intimidation because of their attendance at his schools or lectures. Little else is heard of this proposal and it does not seem to have materialized. It is likely that the project was overwhelmed by the circumstances in 1856–7, by the fact that no funds for it were forthcoming, and because Doudney felt increasingly unsettled about his tenure in Bunmahon.

Despite the proposal for an orphan house, intimidating threats continued. In July 1856, Doudney reported to his readers that three children of one family attending the infant school were withdrawn because the Catholic priest had refused to give a relation of theirs absolution unless they did so.[67] It is not possible to determine the accuracy and validity of these statements, but they do, nevertheless, reflect the high passions prevailing.

Charges of Declining Numbers

While Doudney was absent from the locality in the summer of 1856, the *Waterford News* published a report from a correspondent in Bunmahon claiming that numbers in the different schools had declined considerably in the course of a year. The report claimed that attendance at the infant school decreased from 109 to 10, in the embroidery school from 46 to 13, and that the printing school had only a few occasional employees.[68] The purpose of citing these numbers was to demonstrate the decline of proselytism in the establishments concerned. However, upon his return Doudney was able to refute this portrayal of decline by referring to the reports of a variety of other newspapers including the *Clare Journal* (whose editor had learned his trade in the printing school), the *Cork Constitution*, the *Waterford Mail*, and the *London Morning Advertiser*, all of which indicated that the evidence cited by the *Waterford News* was inaccurate.

In particular a conspectus of these different reports indicates that the infant school had never had an enrollment of more than 70, and that far from declining the embroidery school and printing school (the latter fitted out with new machinery), were thriving with the printing establishment at peak employing up to 40 persons.[69] As to the agricultural school any decline in numbers was attributable to the fact that upon graduating some boys were given employment by local farmers, thus achieving the ultimate objective of the enterprise.[70] Something similar prevailed with the printing school whose object was to train boys in the printing trade and place them in positions with other businesses where they would earn a livelihood, a development which had occurred.[71] Thus in both cases the objective of equipping the children with useful, practical, and employable skills was achieved.

As to declining numbers, Doudney attributed this to the intervention of the priests and to seasonal adjustment for in the summer children were needed to help with farm work. Certainly one family had left and another was about to leave for America. Distinguishing between decline and actual failure, Doudney pointed to a number of indicators in evidence of the viability of the schools. He instanced that £20 per week was given in wages; that 29 pupils were paid in the embroidery school; and that Benjamin

Keach's volume on the parables had recently issued from the printing school.[72] Two boys left the agricultural school during 1856 to work in the mines, driven to do so, according to the instructor, Moore, by persecution.[73] While he conceded that numbers at the printing school had reached their lowest level, yet there were still over 30 employed consistently, while the embroidery school had 29 and the infant school had 19 which altogether, not counting the agricultural school, amounted to a significant total of 78 individuals who were supported entirely or partly by the schools.[74]

Addressing the repeated charges of coercion and bigotry, Doudney again reiterated that everything he did was open and transparent; that while the Bible was publicly read no force was involved; and that the schools had been attended by those who had never gone to his church or heard his lectures.[75] As he often emphasized, Doudney reiterated that if it was numbers of converts he wanted he could have had these by the score, a fact he claimed was well known by the priests.[76] He also disavowed the motive of self-interest charged against him by his opponents, on the simple grounds that if this was the operative principle whereby he proceeded, then he would have chosen a less remote and less expensive (in terms of wages which were made artificially high because of the demand for labour in the mines) location.[77] Anticipating the obvious question as to what his motive was in coming to Bunmahon, Doudney declared that it was simply out of a "desire to benefit our fellow creatures."[78] He left it up to others to judge to what extent he had succeeded in this purpose.

As the year 1856 closed it appeared that continued and increasing opposition to the schools and Doudney's ministry emanated from the priests of the area. At year's end, what was ominous and particularly grieving to Doudney was the public destruction of bibles in the village, though he could not identify the guilty party, yet the act was performed "amid the exultation of some of the inhabitants."[79] The action did not augur well for what was to ensue.

"A Fierce Persecution:" The Kelly Case

The text Doudney adopted for himself and his congregation for 1857 was "My God shall be my strength." (Isaiah 49: 5), and he candidly conceded that "I know not that I ever entered a year with fear and trembling of heart than I do the one about to commence."[80]

As it turned out the year 1857 was to be a defining one in terms of the continued existence of the schools in the area and Doudney's continued oversight of the same. Passions reached a new level of intensity involving continued controversy over charges of proselytism, a suicide, threatening letters, and the public burning of Doudney in effigy.

For a number of years Doudney had been in the habit of meeting and saluting a young man in his walks to and from the village. This man turned out to be Edward Kelly, the brother of Michael Kelly, the local national school teacher, to whom he was also an assistant. Despite the public stance he was subsequently to adopt in the case, Michael Kelly himself was not without blemish. He was the teacher at the Knockmahon boys' school. In June 1858 Kelly was admonished in a report on the state of the school, particularly the low "intellectual proficiency of his pupils and their discipline" and its lack of cleanliness, its bad state generally, and most significantly, because, as the official report stated, "as a teacher [he] seems unworthy of the high position he holds."[81] All this critical assessment amounted to a recommendation that he be dismissed because of his refusal to obey the rules for conducting the school. Already by that date the Kelly family appears to have established somewhat of a dynasty in the local schools. Between them, Michael, Mary, Bridget (both assistants), and Edward Kelly held different positions in the Knockmahon boys and girls schools in the 1850s.[82]

Doudney claimed that Kelly's brother, Edward, came to him about January 1857 at dusk and sought conversion from the Catholic to the Protestant religion.[83] Doudney at first discouraged such a step as he had done with many others whom he suspected of being insincere, acting out of impulse, or from ulterior motives. In Kelly's case Doudney advised that if his desire for conversion had arisen out of a temporary misunderstanding with the priest, then it was better to let it pass and that he should not allow it to influence him to take so important a step so quickly.[84] However, following Kelly's declaration of the seriousness of his intent and that he had weighed the matter before proceeding, Doudney began to instruct him, and Kelly also attended Doudney's evening lectures, a situation apparently only made possible by his hiding behind a curtain so that the priests might not hear of it.[85] Given the circumstances around conversion already alluded to whereby there were constraining forces on either side (on Doudney's part because of the criterion of sincerity, and on the Catholic community's part because of fear and intimidation), Kelly's conversion was both exceptional and controversial.

In time, however, Michael Kelly came to suspect that his brother was receiving such instruction, causing the brother to fear for his life. Doudney's daughter, Emily, later commented that Kelly "became a Protestant, but had to flee the country or he would have lost his life."[86] Given these circumstances, Doudney counselled Edward that he leave the area and go to London, where Doudney undertook to find him employment.[87] Ten days after Edward Kelly's departure, Doudney received a letter from Michael Kelly, dated March 2, 1857, asking whether he had any role in his brother's disappearance.[88] In his reply, Doudney explained what had happened and that the brother had proceeded by his own free will.[89] To this Michael Kelly replied within a week charging that Doudney had taken away his brother to whom he was an only guardian, that Edward was under seventeen years of age, and that on the evening of his disappearance the brother had stolen property from him.[90]

To this charge, Doudney reiterated that Edward had left voluntarily, that he was unaware of his age or the guardianship condition, or of the stolen property. Doudney vowed that if he saw the brother in London, where he was soon to go, he would show him the letter and let him answer for himself and if he wished to return to Bunmahon then that would be his decision.[91]

Further enquiry led Doudney to the knowledge that Edward Kelly was nineteen or twenty years of age, not seventeen as was claimed by his brother. Upon meeting him subsequently in London (to which Doudney had departed on March 10), where he had secured him employment with W. H. Collingridge, Kelly declared that he did not regret the decision he had made, that even if he was given the money to cover the cost of returning to Bunmahon he would not do so, and he promised to write to his brother to declare that nothing he had done was under duress but by his own free will.[92] Doudney also wanted clarification from Edward with regard to the charge of theft brought by his brother. To this Edward conceded that he had taken two or three books belonging to his brother which he was learning from, but that the wages he was owed from being his assistant in the national school would more than cover their value.[93] On all points, therefore, Edward seemed to provide satisfactory explanations for his course of action. However, this was not an end to the matter.

What made the situation concerning the younger brother worse was the news that the Kellys' sister (unfortunately the evidence does not give her first name, but probably Mary, the assistant teacher) had died, a suspected suicide, on the night *before* Doudney returned to Bunmahon from his trip to England.[94] She had been in declining health during the previous year, and although three weeks before her death the doctor had advised that she be admitted to an asylum for her own safety, this advice was not heeded.[95] According to Doudney's daughter in a later account of the case of Mary Kelly, who had also become a Protestant: "we never knew what happened. They made out she committed suicide, but it was impossible in the position in which they found her."[96] Amazingly, although there was firm proof of her long-term illness, her death was attributed to Doudney even though he was absent from the area when it happened.[97] Emily Doudney, recalling the impact the event had, commented that it "caused a great uproar in the village and every feeling was exercised against our dear father."[98] Certainly it was a serious development, not least when viewed in the context of the pattern and nature of crime as a whole in the locality.

In the past, apart from robbery and arson along with petty crimes like drunkenness among the miners, the locality had not been the site of serious crime such as agrarian unrest or murder. In December 1848 the house of William Tobin, a shopkeeper in Ballylaneen, had been broken into, but the majority of cases that came up in the Stradbally petty session court (usually presided over by Colonel Beresford) involved drunkenness.[99] Such petty crimes were doubtless held in check by the presence of police barracks in Knockmahon, Kill, Annestown, and Stradbally.[100] However, the Kelly case was to constitute a serious escalation of community stability that was detrimental to peace and order. Clearly there was a change in attitude towards the Doudneys' presence in the area. Instead of the usual celebrations with bells ringing, bonfires, and cheering that traditionally marked their return from the fundraising trips to England, there was hostility. Emily Doudney records an instance of how this change manifested itself in one case:

> "As they drove through the village not a sound was heard. No one was seen at the doors, it seemed like death; but just as they came to the village cross three great black dogs were let loose at the car on which they were driving."[101]

The novel occurrence of Edward Kelly's conversion, his fleeing to England, his brother's questioning of the circumstance of his disappearance, and his sister's controversial death triggered the beginnings of a more hostile reaction to Doudney. It was the prelude to more serious developments to follow. In the words of Emily Doudney, it was "then that the persecution began in earnest."[102]

Threatening Letters

In the aftermath of the death of Michael Kelly's sister, a series of five or six threatening letters were delivered to Doudney over a period of six months. The first of these was dated May 23, 1857 and its contents were as follows:

> "Mister Doudney, Have your coffin made and your grave dug, for our hands we will wash in your blood. Your well wisher, an ignorant Irishman. Bonmahon."[103]

The death threat contained in this first letter, though specific in its intent and directions, was general in its language. Subsequently, its words were turned into a rhyme and the children sang it as a jingle in the street.[104]

Doudney was warned not to be out after dark.[105] Concerned for his own and his family's safety, he wrote to the lord lieutenant explaining that his glebe house was a half mile distant from the police station where, he emphasized, there was only one Protestant among the complement of men which included a sergeant and four others. In his letter, Doudney pointed out that a comparison of the handwriting of the letters addressed to him from Michael Kelly dated March 2 and March 9 with that of the threatening letter should leave no doubt as to its authorship. Supportive of this deduction Doudney noted that Kelly was "exasperated" because of his brother's departure and because of his sister's death giving him a strong motive to express the sentiments of the threatening letter.[106]

The upshot of it all was that Doudney's request for protection was acceded to for on June 2 the Constabulary Office in Dublin Castle transmitted the request to the county inspector in Dungarvan, J.H. Brackin.[107] Brackin, in carrying out the request, while he considered it an "unfair insinuation" on Doudney's part that he required additional protection because there was only one Protestant among the police force in Bunmahon, arranged for G. Forsythe, a Protestant police officer, to be transferred from Cappoquin to Bunmahon where he was to replace a Catholic constable who was to move to Butlerstown. If necessary a similar exchange of officers could take place between Portlaw and Bunmahon. In addition a reward of £20 was offered by the government for the author of the threatening letter.[108]

The Kelly case generated high emotions among the people towards Doudney. In a letter to Brackin dated June 4, 1857 assuring him of his force's alertness to any threats to Doudney, H.E. Redmond, who was in charge of the Portlaw police station, commented: "There is now certainly a strong feeling against him [Doudney] in Bonmahon, on account of the change of religion and suicide in the Kelly family." More pointedly Redmond concluded that "Mr. Doudney has been the sole cause of a very bad sectarian feeling now existing at Bonmahon." In Redmond's view this hostility began when Doudney distributed "placards" which offended Catholics, however he did not believe that anyone in the area "would attempt bodily injury to him." In addition, it had not been the first time that Doudney had questioned the integrity and motivation of the Catholic members of the police force at Bunmahon who, Redmond assured his correspondent, would perform their "duties faithfully irrespective of creed."[109]

Soon after, Kelly was arrested for issuing the threatening letter. This was a not unexpected development not merely because of the particular circumstances of the case but also because traditionally suspicion fell on teachers as the ones in the community who had the literary skill to write such letters. Kelly's trial took place at Stradbally petty sessions. However, he was released on bail for want of proof, in celebration of which event a large bonfire was lit, Doudney's effigy was paraded about, shot at, and finally tossed in the fire.[110] The violence attendant on this celebration subsided temporarily, however, because one member of the mob inflicted himself with the discharge of a blunderbuss which immobilized him for a few months.[111] The impact this had was later well described by Emily Doudney:

"One day we looked out and saw a crowd of people in the distance and wondered what they could be about. They had actually made an effigy of our dear father and carried him through the village and one man, more bitter than the rest, fired off a blunderbuss. It happened to be an old one and burst and blew off the man's thumb, so seriously wounding him that he had two or three months in the hospital afterwards. You may imagine the effect this had upon the excited crowd—they looked on it as judgment from God and quietly dispersed."[112]

The man who discharged the blunderbuss was unable to recover and eventually ended up emigrating to America where he died.[113]

In the face of the threat Doundey remained resolute, to the extent of preaching in the church in an exposed position before the window through which he could easily have been shot at.[114] Because of these developments and the threats to his life, Doudney initially regarded the threatening letter as a possible sign from God that he should leave Bunmahon, and this was also the consensus of several of his parishioners.[115] Discerning that a clear change had come over the area upon his return from England, Doudney resigned his curacy, though this action was reversed as a result of arguments brought to bear on him by his own congregation.[116]

However, once his decision to stay became known a second threatening letter dated June 13, 1857 arrived just as Doudney was leaving for church on a Sunday morning, the letter giving him one month's notice to leave the area or else his life would be taken.[117] It stated:

"David A. Doudney, you proselitising Orange man Take Notice that if you don't leave Bonmahon in One Month from this date your Self and Family Mark the Consequence this is the last Notice you will Get, your days Are Numbered On this earth Given Under our hand this day [Signed] I CAPT FEAR NOT."[118]

In contrast to the first letter, this one combines sectarian terminology ("proselytising Orange man") with the signature ("CAPT FEAR NOT") of traditional agrarian secret societies notably the Whiteboys. These elements along with a change in the tone of language raised the threat to a new level of seriousness.

Shortly thereafter a third threatening letter dated July 8, 1857, warned him:

> "David A. Doudney you proselytising Orangeman you have got warning to leave this country and take flight to John Bull it is all in vain blame yourself this is the last notice, have your coffin bought, and grave made before this day month Capt Fear not."[119]

Here the language combines elements of sectarianism ("proselytising Orangeman") and of secret societies ("Capt Fear not") with that of xenophobia ("John Bull"). If Doudney had an anti-Catholic tenor in his attitudes and beliefs these were largely based on doctrinal differences, and in no sense was he of violent disposition. This contrasts with the explicitly violent intent of this threatening letter with its expressed anti-English sentiment, sectarianism, and its associations with agrarian secret societies. Clearly the tone and content of the letters evolved from the first one to the last reflecting not merely the extension and development of the threats, but also a certain frustration that the initial one had not met with compliance.

Although the government offered a reward for those responsible for the threatening letters and though the police remained vigilant, those responsible remained at large.[120] Doudney received a fourth threatening letter on September 26, and another arrived in early November, 1857, the latter given to his wife while Doudney himself was absent.[121] This was the fifth threatening letter received by the Doudneys over a period of six months.

The threatening letter was a distinctive instrument of popular protest in pre-famine Ireland. It was used as a weapon to press community or individual grievances typically over land. Its use was intended to gain the amelioration of such grievances, or at the very least to instill fear in the recipient. At a time of change or intrusion, the letter sought to protect local arrangements and traditions.[122] The deployment of the threatening letter in Bunmahon in 1857 was unrelated to its typical use over land issues. Rather it was used to gain compliance and force the exit from the community of one who had provoked its ire. Its use against Doudney was the secular equivalent of the Church's use of excommunication against recalcitrant adherents. In another sense resort to the threatening letter reflected a shift in initiative and responsibility away from the failed efforts of the priests to restrict Doundney's activities, to the more traditional, secular methods of the community itself which held out the possibility of violence.

We do not know what the immediate result of the threatening letters was. Though they obviously generated fear in Doudney's family, yet he remained in the area for about another six months, though he likely was absent in England for part of that time. He did not leave immediately, in part because he did not want to create the impression that he had been forced out.

The threatening letters are an index of the high passions aroused among the majority Catholic community of Bunmahon by the Kelly case. Doudney felt that he was in constant danger of assassination, and the shooting of Rev. Alexander Nixon in Donegal in 1858 proved that such apprehensions were real.[123] Nevertheless, Doudney faced the situation with equanimity and appeared indifferent to his personal safety.[124] Indicative of this was his decision to move the printing operations to a purpose built location adjacent to the new glebe house, and as we have seen above, he continued to seek subscribers for projected new publications.[125]

Despite this positive initiative, Doudney felt that 1858 would be his last year in Bunmahon.[126] Apart from the threatening letters, he felt that his ministry would have more impact if he were a pastor to a greater number of people, rather than among the miniscule congregation at Monksland. Part of this desire was motivated by the on-going resistance that he was experiencing from the Wesleyan Methodists in his community. In February 1858 he commented on their "wretched Arminianism that gnaws like a canker-worm at the root of any little light of those who may have been cradled in it."[127] The issue here was important, for Doudney is referring to the tradition going back to Dutch pastor and theologian Jacob Arminius (1560–1609) who held that people were free to choose for or against faith in Jesus Christ, and that Christians can fall away from such faith. This was in contrast to a more orthodox belief which Doudney would have subscribed to, that faith is the result of predestination, i.e. the belief that before the foundation of the world God had decreed who would have faith and who would not. It is likely that if there had been a sufficiently large and permanent congregation of Wesleyan Methodists in Bunmahon they would have organized their own separate place of worship. As it was they attended the church that was closest to their theological position, i.e. the Church of Ireland, but even that had its flash points as Doudney came to experience.

Cooperation and Support

If the Methodists were prickly, some Catholics, despite all that had gone before, were still prepared to listen to Doudney speak. Thus in March 1858, at the burial of one of his own parishioners, Doudney used the opportunity to speak to the Catholics who were present.[128] In addition, he continued to receive support from readers of the *Gospel Magazine* and others.[129] One such, H. Whitney, who had been a resident of Bunmahon but who had left before Doudney's arrival there, in early 1858 offered words of encouragement to him. Advising him not to fear the threats, Whitney claimed that "the Bonmahon people will not hurt you; they are still the generous, open-hearted people I ever saw them. You have done them good and *they know it*." However, Whitney continued, "each is afraid of his fellow, which is the case all over Ireland. The dear Irish Roman Catholic people love their Protestant neighbours when they find that good will is meant towards them; they see it, aye, and can feel it too, no matter what the evil disposed may do to try and make them think otherwise."[130]

Whitney's remarks are a reminder that we should not believe that relationships between Catholics and Protestants in Bunmahon in the mid-nineteenth century were ones of persistent and pervasive conflict, as the comments of Redmond might imply. The norm was for day-to-day affairs to be civil at least among the common people. There are a number of instances that illustrate this.

Firstly, as we have seen already, it was common for Catholics and Protestants to attend each other's funerals. Shortly after he arrived, Doudney had to officiate at the funeral and burial of a coast guard officer who had been a member of his congregation. His eulogy at the graveside was heard by "a most attentive group" of Protestants and Catholics, one of whom we are told was "much impressed by what he heard."[131] Similarly, it was not uncommon for Catholics to attend Doudney's special church services. Thus at the midnight New Year's Eve service he held in 1854 of the 50 present, about half were Catholics.[132] And in January, 1857, a Catholic was present at one of the Sunday services to hear him preach, Doudney commenting of him that: "He was a man who until recently used to pass me in the street with a scowl and frown, not even returning my salute. Now he is in an inquiring state, and most anxious to be shown the right way."[133] There was general communal celebration when Doudney and his wife returned from one of their regular fundraising trips to England, their daughter later remembering the "bell-ringing, bonfires lit and expressions of welcome after their long absence."[134] Such instances of communal celebration became more difficult as the 1850s proceeded.

Secondly, there was a general attitude of deference and hospitality among the local people especially to visitors and outsiders. In August,

1854 when an Englishman, Peter Sibree, visited the village, as part of a country-wide preaching tour, he fell into conversation with a local Catholic farmer who invited him to visit his farm (of 400 cattle, and 200 goats), partake in a meal, and, by report, "if not a disciple of father Matthew (sic), taste a drop of his best Irish whiskey."[135]

Thirdly, there is evidence of charitableness and giving. Thus in 1855 when a deputation from a new institution in Dublin for deaf and dumb children visited Bunmahon, the boys of the printing school and the girls of the embroidery school made donations for its work.[136]

Fourthly, there was mutual service during times of common experience of disaster. For example, Doudney was responsive to emergencies in the community. On one occasion, he raised the alarm with the coast guard when one of the boys in the printing school had reported to him that a ship was coming in and was in danger of breaking up on the rocks. He encouraged the man in charge of the coast guard, who was lazy, irresponsible and a troublemaker in Doudney's congregation, to send up signals of warning, which he did and this served to steer the ship away from the rocks and onto the beach. Doudney then sent for a bottle of whiskey to warm the coast guard men who were up to their waists in the sea trying to rescue the ship's crew, and had a cart with clothing in readiness for the crew once they were landed.[137] There was another occasion when his alertness served to save a ship in Bunmahon bay from shipwreck during a severe storm, through his providing clothing for the rescued crew, and saving the captain from committing suicide.[138]

On another occasion many were injured by a fire in Bunmahon, the result of an explosion from the blasting powder used in the underground mines. The boat house used by the coast guard was put at the service of the injured, and Doudney provided blankets and other necessities for their use. Although he maintained that his motives in doing so were purely out of common humanity, this was not accepted by the Catholic priest, who refused to talk with him on the matter.[139]

Doudney was sympathetic to human tragedy as it presented itself on a number of occasions during his sojourn in Bunmahon. There was, for instance, the death of three miners in 1855 as a result of the flooding of the mine shaft within a quarter of a mile of Doudney's dwelling which occasioned an outpouring of grief among the wives and children, made worse because it took twenty-six or twenty-seven hours to retrieve the bodies.[140] Recognizing his own limitations in his ability to enter into this level of grief, Doudney admitted: "We wish we had the gift for describing these Irish bursts of feeling, just as they occur. There is so much heart about them, that no pen— especially an Englishman's —can convey; and yet we are often astonished at the reaction. Indeed, were there a continuance of that excess of grief, nature must give way."[141] Doudney was not narrow or exclusive in his application of Christianity, interpreting it as he did in practical terms. Yet his multiple efforts in this regard were misinterpreted or unacknowledged when circumstances changed.

What level of support did Doudney have? His main support base was in England. It was the distribution of funds donated by readers of the *Gospel Magazine* that first brought Doudney to Ireland in 1846, and it was that continuing base of support from the *Magazine* that largely funded his educational initiatives in Bunmahon.

Among his fellow-clergy in the Diocese of Waterford and Lismore and beyond, support for Doudney was minimal. We have seen that the subscription list to Gill's commentary did not include an overwhelming number of local clergy. Some are likely to have disagreed with him on doctrinal grounds, while others were supportive. Rev. W. E. Shaw, vicar of Kinsalebeg, writing from Youghal in February, 1855, was sufficiently impressed with Doudney's efforts to overcome all the obstacles presented to him, that he was moved to say: "I question if any other parish in the south of Ireland has been so signally blessed in awakening the true spirit of enquiry among the Romanists, as to what they should do to be saved! I know of none!"[142]

One consistent supporter was Rev. William Sandford, whom Doudney first came in contact with when he ministered in Templemore during the famine in 1846 and 1847. Sandford was later transferred to Kilvemnon which included Ballingarry, Co. Tipperary, where the events of 1848 unfolded. On a visit to Bunmahon in 1853 Sandford was impressed with what he saw of Doudney's educational initiatives, but more especially at the number of Catholics attending the weekly evening classes, and was encouraged to undertake similar schools in his own area.[143]

Conclusion

Many factors point to the novelty and atypical nature of the religious conflict in Bunmahon. Firstly, it occurred outside the context of the famine. Despite the charges made in the threatening letters, there is no actual evidence of an aggressive proselytism carried out by Doudney. Nor do we have evidence of "souperism" in Bunmahon whereby people were given material rewards like food, clothing, or money in return for a change in their religion.[144]

Secondly, as the 1850s proceeded there was a renewal of profitability in the local mines, so that the religious conflict did not occur at a time of economic depression, in which incidence of poverty might have made people vulnerable. Thirdly, the location itself was outside those areas like Kerry, Doon, Galway, and Mayo where conflict over evangelical efforts occurred.

Fourthly, Doudney made it clear that he was not interested in insincere conversions. Those he believed were sincere (like Edward Kelly) he interviewed to determine levels of sincerity and only then gave encouragement and provision. Those he suspected of having ulterior motives he discouraged and dismissed. Indicative of Doudney's purpose was his flexibility: he was more concerned that people read the Bible no matter what the version, and as we have seen he was prepared to make Catholic versions available for that purpose.

However, despite the exceptionality of context and circumstances, and evidence of communal inter-denominational cooperation, the Kelly case and the ensuing threatening letters—cases in which intervention by the priests was notably absent— made it clear to Doudney that his period in Bunmahon was drawing to a close. It is apparent that the rising level of persecution contributed to his decision to leave Bunmahon in 1858. The reasons for his ultimate departure from the area, however, cannot be ascribed solely to the Kelly case, the threatening letters, the continued viability of the schools, or the accumulated experience of persecution. Wider, more complex factors were at play. These we will examine in the next chapter.

Chapter 8

Facts are Stubborn Things

At the outset of 1858 it became apparent that, due to the persecution and controversies surrounding his various projects, Doudney's days in Bunmahon were numbered. He had a strong sense that it would be his last in Bunmahon.[1] He made clear that he used every effort to continue in his position, but it eventually became apparent that he would have to leave.[2]

His original motive in coming to Bunmahon had been purely unselfish. As he put it in 1852 shortly after the infant school had opened: "It was not the idea of worldly gain that induced us to enter upon the deeply-responsible and laborious work in which we are engaged, but the spiritual welfare of the Lord's Church and people, the temporal good of the youth of our parochial school, and the advantage of the people of this village generally."[3] At the end he could speak of the fact that as a result of his different initiatives, "very many have been rescued from indolence, misery, and vice."[4] It is within the parameters of this motive that any assessment of his success or failure must be made.

As matters transpired, he ended up leaving suddenly. His first official explanation came in a letter to readers of the *Gospel Magazine*, dated at Plymouth, March 30, 1858, followed by a more detailed reflection also from Plymouth, dated May 22, 1858 on his reasons for departure, and in-between an exchange of letters with the parishioners of Monksland.[5] Initially when he announced one Sunday at the end of his sermon that he felt it his duty to resign, the people would not leave the church for twenty minutes. The following day a meeting of the parishioners was convened. The girls of the embroidery school were reported to have said: "We will all become Protestants if you will stay."[6] While this was a touching response, it was not the kind of plea that would have persuaded Doudney to change his mind. However, when the meeting suggested to Doudney that if he left the area just then, it would be attributed to fear which would not augur well for his successor, this was sufficient to cause him to reconsider his decision to depart.

Coincidentally, it was at this point that he received a letter from his rector, Rev. Richard Maunsell of Clonmel, expressive of his shock at Doudney's decision to leave, and requesting a meeting to discuss the matter.[7] At the meeting a proposal for the exchange of Maunsell's parish for Doudney's curacy was made, but this was rejected by the government, something which Doudney again interpreted as indicative that it was not the divine will that he remain.[8] This was his final confirmation that it was God's will that his work in Bunmahon be concluded, though the decision was not without mental and emotional anguish on Doudney's part. There were many reasons that contributed to Doudney's departure from Bunmahon, and these we will now address.

Personal and Emotional Strain

There is no doubt that he had been under constant stress because of his efforts to run his schools with reasonable efficiency, because of his controversy with the priests, and latterly because of the threats on his life. In fact the first reason Doudney gave in his letter of May 22, 1858 as to why he left was the effect the threatening letters had on him. His response to the first of these was to view it as an indication from God that it was time for him to leave, a conclusion he was encouraged in by his parishioners who were concerned for his safety.[9] As matters transpired, Doudney indicated that he would not leave without his family.[10]

Another reason was the obvious mental and emotional toll that the experience of living as a Protestant among the majority Catholic population of Bunmahon involved. In his letter to parishioners after he left, Doudney candidly admitted to them: "my nervous system has been much taxed."[11] As the threatening letters evinced, a strong xenophobic strain of hostility towards Doudney emerged after the death of Mary Kelly that presaged a lack of success to his efforts. This conclusion accords with a wider assessment of the Second Reformation as a whole, in that that movement was a failure since in its most aggressive expression it was directed by an English clergyman, Rev. Alexander Dallas who showed little respect for Irish Catholics either in his declarations or actions. While Bishop Daly might concur with the goals of someone like Dallas, he was at least Irish and knew the circumstances of the people and the country.

While the relative under-employment of the Church of Ireland clergy at the time, particularly those with small congregations, was a consideration, it was a circumstance Doudney recognized as an opportunity for action. He may, however, have taken it to the other extreme. For, in addition to the general stress of dealing with his various undertakings, a variety of other commitments often converged in time. For instance, in August 1852 Doudney was in the midst of seeing through the Gill commentary project and simultaneously building a house to accommodate his infant school while at the same time preparing property set aside for glebe-land.[12] On top of all this was the on-going task of editing the monthly issues of the *Gospel Magazine*. Relief from such a routine was only provided when Doudney went on his regular fundraising tours in England.

More specifically there was the added burden of susbsisting under the glare of public scrutiny. Commenting on this in 1855, Doudney offered his readers the insight that "It is no easy thing… to have one's every motives, and word, and act, maligned; and one's purest intentions set down to selfish ends. It often requires more faith, and more courage, and more self-denial, than we possess, or are wont to exercise, placidly and contentedly to bear with all this."[13] In August 1855 he recorded his feelings about the great responsibility he felt about running the different schools, the financial strain they caused, the "base ingratitude" of those who benefited from the schools, and the "ceaseless" attacks from the priests.[14]

There were also personality conflicts within his congregation and these likely contributed to the level of strain. There was, for instance, the case of the teacher in the scriptural school (who was also the parish clerk) who took notes of Doudney's sermons apparently with the connivance of the clergymen of the two adjoining parishes (likely Stradbally and Annestown) and used them for criticism of him. According to Doudney this man, while purporting to be concerned with the interests of the parish, tried to undermine his power.[15] There was also the person in charge of the coast guard in the area, Clifford, who sat under the pulpit and would "make grimaces, or a certain lisping of the lips" for the purpose of distracting Doudney while he preached.[16] The presence of such individuals, no doubt, did not make for a happy experience of ministry.

The promotion of educational enterprise in Bunmahon is sufficient evidence of the importance Doudney placed on education. Such an emphasis was equally evident in relation to his children. Yet incumbent on this commitment was the strain on family finances in providing a private education (in Wexford and later in Limerick from August 1857) for two of his daughters, which added to the existing cost of educating his two eldest sons, one of whom, David, took and passed the entrance examination for Trinity College in November, 1857, and was later recommended for honors in science.[17]

In all these various manifestations of personal stress, Doudney would have known from Scripture that suffering and trial were part of the believer's lot in this life. Such a realization, however, did not make it any easier in human terms. By 1858 the demands on his composure were great for, in March of that year, he could write: "I have borne the weight as long as it was possible to bear it.

To have grappled with it any longer would have made irreparable inroads upon my health."[18] From Bishop Daly's reply to Doudney's letter of resignation—which Daly thought sudden, unexpected, and to be regretted—we can imply that reasons of health were given as the main motivation for leaving.[19] While other factors were contributory, health and mental considerations were primary in his decision to leave Bunmahon.

Lack of Viability of Schools

As we have seen, Doudney's object in setting up the schools was to provide the children of Bunmahon not only with an elementary education, as in the infant school, but also to furnish them with useful skills as in the printing, agricultural and embroidery schools. Doudney did not intend the schools to be a temporary measure, but he hoped through them "to give permanency to the system of industry and self-reliance."[20]

Some of the educational initiatives, like the printing and infant schools, had been started at a time when the local mines were at a low-point. At the time of his departure, this situation had been reversed in part because of emigration and because an increase in the price of copper boosted demand, which in turn triggered a three-fold increase in miners' wages.[21] Ironically by the time the local mines had recovered, the prospects for the schools seemed inauspicious. Even in mid-1855 the signs were clear: there was only £300 as income from contributors, not all the schools (with 150 enrolled) were self-supporting, and there were mounting expenses (£1200 annually), coupled with the challenge of finding a market for all the items being produced at the schools.[22]

Doudney realised that the only way to boost the prospects of the printing school was to increase sales. Thus on numerous occasions we find him appealing for people to purchase the books, tracts and pamphlets printed at Bunmahon. In the *Gospel Magazine* for

December, 1856 he made an appeal for subscriptions to the *Magazine* to be paid promptly and he exhorted readers to try to extend the circulation of the periodical.[23] While a number of works continued to have large print runs through 1857 and 1858, the quantity was considerably less after 1855 than before it.

Also, as we have seen, there was controversy in the press in 1856 over whether numbers in the schools were on the decline or not.[24] Doudney defended his schools against the accusation of declining numbers of pupils, claiming that he was supporting 150 people, and citing reports from different newspapers for verification of the health of the institutions.[25] We cannot decide for sure what the actual numbers in attendance were, and the controversy in the press over school numbers may have been a reflection of the proselytizing debate then intensifying in Bunmahon.

At any rate Doudney remained undaunted by criticism and drawbacks, and into late 1857 seemed optimistic about prospects for the schools. In the October 1857 issue of the *Gospel Magazine*, he mentions that a charitable donation of £150 had been made to him, and this he used to erect a new building suitable for printing purposes adjacent to the glebe house he had already completed.[26] He maintained that the printing of the *Gospel Magazine* and *Old Jonathan* was insufficient to keep the staff of the printing works busy, so he planned to print Thomas Goodwin's entire works in six volumes, one volume every four months. He urged every reader of the *Magazine* to subscribe to a copy of the new work and to forward their subscriptions immediately. As matters transpired, it proved impossible to secure the necessary number of subscribers for the reprinting of Goodwin's works, and there is no evidence that they were ever printed in Bunmahon.

The reason for the continuing lack of viability on the part of Doudney's schools may lie in the fact that funds were not coming as regularly from readers in England as they had been. Certainly after about mid-1857, sums of money for the support of the Bunmahon schools are only occasionally acknowledged in the *Gospel Magazine*.

If the schools could not be sustained, then there was insufficient occupation to keep Doudney in Bunmahon, enjoining him to seek employment elsewhere. Nevertheless, in the end 26 persons employed in his schools (19 Protestants, 7 Catholics) had to leave the locality, Doudney making provision for several of them to go to Canada.[27]

Costs

Related to insufficiency of orders for the printing school, was the issue of costs. For the first few years it seemed as if the aim of self-sufficiency might be achieved. The printing school, for instance, had considerable success in its early years. When the printing of Gill's *Exposition* was undertaken, at least 2,000 subscribers were secured. This number was sufficient to ensure that all expenses would be covered, and it even allowed Doudney a surplus which he put towards the cost of completing a new glebe house. After the issuing of Gill's commentary, Doudney admitted that the printing school did not pay its way, due to the cheap rate at which the books were issued, increases in paper prices, and rising labour costs. The total cost of transporting Gill's commentary by land reached £300 (equivalent to almost four years of his annual clergyman's salary of £85), and in addition the freight by sea to London for the final volume of the set was calculated at just under 2d. per copy.[28] So far as the printing works are concerned, it cost him more to have Gill's commentary printed in Ireland than it would have in London.

By the summer of 1855 it was apparent that since the completion of Gill's commentary, the printing school was not able to meet its expenses due to the different nature of works being printed which had increased the expenditure and also because of the economic depression caused by the Crimean war.[29] There were increases in the cost of paper and contemporaneously a rise in labour costs, all of which combined to create a lack of viability in the printing establishment since the completion of Gill.³⁰ By March, 1856 the wages for all the schools totalled £100 per month.³¹ By 1857 a total of £2,000 was needed yearly to pay the wages of the schools, the cost of materials, rent, and other sundries.³² He claimed to have spent £1,000 from his personal funds on the Bunmahon projects.³³ Given this outlay, the long-term prospects for the printing establishment were perilous.

It was clear to Doudney at the point when the work then in hand, Keach's *Metaphors*, was completed, that he would have to retract the printing output otherwise the demands of existing deficits and the cost of labour would make the enterprise untenable.³⁴ The order for republishing Keach was made by Collingridge, not because a new edition was needed, but as a means of providing employment for the schools.³⁵ Such a strategy did not make business sense in the long term as it meant the accumulation of product that was not being disposed of.³⁶

The need to raise funds for the schools, largely through preaching and speaking engagements, necessitated Doudney's absence in England, often for lengthy periods of three months at a time. Such a trip in 1854 was occasioned because he found that expenditure on the schools exceeded subscriptions and financial support in the amount of £200.³⁷ In November 1855 a total of £395.15s.5d. was acknowledged in the *Gospel Magazine* as having been received for the funds of the infant, embroidery, and agricultural schools.³⁸ In February, 1856 Doudney was in Portsmouth at a public meeting soliciting funds for the schools which he claimed needed £800 to operate.³⁹ However, in February 1857, only £50.7s. was acknowledged, reflecting contributions in the months up to that point.⁴⁰ Clearly sales of books from the printing school were not meeting the expenditures invested in their production.

Despite the charges levelled against him that he was a well-paid agent of various societies, that he was the recipient of constant funds from England and America, that he was making £500 annually from the printing works and £100 for every convert, it is apparent that Doudney's projects were ceasing to be viable.[41] To his mind his departure would have at least one positive result in that it would demonstrate that the position he held in Bunmahon had been of no personal financial benefit to him.[42] On the contrary, he had lost heavily on the entire enterprise.

Distribution Challenges

What exacerbated the financial difficulties were the challenges of distribution associated with location. Because of Bunmahon's remoteness the cost of bringing in supplies for the printing works particularly added to the expense. Another challenge was the defects and unreliability of the transportation and communication network between Bunmahon and the port of Waterford, a distance of fifteen miles. Illustrative of this was the occasion of the publication of Keach's *Metaphors* in early 1855. Doudney had worked until four o'clock in the morning in order to meet the deadline of sending the volumes of Keach to Waterford only to find that a dispatch of other volumes sent three weeks earlier was still in storage there. He discovered that messengers were aware of this and of the fact that a steamer for London was taking in her cargo, but yet they made no effort to have the volumes loaded.[43] Inefficiency, or what Doudney characterized as the "want of promptitude and business-thought" at the port was exacerbated by duplication in the transportation infrastructure. He complained particularly of the fact that in many cases the mail was conveyed on the common road because it was cheaper than on the railways which ran through the same district.[44]

Similar delays bedeviled the *Gospel Magazine*. As a monthly publication, it was critical that it reach subscribers in a timely fashion. However, there appear to have been regular delays due to the remoteness of Bunmahon and the inadequacy of the transportation arrangements. To mitigate these and also to save the village postmaster the task of stamping so many issues of the magazine (numbering about 2,000) and the labour of a messenger carrying them, it became Doudney's practice to send them directly by donkey cart to Kilmacthomas, four miles away. But there were typically persistent delays in having the magazine dispatched from Kilmacthomas, the excuse being that there was no room in the car. The result of all this was that there were delays in getting the magazine to subscribers causing the blame to be directed at Doudney.[45] Inadequacies in the transportation infrastructure and distribution system inhibited the efficiency of the printing operation.

Parish Reorganization

In his letter to parishioners dated March 30, 1858 explaining his departure, Doudney mentioned parish reorganization first as his reason for leaving.[46] Twice, Doudney says, proposals for an adjustment of the parishes in the area had been proposed, and had these been sanctioned, he would have remained in Bunmahon.[47] He explained that his decision to leave "may be said to have originated some three or four years ago when the proposed arrangement of the parishes were negatived... Had the proposed arrangement been carried out it would most probably have fixed me with you for the residue of my days."[48]

The first of these proposals was in November 1853, when the death of a clergyman in a neighbouring parish (unstated but likely either Annestown or Stradbally) led the parishioners to send a memorial to the bishop favouring Doudney as permanent successor.[49] Over a year later in December, 1854, after he had returned from another preaching tour in England, Doudney heard that a clergyman in the neighbourhood (likely Dungarvan) died as a result of contracting fever during the course of his parish duties.[50] This presented another opportunity. Though nothing came of these proposals, they did create a sense of unsettledness about his continuance as the curate of Monksland, but by the end of 1854 he was sufficiently encouraged by the spiritual advancement of his own congregation and his firm aversion to removal, to believe that he was meant to continue where he was.[51]

The second and most radical of the proposals for parish reorganization took place in the period 1857–8 following Doudney's agreement to accede to the wishes of his parishioners to continue for one year after he first announced his decision to leave in 1857. The background related to the status of Monksland parish being united to that of Inislounaght, west of Clonmel, Co. Tipperary, thirty miles or so away. The River Mahon separated the ecclesiastical parishes of Monksland in the east and Stradbally in the west. The river also divided what was in essence a continuos settlement: Bunmahon to the west in Stradbally parish, and Knockmahon to the east in Monksland. Because of its proximity, the Protestants of Bunmahon attended the church in Monksland, rather than the actual one for their parish in Stradbally, four to five miles away.

This anomalous situation led the vicar of Stradbally, Rev. George Tierney Roche (1837-59), to remark to a parishioner that it was his belief that the death of the rector of Inislounaght (who was then in his eighties) and on his own death (he was also advanced in years), would present the opportunity for a rearrangement of the parishes. This would involve detaching Monksland from Inislounaght, and Bunmahon from Stradbally, and uniting them as one new parish.[52] Roche was supportive of this change as it would ensure the continuity of Doudney's work in the area.[53]

When Doudney related these suggestions to Bishop Daly, the latter was initially supportive of anything that would contribute to Doudney's continuance in the locality, but indicated that for the plan to succeed it would be necessary for Roche to resign from his position in Stradbally.[54] Responding to this condition, Doudney suggested that Roche would need to be provided with something equivalent to support himself, but at the time the bishop had no parish to offer Roche. Later, however, when a vacant parish did present itself, Daly offered it to another clergyman who refused it, whereupon he contacted Doudney saying that he was willing to support the proposal about Stradbally. The condition was that if the crown gave Doudney Monksland and the Duke of Devonshire (the patron of the parish) gave Stradbally to Daly's nominee, then the bishop would give the vacant parish to Roche.[55]

Upon receipt of this information Doudney immediately set out for Lismore, the seat of the Duke of Devonshire, passing through Stradbally and Dungarvan en route and meeting the curates of each. To one of them, the curate of Dungarvan, Rev. William Elliott Shaw (1850–54), whom Doudney knew, he mentioned the developments regarding Stradbally, and indicated his support for Shaw's appointment to Stradbally upon its becoming vacant. This, however, created jealousy in the curate of Stradbally, Rev. Benjamin C. Fawcett (1853–56), the assistant to Roche, who had not been that many years in the diocese and who was then driven into opposition to Doudney likely because he saw his natural expectations of promotion being stunted. What made this development all the more awkward for Doudney was that it was the practice of Bishop Daly to spend his summers at Stradbally, giving him a personal interest in how matters stood with the parish.

At any rate Doudney reached Lismore where he obtained an assurance from the Duke of Devonshire's agent that if Bishop Daly did not insist on influencing the outcome at Stradbally, then he (the agent) would recommend to the duke that the course of action as proposed be adopted.[56] In furtherance of his case, Doudney then journeyed to Dublin to petition the lord lieutenant, who in commending the work at Bunmahon communicated an understanding that he would be supportive of the proposed changes to the parishes. Doudney then sent a telegram to the vicar of Stradbally, Roche, who was by that stage in Brussels, and arranged to meet him in London where they conferred with the London agent of the Duke of Devonshire. The agent agreed with the opinion of his Irish counterpart, i.e. if Daly did not insist on the presentation to Stradbally, then the duke would be advised to agree to the changes contemplated for the parishes.

However, when Doudney communicated with the bishop again he insisted that his having the presentation to Stradbally was a non-negotiable in the proposed changes.[57]

Doudney returned from London disappointed at these developments, and on his way to Bunmahon called to see the bishop in Waterford. Doudney communicated the conversation he had had with Shaw about Stradbally, but neglected to ask Daly if he would confirm the appointment if the duke gave him the living of Stradbally. Later back in his home in Bunmahon, Doudney was assured by a personal friend of the bishop who was staying with the Doudneys at the time, that Daly would approve of the appointment if it were made. On the strength of this assurance, Doudney on a Saturday evening sent a messenger to Shaw in Dungarvan to apply to the duke, and on the following Monday Doudney travelled to Waterford to determine if the bishop would confirm the appointment if the duke gave it to Shaw. But when Doudney communicated that on the basis of the bishop's seeming approval of Doudney's suggestion of Shaw's candidacy for Stradbally (deriving from their interview the previous Saturday), he had in the interim contacted Shaw with a view of suggesting his name to the duke. When Doudney revealed this the bishop was "vexed" and declared that by his action Doudney had taken the appointment to Stradbally out of Daly's hands.[58]

A few days later Doudney received a letter from Shaw indicating his appointment to Stradbally by the Duke of Devonshire, which Doudney brought to show Daly in Waterford, who still insisted on his right to present to the living of Stradbally.[59] Daly eventually gave the Stradbally position to Rev. Richard Henry Smith, conditional on his acceptance of the fact that if Doudney succeeded in the parish reorganization as proposed within six months, then he would have to relinquish the parish.[60] Doudney, however, took the bishop's rigid stance as a firm indication that that was the end of his personal efforts to pursue the route of parish reorganization as a means of staying in Ireland, and he reassured the new appointee to Stradbally on that score.[61]

The intricacies and vacillations of ecclesiastical patronage and appointment should not blind us to the fact that, though unsuccessful in the attempt, Doudney made every effort to perpetuate his presence in the area. The entire episode makes explicable the later comments of Doudney's daughter Emily that "The Bishop made favourites among his clergy. One of these was a great enemy to father. He was jealous of his now rising reputation. He did his very best against him, so altogether poor father felt his work was done."[62]

A related factor to the above was the consideration that Doudney was always dissatisfied with the small size of the congregation that he ministered to in Monksland parish. He may have thought that a reorganization of the parishes might serve to enlarge his congregation, thus making his ministry and preaching more extensive. As things stood he had only 50 Protestant parishioners including children, with an average Sunday attendance of 70 or 80, the supplement being made up of those who came from the outlying areas of the adjoining part of the parish of Stradbally, that is, those in the village of Bunmahon.[63]

Then in 1857, as we have noted, after Doudney had first indicated his intention of resigning, following the Kelly episode, and his promise to reconsider his decision in light of representations from a few of the parishioners that it would not be wise to give the impression that he was leaving out of fear, he received a letter from the rector of the parish, Rev. Richard Maunsell who resided in Clonmel to come and talk the matter over with him.[64] He did so and during the conversation with Maunsell, who was then aged 85 years and therefore not likely to live much longer, proposed that he was willing to exchange his living for Doudney's small sinecure, so that he could continue to remain engaged in his educational work, but the government (in the person of the lord lieutenant, the Earl of Carlisle, in whose gift the parish was) refused to approve this proposal.[65] In the case of Maunsell's death, that would mean Doudney's removal and the crown would reappoint to both positions.

Doudney interpreted this as a sign that his ministry in Monksland parish was not to continue.

There is no further evidence of parish reorganisation at this time. Curates continued to be appointed to Monksland (Doudney's successor was Patrick J. Lee (or Leo)) up to 1867 when, for a short period, the parish was made independent, but only until 1875 when it was united to Stradbally parish, a year in which Inislounaght was also united with Clonmel.[66] The failure of efforts at parish reorganization to materialize was yet another indicator to Doudney that his time in Waterford was expiring.

Difficulties with Bishop Daly

Writing in 1892, over thirty years after he left Bunmahon and twenty years after Robert Daly's death, Doudney candidly stated: "The simple cause of my leaving [Bunmahon] was the impediment thrown in my way by my Bishop."[67] In the immediate aftermath of the break-up of the printing establishment, Doudney made a candid public admission in the *Gospel Magazine* which was reproduced in the *Waterford Mail* that his reason for leaving was as follows: "I was refused the time in England which was absolutely necessary for the collection of funds and disposal of work."[68] The newspaper reported Doudney as claiming that Daly refused him the leave of absence of three months at a time from his parish duties to organise his financial collection system in England and to gain a wider interest in his work.[69] The newspaper was sympathetic to Doudney's plight, commenting: "We are sorry to think that one who had encountered great opposition from without, should have to complain of, and attribute his removals [sic] to the want of sympathy, and to the obstacles put in his way by his ecclesiastical superior."[70]

As we have seen, funds from England were essential if Doudney's schools were to succeed, but from mid-1857, these funds were not being forwarded as plentifully nor as regularly as formerly, though initially the prospects had seemed favourable. What exacerbated the situation was Doudney's inability to secure a substitute minister to cover for him when he was away.[71] Added to this circumstance was Bishop Daly's understandable insistence on his clergy being resident on a continuing basis.

In 1857, following the notice he gave to his parishioners of his intention of leaving, his decision to reconsider, and the negative outcome on the parish reorganization proposal, an unexpected gift of £150 allowed Doudney to erect a new building for the printing school, a sign to his enemies that it would not be fear that would force his departure.[72] The counterpart to this positive development, of course, was that he required continued work for the printing school, however, and for this reason thought it prudent to pay a personal visit to his various collection agencies in England, and this caused some rancour with his bishop who eventually refused him such extended absences from the parish.[73]

Added to this may be Doudney's independent attitude towards Daly's preference for missionary societies as one of the main instruments for advancing the evangelical cause. As we have seen Daly was a firm supporter of such societies as the Irish Society, though Doudney tended to eschew involvement by such societies in his efforts in Bunmahon, and it was only after his departure that branches of such societies were established in the area. All this suggests Doudney's independence of action, something that may not have sat well with his bishop.

However, the suggestion of the *Waterford Mail* that Doudney's final departure from Bunmahon was due to a lack of sympathy for his aims on the part of Bishop Daly, cannot be sustained for, as we have noted, Daly was the most staunch proponent for the advance of Protestantism in Ireland and, on this basis, would not have hindered Doudney's efforts.[74] Indicative of the fact that there was no personal rancour between the two is the fact that in later years after Doudney had departed from Bunmahon and settled in to his long ministry in Bristol, they had the occasion to meet in London and were reconciled.[75]

Doctrinal Differences

In the short term, however, relationships with Bishop Daly combined with the controversy over the succession to Stradbally, were exacerbated by doctrinal differences particularly over the subject of particular redemption. This theological position held that Christ's death on the cross was only for an elect group who alone would share in its blessings. Upon Doudney's first meeting with the curate of Stradbally, wanting to know his doctrinal position, he sounded him out as to his views on particular redemption.

This was a topic that Doudney already had an inkling of what the prevailing local view was. For, back in 1847 on the day before his ordination examination, Doudney had been asked by Bishop Daly as to his views on particular or limited redemption. Doudney replied that he favoured particular redemption and this turned out not to be the bishop's view though he indicated that he respected many of those who held it.[76] Later Doudney was informed by acquaintances in England that Bishop Daly had indicated that he would never ordain another man who adhered to the doctrine of particular redemption. In an interview with Daly at his summer residence in Stradbally, the bishop flatly denied having made such a statement.[77]

Despite the bishop's assurances, Doudney discerned that a change in Daly's attitude to him dated from this experience. Prior to that, he had never objected to Doudney spending time in England raising funds for the educational projects. Ultimately Daly would have found such absences difficult to reconcile with his avowed policy of resident, engaged, and active clergy in their parishes. Yet, in seeming contradiction to his previous conviction, when it came to the bishop's next appointments to vacant parishes, he appointed two candidates whom he knew held views favourable to particular redemption.[78] On this issue, at least, Daly was not consistent.

Departure from Bunmahon

The foregoing provides a catalogue and review of some of the factors that contributed to Doudney's departure from Bunmahon. With a majority of the Catholic population deeply hostile towards him because of his alleged attempts to use his schools to gain converts to his faith, with funds for the schools themselves not being as forthcoming as before, with a lack of support from most of his fellow clergymen in the diocese of Waterford and Lismore, and with the rising levels of xenophobia and sectarianism expressed in threatening letters, by early 1858 departure seemed the most hopeful option for Doudney and his family.

While all these factors contributed to his reasons for departure, yet in the end it was not an easy decision. In this vein, referring to his resignation Doudney later communicated to his parishioners the view that "at the same time, it has caused me an amount of pain and anguish, mentally which words cannot express, nor heart conceive."[79] Sometime early in 1858—we are not sure of the exact date, but at least before March—Doudney abruptly resigned his curacy in Monksland and decided to depart for a new life in England. His initial announcement of resignation in 1857 evoked such an emotional response in his congregation that he reversed his original decision, but the circumstances of that year and the continuing difficulties of the schools made his final decision to resign in 1858 an irreversible one.[80]

Before he left, Doudney had a number of matters to attend to. On May 13, 1858, there was a sale at the glebe in Bunmahon of various household furniture and effects.[81] In June 1858 local newspapers reported that the types and presses had been returned to England, thus pointing to the effective ceasing of the printing operation in May 1858.[82] These were shipped to the firm of Collingridge in London.[83]

Premises of W. H. Collingridge, Long Lane, London.
Source: Credentials, 183.

While Doudney's successor, P.J. Lee (or Leo), continued in the glebe house he had erected, under the act of disestablishment (1869) he had to leave and the house and lands were sold to the main grocer in Bunmahon, James Watts.[84] Doudney's interest in the property he leased from the College of Physicians was purchased by the Mining Company of Ireland.[85] The welfare of the pupils who attended the schools was also attended to. Doudney's wish was to obtain passage to Australia, Canada and America for some of the elder boys and girls, and he recounts that six girls and one young man from the printing school left for New York at a cost of £50.[86]

Later Career

Doudney had spent a little less than twelve years in Ireland, equivalent to about one-quarter of his life to that point. He departed from his curacy in Monksland sometime between May and July, 1858.[87] Although he long had a desire to minister to a larger congregation than he had in Monksland, he had no immediate prospects and did not know where he would go next. This fact served to dispel the notion that he left Bunmahon in order to advance to a better church position.[88] However, within a year, he took up a new position as curate of St. Luke's, Bedminster, Bristol, a parish where he was responsible for between 6,000 and 7,000 people, but with an actual Sunday congregation of 1,600.[89] There he was to remain for thirty-two years (until his retirement from the ministry in 1890 when he was aged 79 years) during which time he oversaw the building of a new church, schools, soup kitchen, mission hall, and vicarage, at a total cost of £50,000.[90] We know that he started a printing works in Bristol from which a number of tracts and devotional works were issued including *Old Jonathan*, which he had begun while in Bunmahon and of which he was editor for thirty-six years.

Doudney also continued his editorship of the *Gospel Magazine*, and in 1866, to celebrate the centenary of its foundation he was presented with a watch and £400 at a function in London.[91] While we have noted that Doudney's domicile in Templemore acted as preparation for his work in Bunmahon, it can also be said that his time in Bunmahon was a time of training for his later work in England, a fact he later acknowledged.[92]

Doudney's links with Ireland, however, were not severed immediately upon his departure from Bunmahon. In July, 1861, at the opening of the new Protestant Hall in Waterford, several letters were read, including one from Doudney enclosing a cheque for £25 which, with the £75 already given would make up the £100 he had promised to donate for the new hall.[93] In the summer of 1864 Doudney returned to Ireland for the purpose of visiting his former parishioners, in August he visited Tramore and in the church there delivered sermons morning and evening, and later that month visited Lord Roden at Tollymore Park, Co. Down.[94] He returned again in September 1866, and again in June 1874 when he visited

Waterford, Tramore, Annestown, and Bunmahon.[95] Also one of Doudney's sons—who, like himself, had the initials D.A.D.—was still studying in Ireland. The twenty-year old son entered Trinity College on November 6, 1857, received his B.A. in 1861, and his M.A. in 1864. In 1865, he was appointed to a church position in Carlisle.[96] In 1867 Doudney senior was himself the recipient of a DD (Doctor of Divinity) degree from the University of Giessen in Germany in recognition of this work.[97]

He remained an active observer of the Irish scene, to the extent that a year before his death he published, *Ireland: its priests and its people* (London, 1892), which was meant to coincide with the general election of that year when home rule for Ireland was still the central issue. The book consisted of previously published pieces on his experience in Ireland, particularly in Bunmahon.

Family vicissitudes did not cease after Doudney's removal to Bristol. Shortly after, in 1861, his eleven year-old son was reported as having run away from school at Clapham near London, as he was homesick for Bristol; later in the winter of 1862–3 his daughter Emily experienced an attack of bronchitis but recovered; another young daughter, Helen, died and was buried in Monksland churchyard; and later again three other children contracted scarlet fever, to which one of them, Alice (his third daughter) succumbed.[98] At this time also Doudney himself narrowly escaped accidental death on two occasions, and in 1868 a fall in a timber yard incapacitated him.[99] To add to his anguish in the same year, his second wife, Eliza, died of apoplexy in her fifty-seventh year.[100] Another source of sorrow was the emigration of his three sons, Edwin, Montague, and Arthur, and although Edwin returned, he never saw the other two again.[101] Another blow was the sudden death of his brother-in-law, Rev. G.D. Doudney of Plymouth, with whom he had been close for forty years.[102] All these events seemed to augur the end of his ministry (added to by a fire in 1871 which destroyed the interior of St. Luke's) but, in fact, he was able to continue for an additional twenty years.[103] In this period, he was encouraged by the marriage of his daughters, one in 1870, the other in 1877; by the settlement of his son Edwin in a medical practice; and by his third marriage to Kate Bell, a year after his second wife's death.[104]

The elder Doudney continued in his curacy at St. Luke's, Bedminster until 1890, when he resigned. In 1890 also, he received a gift of £1,000 in commemoration of his fifty years as editor of the *Gospel Magazine*.[105] To spend his retirement, Doudney moved to Southsea where he died peacefully on April 21, 1893, at the handsome old age of eighty-two years.[106] Although he came of a large family, all passed away before him, leaving him to feel their loss. His life indeed had been long, colourful and eventful.

D. A. Doudney in 1892 the year before his death.
Source: *Memoir* frontispiece.

Legacy in Bunmahon

While much is made of the so-called devotional revolution in Ireland, what is little appreciated is how Protestantism might have contributed to this. A heightened seriousness among Catholic clergy and laity alike as a result of Doudney's witness is perhaps exemplary of this. The result of Doudney's presence in Bunmahon, despite his anti-Catholic rhetoric, was that there was a heightened sense of religiosity among Catholics pertaining to the norms of belief and practice. This was the case even where the priests were concerned. The priest given responsibility for the new chapel opened at Saleen in 1854, Rev. Roger Power, instead of criticizing Doudney and his schools, preached from the Bible, referring to Jesus Christ (rather than the saints) and treating of topics like predestination.[107] One can add to this the numbers who attended his schools, services, and evening lectures, who witnessed his community service in times of tragedy and danger, and those who benefited from his emphasis on biblical literacy. Ironically then, while the result of Doudney's ministry in the area was not large numbers of Catholics becoming Protestants for the number of converts was insignificant, but rather it was to make them better Catholics!

On the other hand, religious conflict in Bunmahon did not cease with Doudney's departure. In 1860 Bishop Daly established branches of the Society of Irish Church Missions in Bunmahon, Knockmahon, and Kilmacthomas; while branches of the Irish Society were also established in the locality in the same year.[108] It is interesting to note that these developments only occurred after Doudney's departure, suggesting that he had resisted such an approach by the bishop while he was curate of Monksland. At any event Daly's action elicited a response from Catholic interests whereby a Redemptorist mission came to the area, though the Redemptorist priests concerned in the mission declined an invitation to a debate with local Church of Ireland clergy, a group which did not include Doudney's successor, Rev. P. Lee (or Leo).[109] In response to the Redemptorists' non-appearance for debate the Church of Ireland clergy issued a pamphlet entitled *To the Roman Catholics of the County of Waterford*, issued in Bunmahon by the Irish Society branch there and arguing against certain Catholic doctrines.[110]

The arrival of a team of Jesuits in Bunmahon in July 1861 elicited another invitation from the Church of Ireland clergy of the district for open debate, but this was apparently also declined.[111] In that year also a mission of six weeks' duration was conducted in the local chapel in August, 1861, by Father Dickson, assisted by five other missioners.[112] The utilization of a mission as a strategy by the Catholic Church to counter the advances made by Protestant missionary societies in Ireland, dates to the decade of the 1850s.[113] The specific deployment of missioners in Bunmahon in the early 1860s demonstrates the seriousness with which Daly's initiative was taken by the Catholic authorities. Although they demurred to engage in open debate with their Church of Ireland clerical opponents, the arrival of the Redemptorists and Jesuits in the area in 1860–61, is indicative of the bolstering of local clerical resources to battle an aggressive Protestantism under Daly.

Conclusion

Clearly the reasons for Doudney's departure are not confined to what might seem like the obvious one of a response to the threatening letters. Apart from the mental, emotional and financial strain associated with his family and the different educational enterprises, there were many other reasons that contributed to his departure. While he made protracted efforts to assist in bringing about a rearrangement of the parishes of Stradbally and Monksland that would have more rationally reflected the concentration of the Protestant population and which would have allowed for his continuance in the area, such efforts were neutralized by apparent vacillation on the bishop's part. By this juncture Doudney's relationship with Daly had been strained over the former's absences in England for fundraising and over doctrinal issues.

Chapter 9

Conclusion

This study has addressed the issue of religious conflict in the mid-nineteenth century in the copper mining community of Bunmahon, Co. Waterford. Central to a consideration of the issue was the presence in the area of an English evangelical clergyman, David A. Doudney. We have noted that there were three formative influences in his life prior to coming to Ireland: his religious upbringing, his background in the printing business, and his experience of multiple family bereavements. Though he was raised in humble economic circumstances, Doudney's childhood was imbued with a strong religious fervour. A life-changing conversion experience when a teenager made religious imperatives real. Thereafter he was more keenly aware of God's provision for his life. The vital Christianity that emerged stressed the interconnectedness of faith and the circumstances of life, dependence on divine providence, and a transparency of belief. He was led to pursue a call to active ministry which came about in providential circumstances, a decision affirmed by the dissolution of his printing business, and ultimately led him to come to Ireland in 1846.

What made Doudney different as a clergyman was that he had a background in the printing trade. Normally those entering the ministry of the church had a university education, typically to bachelor's level, though after 1833 in Ireland this changed.[1] In its absence, it was the prerogative of the bishop in any particular diocese to ordain whom he wished, and it was the undertaking by Bishop Daly to exercise this right that brought Doudney to

Ireland. Bishop Daly's experience of controversy with the Osbornes over the scriptural school coupled with the fact that Doudney's predecessor as curate—Thomas Power—was a local (possibly the son of William Power the board of guardians' representative for Stradbally), may have influenced him to choose a complete outsider like Doudney, as successor in the curacy. The fact that Doudney had skills in printing (along with skills in writing and editing) meant that his interpretation of what was involved in being a clergyman was different than the norm in the Church of Ireland at the time, for he viewed his work more broadly than was traditionally the case with clergymen. Such breadth of interpretation as to the parameters of ministry was to benefit the population of Bunmahon but it was also to provoke a hostile response.

Doudney was thirty-five years old when he came to Ireland, and while he possessed a keen sense of divine leading and providence, he must nonetheless have been burdened with sorrow given his recent experience of family loss. All too often the picture presented of those active in evangelical ministry in nineteenth century Ireland is construed as consisting of one-dimensional, wooden personalities untroubled and serenely engaged in their task, with little attempt to delve into their personal circumstances and background. In contrast, Doudney emerges as one who had to deal with deep sorrow given the fact that by the time he came to Ireland, he had lost three out of his four children along with his wife. Add to this the fact that by 1846 his printing business had gone under. Though he had remarried and started another family, the legacy of personal loss must have been immediate and indeed was to continue long into later life.

Such experiences of bereavement must have predisposed him to be sympathetic to the plight of others. There could have been no better time to exemplify this than in famine-stricken Ireland in the 1840s, and it was demonstrated by his time in Templemore, Co. Tipperary. Engagement in famine relief, in teaching, and in visitation in the locality made a material difference to many, a spiritual difference to some, and was a life-changing experience for Doudney. He admitted that the suffering and deprivation he witnessed overshadowed any sense of his own personal loss. Through direct contact in the context of famine, he grew in his appreciation of the Irish people, but he also came to experience at first hand the opposition which his activities evoked among the Catholic authorities. As a whole, these experiences in Templemore were to prove formative and preparatory to the situation he would face in Bunmahon, though in more divisive ways.

By the time he came to Bunmahon in late 1847, the area had undergone major changes due to the more intense exploitation of the rich and extensive copper ore deposits that had begun two decades earlier. This transformed the locality from a sleepy bathing place to a bustling mining centre. This transformation was in part directed by the Osborne family, who despite their absenteeism, articulated and implemented a broad social vision which resulted in educational facilities, housing for miners and others, a new church, and funding for a temperance hall. Against this, the Catholic Church, admittedly more limited in resources, was remiss in responding rapidly to emergent pastoral needs in the area. By 1840 there was no Catholic chapel in the immediate area of Bunmahon or Knockmahon, and not until 1854 did it materialize, and then only because the former temperance hall was adapted for use.

Major investment in extraction, the arrival of a skilled and unskilled workforce, and the growth in population, all contributed to reducing the traditional remoteness of the area. The mines proved highly profitable reflected in the provision of a livelihood to 1100 persons by 1840, competitive wage rates, a sharp increase in property values, and in rising demand for housing. Its negative by-products included multiple social evils like overcrowding and drunkenness, problems addressed in part by the opening of a temperance hall in 1840 which resulted in an increase in productivity, restoration of order, and a commensurate increase in savings.

Intense industrial production meant that when decline occurred in 1843–4, the result was unemployment, depopulation, insolvency, falling incomes, and slumped property values. This experience—occurring before the famine hit in 1845—exacerbated an already dire situation where a sharp increase in population was not matched by the provision of sufficient housing stock leading to overcrowding, coupled with the perennially high cost of potato ground and plots. Even prior to the famine's arrival in the area the local population was highly vulnerable given its dependence on the profitability of the copper mines. Already familiar with famine conditions from his time in Templemore, Doudney became involved in efforts to obtain funds for a hospital in the locality. The famine exacted its toll in terms of population loss and emigration. On the other hand, from the early 1850s the copper mines experienced renewed prosperity.

Sectarian animosities pre-dated Doudney's arrival in the area. In particular, the sensitive issue of education had emerged to be a source of controversy prior to his arrival. The particular issue over whether a scriptural or parochial school could be erected within the church grounds brought into the public arena a sharp difference of opinion between Doudney's patron, Bishop Daly, and the local landowners, the Osbornes. For this reason it had wider implications, not least because of the status and profile of those involved in the controversy.

The episcopal leader with oversight of the Church of Ireland population of the area was Bishop Robert Daly, the chief proponent for the advancement of evangelicalism and the conversion of Catholics in Ireland in the mid-nineteenth century. Daly was prominent in promoting the activities of societies involved in such goals and was forthright in instilling high expectations among his clergy to the same end. On the other hand, the Osbornes were liberal Protestants, sympathetic to Catholic claims, and proponents of the new national system of education. The family had already sponsored the establishment of a school under the state-run national system of education, whereas Daly favoured supplementing this with a new school in the church grounds where education would be scripturally-based. At the end of a very rancorous exchange, Daly's preference prevailed.

Given Doudney's background, experience, and life circumstances, it became clear that his ministry in Bunmahon would be different than what was conventionally the case with clergymen elsewhere in the Church of Ireland. Given the paucity in numbers of his congregation (less than 100), he had time available to invest in the service of the wider community. This took the form of developing a range of educational and industrial projects for the children of the area. Though apprehensive about the prospect (given the fact that he was English and Protestant), despite offers to move to better situations in England, and despite rumours of massacre in 1848, Doudney in time proceeded with founding a printing school initially intended to assist the elder boys in the parochial school adjoining his church, but also for Catholic youth of the area. Starting with the daunting task of republishing Gill's commentary followed by other works, despite challenges around distribution and delivery, coupled with the long-term financial viability of the enterprise, youth of the locality acquired a practical new skill, earned wages that contributed to the local economy, and in a few select cases proceeded to important careers. Among the other educational and industrial initiatives the embroidery school enjoyed most success, the agricultural school least, while the infant and embroidery schools were the focus of a sharper sectarian animus that erupted in mid-1855. In all this Doudney had a genuine concern for the well-being of the inhabitants, his daughter Emily noting how "he loved the people over there. His heart throbbed with pity for them, and what changes he wrought during the twelve years he was over there."[2]

As matters transpired these initiatives were a challenge to the control held over their flock by the priests of the area, who clearly felt threatened by Doudney's presence. However, their repeated attempts to prohibit attendance at his schools through altar denunciations and curses had little effect. The more extreme sanction of excommunication was resorted to in the summer of 1853 as the final effort to discipline those Catholics who were sending their children to the infant school. The excommunication failed to have its desired effect rather it had a contrary outcome in that it caused an undermining of priestly authority, evidenced in the continuing attendance by Catholics at the funerals of Protestants and their interest in the Bible in defiance of their priests who then adopted it also. These developments may have quickened the opening of a renovated hall to be a new Catholic chapel in Bunmahon in 1854, thereby giving the Catholic Church a more visible presence in the area.

Inevitably the charges brought against Doudney's educational schemes focused on their alleged proselytizing intent. From the time they were initiated there were suspicions about the printing school, the infant school, and the embroidery school that they were a cover for proselytizing. However, it is clear from his own statements that Doudney was not concerned in overt proselytism or its derivative, souperism. He made it clear that his status as a priest demanded that he welcome persons who were sincere in their desire for conversion, but that he turned away those who were only interested in nominal conversion because of what they could gain from it materially. Doudney was interested in encouraging a more vital Christianity, in opposition to the nominalism he found around him whether among Catholics or Protestants. This stance contrasted sharply with the approach of clergy in the west of Ireland where hundreds were accepted seemingly indiscriminately as converts.

Doudney's efforts to provide a useful education in various skills for the young people of Bunmahon could not succeed permanently due to the suspicion that reigned over his motives and because in an area where most of the population was Catholic, an English evangelical clergyman could not hope to achieve his aims with long-lasting success because of prejudice. The result was that Doudney's schools, in the short span of their existence, while they may have served the needs of his own parishioners primarily, did not appeal at a popular level to the Catholics of the district. By all accounts, it was the national school system which, by March 1853, had four schools under its auspices in the Bunmahon-Knockmahon area, that had most appeal.

In the end it was not the issue of attendance of Catholic children at Doudney's schools that served to heighten the sectarian tension in the area from 1855 onward. Rather it was a succession of controversies over admission to the Kilmacthomas workhouse which brought to the fore again the charge of proselytism. In his defence Doudney reiterated his concern to encourage sincere Christianity over nominalism. As events transpired such a distinction was to be elusive at popular level in the context of Bunmahon in the 1850s. While he noted that many had contemplated making a decision in favour of such a course of action, he recognized that fear and intimidation were constraining factors.

On the other side, within the Catholic polity itself, the failure of the excommunication in June 1853 and of the predicted transformation of August 1855, indicated the limitations on traditional clerical power and a concomitant decline in deference between priest and people. Nevertheless, ostracism and exclusion followed for those who attended Doudney's schools. Clearly there was division among the local Catholic community between those in a minority who saw the benefits of Doudney's schools, and those who complied with clerical admonitions and opposed them.

There were clear acts of provocation on the part of Catholics towards Doudney such as the deliberate destruction of bibles, lack of hospitality, and intimidation. He was the object of threats to his life, bigoted opposition, and a narrow and misplaced sectarianism. Even at the level of humanity, he was shunned. On one occasion, shortly after he had arrived in the area and before he had found a house to reside in the parish itself, he was thrown from his horse, but no one in a nearby farmhouse came out to help him even though they had witnessed his fall.[3]

There was an array of other factors that contributed to Doudney's departure from Bunmahon, and not merely the violence threatened in the letters. His period of residence in the area induced an emotional strain given the multiple responsibilities he had between his church, his small congregation which included a disruptive element of Wesleyan Methodists, the health and safety of his family, and the financial viability of his schools along with the associated distribution challenges at the printing works. Added to this was the sense of exclusion because of his minority status as an Englishman and a Protestant in a predominantly Catholic region. On the other hand, Doudney's sincere desire to remain in the area was demonstrated by his attempts to pursue the opportunities of parish reorganization, attempts that were subsumed in the nuances of ecclesiastical patronage and episcopal vacillation. Clearly relationships with Bishop Daly had become strained over the course of Doudney's tenure in the locality. While Daly was initially supportive of Doudney's presence, relationships between the two deteriorated over Doudney's regular absence in England raising funds for his schools and Daly's reasonable expectation that clergymen in his diocese be resident. This division extended itself into doctrinal differences. At diocesan level, Doudney received little support from fellow clergy in Waterford and Lismore, his main source of support being the readership of the *Gospel Magazine* in England.

Doudney was not without blemish himself. There is no doubt that he articulated a strong anti-Catholic rhetoric characteristic of the Victorian age. This was directed particularly against the doctrines and practices of the Catholic Church, which he viewed as fabricated, superstitious, and oppressive to its adherents. He was particularly wary of priests whom he saw as a grasping class of individuals, using the institutional church, its rites and ceremonies as a means of exploiting and controlling the people in their need, and keeping them in ignorance.

Yet at the level of personal relationships Doudney exhibited a charitable disposition. He employed Catholic youth in his schools with many of them (particularly those in the printing school) proceeding to secure good positions. He helped people emigrate. He was available to participate in rescues. He was proactive in getting a much-needed dispensary for the area. He sought to promote industry and self-reliance.

Local passions came into focus more pointedly in early 1857 over the Kelly family, in particular relating to the departure of the younger brother and the apparent suicide of his sister. A succession of threatening letters addressed to Doudney ensued over the months from May to November 1857. While Michael Kelly was acquitted of issuing the first of these, they continued to be issued over the next months but did not deter Doudney from remaining in the area, at least in the short-term.

In assessing Doudney's tenure in mid-nineteenth century Bunmahon we should distinguish between his public and private attributes. As to the former, the description used by Anthony Trollope of a Church of Ireland evangelical clergyman of the time, is perhaps apposite and summative: "He was most zealous and conscientious, but a most indiscreet servant of his Master. He made many enemies but few converts."[4] As to the personal dimension, perhaps the final verdict on him should be left to those closest to him, i.e. his own family. In their estimation of their father his two children who wrote the *Memoir* concluded about him: "He had his faults, and no one would have been more ready to acknowledge them than he; and he had some noble virtues, for which he would have given all credit to the grace of God."[5] Of his virtues they mention his "tenderness," his "forbearance," his "overflowing sympathy," his unselfish and remarkable generosity," and his "unfailing interest and love."[6]

Monksland church closed in the mid-twentieth century, the Protestant population having declined over the years, while St. Luke's Bedminster, Bristol, a much larger edifice than the humble church in Knockmahon, where Doudney ministered for thirty years after leaving Ireland, was demolished in 1970.

Contemporary local initiatives to promote tourism and revitalization have focused on the geological and cultural heritage of the area, are based on the premise of self-reliance and local resources, and are centered on the church building where Doudney ministered. The attributes of self-reliance and entrepreneurship which these initiatives exemplify, were also ones that Doudney espoused with his various enterprises in the locality, but which were resisted.[7] Instead of being denigrated, Doudney should be remembered as an inspiration to such efforts.

Abbreviations

Cowman, *Making* D. Cowman, *The Making and Breaking of a Mining Community: The Copper Coast, County Waterford 1825-1875+* (n.p., 2006).

Credentials D. A. Doudney, *The Credentials, Call & Claims of the Christian Ministry with details of the author's labours in Ireland during a period of eleven to twelve years* (London, n.d. [c.1883])

Ireland D. A. Doudney, *Ireland: its priests and its people* (London, 1892).

Retracings D. A. Doudney, *Retracings and Renewings or Gleanings from a journal extending over nearly half a century* (London, 1878).

GM *The Gospel Magazine and Protestant Beacon*

Memoir	*Memoir of the Rev. D. A Doudney, D.D.* [by D.A. Doudney & Mrs. H. O. Adams] 2nd ed. (London: Collingridge, 1894).
NA	National Archives of Ireland, Dublin
NLI	National Library of Ireland, Dublin
PO	D. A. Doudney. *Pictorial Outing of the Rise and Progress of the Bunmahon Industrial, Infant and Agricultural Schools.* [Bunmahon 1855]
RCB	Representative Church Body Library, Dublin
RCPI	Royal College of Physicians of Ireland, Dublin
RLFC	Famine Relief Correspondence (NA)
WM	*The Waterford Mail*

Endnotes

Chapter 1

1. *Memoir of the Rev. D. A. Doudney, D.D.* (London: Collingridge, 1893). A second edition was published in 1894.
2. Ibid., 2–3.
3. Ibid., 2.
4. Ibid., 7–8.
5. Ibid., 8. It is clear that while Doudney considered his father's disposition "at times a little too strict and inconsiderate," he later understood that such behavior was motivated by love (ibid., 9).
6. Ibid., 1. The experiences of the two boys, John Doudney Lane and David Alfred Doudney, who were the same age, is recounted in the book authored by Doudney entitled, *Try and Try Again*. Lane later went on to be a successful student at the University of Cambridge, was ordained, and had a fruitful ministry in the Cambridge area: ibid. 3–5.
7. Ibid., 16; David Alfred Doudney, *The Credentials, Call, and Claims of the Christian Ministry…*(London, n.d. [c.1883]), 38.
8. *Memoir*, 16–17. Reading Doddridge also influenced William Wilberforce, the abolitionist, to devote his life to Christianity.
9. Ibid., 17–18.
10. Ibid., 19–21.
11. Ibid., 21. Doudney was instrumental in persuading his employer not to dismiss the entire workforce: Ibid., 22–23.
12. Ibid., 29.

13 Ibid., 30.
14 Ibid., 68.
15 *Credentials*, 177.
16 *Memoir*, 81.
17 As early as 1844 he had experience of giving a spontaneous sermon: *Memoir*, 138–9.
18 For these and other providential events illustrating Doudney's call to ministry: *Memoir*, 81–89; *Credentials*, 87–88. Roden: "Jocelyn, Robert, third earl of Roden (1788–1870)," John Wolffe in *Oxford Dictionary of National Biography*, ed. H. C. G. Matthew and Brian Harrison (Oxford: OUP, 2004); online ed., ed. Lawrence Goldman, January 2008, http://www.oxforddnb.com.myaccess.library.utoronto.ca/view/article/39661 (accessed June 12, 2013).
19 *Memoir*, 86–87; *Credentials*, 197–9.
20 This was despite the introduction in 1833 of a mandatory two-year programme of study in divinity at Trinity College Dublin, the Irish centre for the training of ordinands: Thomas P. Power, "'Of No Small Importance:' Curricular Change in the School of Divinity, Trinity College Dublin, 1790-1850" in Thomas P. Power (ed.), *Change and Transformation: Essays in Anglican History* (2013), 140-183.
21 *Memoir*, 88–89; *Credentials*, 178–180. Material and machinery purchased for £7,000 sold for only one quarter of that amount.
22 *Credentials*, 181–2.
23 *Memoir*, 89; *Credentials*, 208, 212.
24 *Credentials*, 266–70.
25 Ibid., 270.
26 *Memoir*, 3.
27 Ibid., 14.
28 Ibid., 14–15.
29 Ibid., 28, 30.
30 Ibid., 28.
31 Ibid., 77.

32 Ibid., 44.
33 Ibid., 1–2, 9.
34 For the foregoing incidents: Ibid., 24.
35 Ibid., 26–27.
36 Ibid., 29.
37 Ibid., 33–35.
38 Ibid., 36–37. Rev. Draper was likely Bourne Hall Draper (1775–1843), a minister in the Baptist Church, and the author of hymns (www.hymnary.org). Like her father, Miss Draper, was an author, producing a work entitled, *The Breakfast Table Companion* (ibid., 37).
39 *Credentials*, 45.
40 *Memoir*, 42, 48.
41 Ibid., 48, 49; *Credentials*, 69–70.
42 *Memoir*, 49.
43 Ibid., 52–55.
44 Ibid., 78. For the providential nature of the marriage, see ibid., 78–80. See also *Retracings*, 147.
45 Ibid., 78.
46 *Ireland*, 59.
47 *Memoir*, 78. They were Emily (b. 1844), Edwin (b. 1846), Augustus Montague (b. 1850), Charles William (b. 1852), Arthur Searle (1853), who supposedly drowned in the South Seas, and Marion (b.1856). Alice (b. 1846) died in 1863, and Helen (b. c.1849), only survived birth a couple of hours.
48 *Retracings*, 120–121; *Credentials*, 214.
49 *Memoir*, 90–91.
50 Ibid., 91.
51 Ibid., 92.
52 Ibid., 93; *Credentials*, 217; Thomas P. Power, *Land, Politics, and Society in Eighteenth-Century Tipperary* (1993), 53–4.
53 *Memoir*, 106.
54 *Credentials*, 252.
55 *Memoir*, 94; *Credentials*, 217.

56 *Memoir*, 94; *Credentials*, 217.
57 *Memoir*, 95; *Credentials*, 218.
58 *Credentials*, 253.
59 For Sandford, see H. Cotton, J.B. Leslie, & W.H. Rennison (revised and updated by I. Knox), *Clergy of Waterford, Lismore, and Ferns: Biographical Succession Lists* (Dublin: RCB, 2008), 379. He was later rector of Kilvemnon (1853–74) and of Clonmel (1847–82): ibid.
60 *Memoir*, 96.
61 Ibid., 96; *Credentials*, 220.
62 *Memoir*, 96–7.
63 Ibid., 103–4.
64 Ibid., 104.
65 Ibid., 105.
66 *Try, and Try Again*, 147.
67 *Memoir*, 107; *GM* 7 n.s. (1847), 40, 55, 58, 92, 194, 240; 53 (1853), 176; *Credentials*, 240–1; *Try and Try Again*, 147.
68 *GM* 7 n.s. (1847), 190.
69 *Credentials*, 222.
70 Ibid., 223.
71 *Memoir*, 109; *GM* 7 n.s. (1847), 334.
72 *Memoir*, 109–110.
73 Ibid., 110.
74 Ibid., 112–3.
75 Ibid., 111–2.
76 Ibid., 125–8. Among other works, he was the author of *Sermons and Outlines of Sermons* (London, 1849), intended for the use of young clergy.
77 *Credentials*, 264–5.
78 *Memoir*, 98. The feeling was reciprocal, for a couple of years later on a return visit to Templemore, he was mobbed by well-wishers: ibid.,115.
79 *Credentials*, 222.
80 Ibid., 264.

81 Ibid., 223.
82 *Memoir*, 106.
83 *Credentials*, 246.
84 Ibid., 250.
85 Ibid.
86 Ibid., 259.
87 Ibid.
88 Ibid., 256.
89 *PO*, 9.
90 Ibid.
91 *Credentials*, 256.
92 Ibid., 257.
93 Ibid., 258.
94 *Try and Try Again*, 159.
95 *Credentials*, 257–8.
96 Emily's Story, 2.
97 *Memoir*, 116; *Credentials*, 225, 459–61. The examination was a nerve-wracking and rigorous affair (*Credentials*, 460–62). It was suggested of Daly that he experienced difficulty finding prospective candidates with education to serve as clergymen in his dioceses, so he had to resort to ordaining those without the required academic education (J. Godkin, *Ireland and Her Churches*, (1867), 331).
98 *GM* 51 (1851), 360.
99 *Credentials*, 226, 296. His wife and children David, Edwin, and Emily joined him in 1847. They lived adjacent to the Palliser family in Annestown House: Emily's Story, 1–2. He had moved closer to Bunmahon by October 1848: *Credentials*, 290.
100 T. Power, "Notes on a Forgotten Co. Waterford Religious House," *Decies* 9 (1978), 28–33.
101 HC *Papers relating to the state of the established church* 1820 (93), ix, 250.

Chapter 2

1. *Retrospections of Dorothea Herbert*, 2 vols. (London, 1929-30), ii, 299–300, 310–13, 326, 363, 374, 387.
2. *Ireland*, 77.
3. Copy rental of Bunmahon, 28 June 1841 (RCPI 4/3/4/1/7); R. Douglas to W. Stanley, n.d. [c. Feb. 1847] (NA RFLC 7/27/ [70]); W. Nolan and Thomas P. Power (ed.) *Waterford: History and Society* (Dublin, 1992), 523.
4. Report of Charles Farran to the College of Physicians, 11 May, 1848 (RCPI 4/3/6/4, p.1). The Power-O'Shee family derived from the marriage in the eighteenth century of Elizabeth Power of Gardenmorris and John O'Shee of Sheestown, Co. Kilkenny.
5. J.D.H. Widdess, *A History of the Royal College of Physicians of Ireland, 1654– 1963* (Edinburgh, 1963), 145-9.
6. J. Burtchaell, "19th Century Society in County Waterford," *Decies* 31 (1986), 39-40.
7. Widdess, *History*, 145, 148.
8. Lewis, *Topographical Dictionary*,1st ed. 1840, i, 215. The Osborne estate in counties Waterford and Tipperary comprised over 13,700 acres (statute) in the mid-19th century and produced a yearly rent of almost £6500 (NA D 5998). (This does not include Knockmahon, however). The townlands of Templevrick, Lisnegeragh, Killaghmolan [Kilmoylan], and Shankill (1275 acres) were sold by the Duke of Ormond to Sir Patrick Dun who bequeathed them to the College of Physicians which in turn leased them to Power-O'Shee, who sublet the ground near the mines in small plots at £2-£4 per acre. In 1824 Power-O'Shee had about 24 years remaining on his lease (NLI Ms 657 Minutes and proceedings of the Hibernian Mining Company). For the general circumstances surrounding the disposal of the Ormond estate, see Power, *Land, politics and society*, 76–82.
9. NLI Ms 657 Minutes and proceedings of the Hibernian Mining Company (Report of Henry Price, 6 Oct. 1824).
10. NA D 6049.

11 Cowman, *Making*, 11.
12 Ibid., 20–23.
13 NA D 6086, D 6088, and D 6186. The Osbornes demanded one-tenth of the ore extracted. In one case (D 6088) the company undertook to employ 6 miners for at least 150 days per year. See also D 5998 and D 6091. In the 1870s the Osborne estate in Waterford (just under 9,000 acres statute) was valued at just over £4000: E. Broderick, *Waterford's Anglicans: Religion and Politics, 1819– 1872* (Newcastle-Upon-Tyne, 2009), 15.
14 Hall, *Ireland*, i, 314; R. Kane, *The industrial resources of Ireland* (1844), 180.
15 Kane, *The industrial resources*, 181; R. Purdy to O'Brien Adams, 20 Nov 1840 (RCPI 4/3/3/8).
16 Lewis, *Topographical Dictionary*, 2nd ed. 1849, i, 207; cf. S.C. Hall, *Ireland its scenery and character*, 3 vols., i, 314.
17 "Knockmahon Mines Statement of [Expendit]ure, Returns, and Profits…" (RCPI 4/3/3/8).
18 Report of Charles Farran to the College of Physicians, 11 May, 1848 (RCPI 4/3/6/4, p.3-4).
19 *WM* 13 Jan. 1849.
20 For this paragraph see, Cowman, *Making*, 1; idem, "Survival, Statistics and Structures: Knockmahon Copper Mines, 1850-78," *Decies* 46 (1992), 10-20; *WM* 6 Jan. 1856.
21 For summary description of the work involved see [Cowman], "Life and Work in an Irish Mining Camp c.1840: Knockmahon Copper Mines, Co. Waterford," *Decies* 14 (May, 1980), 33–4.
22 [Cowman], "Life and Work," 33.
23 Ibid.
24 [Cowman], "Life and Work," 36–8; Cowman, *Making*, 57, 85-6. Adding to the population mix was the settlement of shipwrecked sailors: Cowman, *Making*, 86.
25 Cowman, *Making*, 9, 28; [Cowman], "Life and Work," 30.
26 Kane, *The industrial resources*, 181; R. Purdy to O'Brien Adams, 20 Nov 1840 (RCPI 4/3/3/8).

27 Thomas McDonagh, Moate, Westmeath to Jonathan Labatt, 1 June, 1841 (RCPI 4/3/3/8).
28 RCPI 4/3/3/8.
29 Report of Charles Farran to the College of Physicians, 11 May, 1848 (RCPI 4/3/6/4, p.5).
30 Cowman, *Making*, 26.
31 [Cowman], "Life and Work," 30; Cowman, *Making*, 28.
32 *Credentials*, 488.
33 Thomas McDougall to J. Labbatt, 2 July 1841 (RCPI 4/3/3/8).
34 *GM* 53 (1853), 227. For the challenges boats from Swansea faced in loading the copper ore, see *Memoir*, 121.
35 Report of Charles Farran to the College of Physicians, 11 May, 1848 (RCPI 4/3/6/4, p.2–3).
36 For the foregoing paragraph see Report of Charles Farran to the College of Physicians, 11 May, 1848 (RCPI 4/3/6/4, p.4–5).
37 Report of Charles Farran to the College of Physicians, 11 May, 1848 (RCPI 4/3/6/4, p.8–9).
38 Hall, *Ireland*, 2nd ed. 1849, i, 207; Cowman, *Making*, 38.
39 Doudney, *Try and Try Again*, 157–8.
40 Cowman, *Making*, 38.
41 Ibid., 38–9. The village was subject to regular sandstorms which acted to bury the mud huts: Emily's Story, 7.
42 *GM* 53 (1853), 227; *Ireland*, 49.
43 Cowman, *Making*, 39, 45.
44 For the foregoing, see *Report of the total temperance society founded at Mount Sion in the City of Waterford on the 10th day of November 1839 by the Rt. Rev. Dr. Nicholas Foran* (Cork, 1840).
45 Kane, *Industrial resources*, 388; Cowman, *Making*, 39.
46 [Cowman], "Life and Work," 35. In 1851 he resided at Mount Patrick, townland of Ballyvaden, parish of Monksland, in a house he leased from Power-O'Shee.
47 Ibid.; *GM* 53 (1853), 227; *Memorials of the life and character of Lady Osborne and some of her friends*, 2 vols. (Dublin, 1870), ii, 108; *WM* 15 Dec. 1847; *Ireland*, 49; Cowman, *Making*, 35,

41. Rev. Power died in an accident while raising the funds in America: Cowman, *Making*, 41.
48. Kane, *Industrial resources*, 288.
49. Morrissey to J. Labbatt, 12 May, [18]48 (RCPI 4/3/3/11).
50. Cowman, *Making*, 42.
51. M. Purdy to A. Kennedy, 27 Mar. 1837 (RCPI 4/3/3/8). The college's unwillingness to contribute to improvement generally, contrasts with that of another institutional landowner, Trinity College Dublin (see R.B. McDowell & D.A. Webb, *Trinity College Dublin, 1592-1952: An academic history* (Cambridge, 1982), 101).
52. J. Labatt to [C.] Farran, 8 Jan. 1846 (RCPI 2/3/2/3)
53. Kane, *The industrial resources*, 1st ed., i, 215.
54. C. Farran to J. Labbatt, 28 Mar. 1848 (RCPI 4/3/3/11).
55. P. Power, *Parochial History of Waterford and Lismore During the 18th and 19th centuries* (Waterford, 1912), xv, 121.
56. D. Kerr, *Peel, Priests, and Politics: Sir Robert Peel's Administration and the Roman Catholic Church in Ireland, 1841-1846* (Oxford, 1982), 12–13, 331; M.R. O'Connell (ed.), *The Correspondence of Daniel O'Connell* (Dublin, 1973-), 7 vols., iv, nos. 1629, 1631, 1713, v, no.2188, vi, no. 2563, vii, no.3173.
57. Kerr, *Peel*, 330–331.
58. Ibid., 33.
59. HC *An account of the salaries and emoluments of the different curate in each and every benefice in Ireland* 1833 (721), xxvii, 18; Broderick, *Waterford's Anglicans*, 56.
60. *Ireland*, 46; *Credentials*, 214, 282; Broderick, *Waterford's Anglicans*, 56.
61. S. J. Connolly, *Priest and People in Pre-Famine Ireland* (Dublin, 1982), 48. The average income of a parish priest (exclusive of maintaining a curate) at this time was £65 (Ibid.).
62. Connolly, *Priests and People*, 50–51.
63. Waterford Diocesan Archives, Bishop Dominick O'Brien papers, Box 6B (1855–60): Rev. Roger Power, Mount Patrick to Bishop

O'Brien, 21 June [18]56; Rev. Michael Power PP, Stradbally to [Bishop O'Brien], 8 July 1856.

64 Details on the chapel from Waterford Diocesan Archives, Bishop Dominick O'Brien papers, Rev. Roger Power, Mount Patrick to Bishop O'Brien, 21 June [18]56. Although the chapel came into existence in 1854, it was not noted in a listing of Catholic chapels in the area: *Key to the Catholic Ecclesiastical map of Ireland* (Dublin, 1859), 18. Rev. Roger Power was also the Catholic chaplain to the workhouse in Kilmacthomas, a position he resigned in December 1856 in a dispute over his salary: G. Crotty, "Kilmacthomas Union: the administration of poor law in a County Waterford workhouse, 1851-1872," *Decies* 64 (2008), 129, 131.

65 Indenture between Dame Catherine Osborne and David Colquohoun and John Murray, churchwardens, 31 May, 1830 (NA D 6214); RCB Ms. 138/6/4 (architectural drawing of "Bunmahon church" by James Pain).

66 *WM* 22 Feb. 1845.

67 C Farran to J. Labbatt, 5 Sept. [1848] and 25 Apr. 1849 (RCPI 4/3/3/11); Cowman, *Making*, 48–9; Emily's Story, 3.

68 Cowman, *Making*, 28, 79-80.

69 Mrs. [C.I.] Osborne, *Memorials of the life and character of Lady Osborne and some of her friends*, 2 vols. (Dublin, 1870), i, 97, 123 (quote). Her decision to support the National Board was the result of her attendance at Exeter House— the centre of the evangelical movement in London—where a meeting to oppose it was held: ibid., i, 174. She was also influenced in her views through correspondence with Richard Whately, archbishop of Dublin: Ibid., ii, 206–281.

70 NA D 6214 mentions that the land laid out for the church was bounded on the west by the ground allocated for a school house.

71 NA ED 1/86/35.

72 Foregoing from HC *Reports from commissioners on the employment of children (Mines)*, xvi (1842), 862–4.

73   NA ED 1/86/35.
74   Ibid.
75   Ibid.
76   Ibid.; *Irish Catholic Directory* (Dublin, 1850), 303.
77   NA ED 1/86/49. The curate of Monksland in 1839 was Rev. Thomas Garde Durden: Cotton, Leslie, & Rennison, *Clergy of Waterford,* 128.
78   NA ED 2/183; ED 1 /86/109/2A. The local curate of Monksland would have been Doudney who arrived in late 1847, though a recent list gives Thomas Power as the curate between 1844 and 1850, and Doudney as the curate of Monksland *and* Kilbarrymeaden (Cotton, Leslie & Rennison, op.cit., 128, 242), and elsewhere in the list Power is given as curate of Monksland, 1843-7 (ibid., 363). Responsibilities for Kilbarrymeaden were minimal since according to a survey of 1833, while occasional services were held, there was no church located in it: TCD Mss 2770–4/899; *Decies* 8 (1978), 31.
79   RCB 154/1/1/1 Church Education Society, Committee Proceedings, 1839–44, p. 420; 154/1/1/2 Committee Proceedings, 1844-48, pp. 166, 222, 504, 557; 154/1/1/4, 1852–8, pp. 102, 324; School Inspections, 1846-57, p.66; *Eight report of the Church Education Society for Ireland being for the years 1846 and 1847* (Dublin, 1847), 22, 31.
80   *Substance of a speech delivered by the Bishop of Cashel etc in the House of Lords, 17th June 1845 on presenting petitions on the subject of National Education* (Waterford, [1845]), 15 (This is also available online at http://hansard.millbanksystems.com). There were reported cases in the summer of 1843 of Protestant children being verbally abused by the other children which was the cause of "much dissension and unhappiness" between the parents: Ibid., 16.
81   Ibid., 16.
82   The controversy can be followed in the *WM* 22 Feb. 1845. Unless otherwise indicated, the following draws on this source.

83   NA D 6214.
84   *WM* 22 Feb. 1845.
85   D. H. Akenson, *A Protestant in Purgatory: Richard Whately, Archbishop of Dublin* (Hamden, Conn., 1981), 198–9.
86   *WM* 24 Nov. 1848. The three churches were the Cathedral, St. Olave's, and St. Patrick's.
87   Robert Bell, *Some thoughts on the past history and present position of the question at issue between the adherents of the government system and the supporters of scriptural education* (Dublin, 1850).
88   *WM* 22 Feb. 1845. Osborne's claim as to the absence of sectarian animosities was not entirely accurate as the local response to the conversion of Laurence Lynch in 1837 demonstrated: see Chapter 6, n.43.
89   Ibid.
90   Ibid. Another source states that the petition was written by 33 fathers of families (*Substance of a speech delivered by the Bishop of Cashel*, 17).
91   Quoted in *Substance of a speech delivered by the Bishop of Cashel*, 17.
92   *WM* 22 Feb. 1845.
93   *Sixth annual report of the Church Education Society for Ireland* (Dublin, 1845), 58. In 1856, in submitting a report on the two national schools in Knockmahon, Rev. Roger Power, commented that: "There are no Protestants attending them." Waterford Diocesan Archives, Bishop Dominick O'Brien papers, Rev. Roger Power, Mount Patrick to Bishop O'Brien, 21 June [18]56.
94   Printed annual reports for the Church Education Society for the respective years. The school continued on into the 1870s at least.
95   Cowman, *Making*, 53.
96   Ibid., 53–4.
97   NA ED 2/46/14; 2/183/18.
98   NA ED 2/45/70 sub 12 June 1844; ED 2/46/17 sub 30 Oct. 1849; Cowman, *Making*, 48. After 1852 when he resigned as

mine manager, Petherick was only irregularly present in the locality.

99 NA ED 1/87/88/1; 2/183/65.
100 Waterford Diocesan Archives, Bishop Dominick O'Brien papers, Rev. Roger Power, Mount Patrick to Bishop O'Brien, 21 June [18]56.
101 Cotton, Leslie & Rennison, *Clergy of Waterford*, 363.
102 G. D. Burtchaell and T U. Sadleir, *Alumni Dublinenses* (London, 1924), 679.
103 NA ED 1/86/47.
104 Ibid.; *Irish Catholic Directory* (Dublin, 1850), 303. His curates in 1850 were Thomas Casey and M. Dooley (ibid.). They were still in the same position in 1860 (*Irish Catholic Directory* (Dublin, 1860), 192).
105 Ibid.
106 Cowman, *Making*, 52.
107 NA ED 1/86/47. The subsequent history of the school can be traced in NA ED 1/87/85/1-2, 2/45, 2/183.
108 Waterford Diocesan Archives, Bishop Dominick O'Brien papers, Rev. Roger Power, Mount Patrick to Bishop O'Brien, 21 June [18]56.
109 HC *Appendix to 16th Report of the Commissioners of National Education (Irl.)*, xxv (1850), 89.
110 NA ED 1/87/5/1A.
111 HC *Appendix to 16th Report of the Commissioners of National Education (Irl.)*, xxv (1850), 89.
112 For its later history see NA ED 1/87/5/2A; ED 2/46; RCPI 4/3/7/2/5.
113 NA ED 2/45/44 under 9 June 1838. This formed part of a report sent to Lady Osborne.
114 Corish, *Irish Catholic Experience*, 208.
115 For these quotations see HC *Reports from Commissioners on the Employment of Children (Mines)* xvi, (1842), 862–4.
116 Cowman, *Making*, 96.

117 Cowman, *Making*, 98–9.
118 Burtchaell, "19th Century Society," *Decies* 31 (1986), 40; *GM* 53 (1853) 226.
119 D. Mhic Mhurchu, "Phillip Barron: Man of Mystery," *Decies* 2 (May, 1976), 10–15.
120 *Ireland*, 48.
121 *Credentials*, 495–6.
122 *Ireland*, 17.
123 [D.A. Doudney], *Recollections and remains of the late Rev. George David Doudney* (London, 1866), 71–3. He was married to Alfred Doudney's elder sister (ibid., 4). Foley later went with George Doudney to Donegal, stayed a few months, and later worked as a Scripture reader among Irish people in the north of England: Ibid., 73; *Retracings*, 122.
124 *WM* 1 Oct., 26 Nov. 1851; D. Foley, *A missionary tour through the South and West of Ireland, undertaken for the [Irish] Society [for Promoting Scriptural Education]* (Dublin, 1849).
125 *Recollections and remains*, 42, 77–8.
126 Ibid., 81, 83, 88. Doudney was ordained by the Bishop of Derry (ibid., 42, 81); *Retracings*, 133. He acquired the facility of preaching in Irish and this attracted some Catholics to his services: Ibid., 84; *WM* 21 Aug. 1850, 26 Nov. 1851. D. A. Doudney was present and spoke at the laying of the foundation at Dunlewey (*WM* 21 Aug.1850).
127 [Cowman], "Life and Work," 39.
128 Cowman, *Making*, 62.
129 Ibid.
130 [Cowman], "Life and Work," 39.
131 Constabulary returns for farms in Ballylaneen, Monksland, May 1846 (NA RLFC 4/29/40).
132 Constabulary returns for Kilmacthomas and Bunmahon, 25 Aug. 1846 (NA RLFC 5/29/4).
133 [Cowman], "Life and Work," 39; resolution passed at a meeting of the Kilmacthomas and Bunmahon relief committee, 11 May,

1846 (NA RLFC 3/1/2212). Only in 1848 was a special fever "shed" and a medical depot (1849) opened in Bunmahon: D. Cowman & D. Brady (ed.), *The Famine in Waterford* (Dublin, 1995), 121, 123.

134 [Cowman], "Life and Work," 39; Cowman, *Making*, 65.

135 J. Labbatt to Rev. James Power, 9 May 1846 (RCPI 2/3/2/3 Copy letter book, 1845-1861). Government was aware of the college's obligations, see NA RFLC 7/27/[70].

136 NA RLFC 6/29/7. In the period, the committee paid over £1236 for the purchase of meal; Cowman & Brady, *Famine*, 52.

137 Ibid.

138 [Cowman], "Life and Work," 39; Cowman, *Making*, 65.

139 Rev. J. Power to W. Stanley, 18 Feb. 1837 (NA RLFC 3/2/29/18).

140 Ibid.

141 R. Douglas to W. Stanley, 20 Feb. 1847 (NA RLFC 3/2/29/18).

142 *Transactions of the central relief committee of the Society of Friends during the famine in Ireland in 1846 and 1847* (1852), 183.

143 Cowman & Brady, *Famine*, 218.

144 Rev. J. Power to W. Stanley, 14 Mar. 1847 (NA RLFC 3/2/29/18); and "A list of the subscribers to the soup kitchens at Bonmahon and Kilmacthomas," 22 Mar. 1847 (NA RLFC 3/2/29/18). The total amount for the Kilmacthomas area was £83.18s.10d.

145 Subscription list dated 22 Mar. 1847 (NA RLFC 3/2/29/18). The total amount for the Bunmahon area was £118.18s.6d. in addition to which there was £20 from the Strangmans of Waterford and £20 part of a donation from the Catholics of Liverpool.

146 Rev. J. Power to [ ], 27 Mar. 1847 (NA RLFC 3/2/29/18). See also the list of additional subscribers (£54.7s.6d. total) in ibid.

147 *Personal recollections of the Right Rev. Robert Daly, DD, late bishop of Cashel at Powerscourt and Waterford by an old parishioner* (Dublin, 1872), 38. Daly insisted that the local curate of Stradbally take a holiday of a month or six weeks and he would

assume his duties including Sunday services, visiting the school, and attending to the poor (Madden, *Memoir*, 355).

148 Mrs. H. Madden, *Memoirs of the late Right Rev. Robert Daly DD, Lord Bishop of Cashel* (London, 1875), 253, 275, 277; *Personal recollections*, 34. Already he had a reputation for giving charity, caring for the sick, and dispensing general welfare for the less well off when he was rector of Powerscourt, Co. Wicklow (*Personal recollections*, 17, 24, 26).

149 He contributed, for instance, to the Association for the Relief of the Sick or Indigent Protestants of Waterford (RCB Ms 627/1 Account book, 1835–1863, under 19 April, 1853). The association was devoted to the provision of coal tickets, coffins, and weekly payments.

150 *WM* 1 Jan. 1848.

151 Cowman, *Making*, 66–67. In the summer of 1847, of 3,500 applications for relief only 1400 could be met before the food supply became exhausted: Ibid., 67.

152 Cowman, *Making*, 67–8.

153 Farran to J Labbatt, 25 Apr. 1849, 6 Aug. 1850 (RCPI 4/3/3/11, 4/3/3/12).

154 *GM* 55 (1855), 439.

155 Cowman, *Making*, 72.

156 Farran to Labbatt, 11 June [18]49 (RCPI 4/3/3/11), same to same, 16 July 1850 (RCPI 4/3/3/12).

157 Petition of Patrick Power, David Power, John Shanahan, Michael Meany, Pat Magrath, tenants of Kilmoylan, Co. Waterford, [c.22 Mar.], 1848.

158 C. Farran to J. Labbatt, 15 Mar. 1848 (RCPI 4/3/3/11).

159 Farran to J. Labbatt, 16 July 1850 (RCPI 4/3/3/12).

160 Rents and arrears for the year ending September, 1852 (RCPI 4/3/4/1/14).

161 Ibid.

162. Return of arrears of poor rates for Bunmahon, Templevrick, and Ballynard, n.d. [c.1848] (RCPI 4/3/3/11). Of the total arrear of £27.3s.10d., Bunmahon accounted for almost half at £12.13s.6d.
163. Report of Charles Farran to the College of Physicians, 11 May, 1848 (CPSI 4/3/6/4, p.15).
164. [Cowman], "Life and Work," 39; Cowman, *Making*, 68.
165. Cowman, *Making*, 81.
166. Ibid., 81–2.
167. D.A. Doudney to W. Stokes, 4 Jan. [18]50 (RCPI Estate Correspondence, 4/3/3/12). Doudney's wife had contracted cholera in August 1849: *Retracings*, 129. His wife Eliza's health was the other cause of his unsettledness in Bunmahon: *Retracings*, 130, 146.
168. Same to same, 6 Jan. [18]50 (RCPI 4/3/3/12). What made the situation more pressing was that tenants on estates whose landlords did not subscribe to the fund were not entitled to medical relief: Walker to Stokes, [1850] (RCPI 4/3/3/12).
169. Ibid.
170. Stokes to Doudney, 8 Jan. [18]50 (RCPI 4/3/3/12).
171. Doudney to Stokes, 25 Feb. [18]50, J. Labbatt to Doudney, 9 Mar. 1850, Doudney to Labbatt, 12 Mar.1850 (RCPI 4/3/3/12).
172. Doudney to J. Labbatt, 12 Mar. [18]50 (RCPI Estate Correspondence, 4/3/3/12).
173. *GM* 53 (1853), 226.
174. *Substance of a speech delivered by the Bishop of Cashel*, 16.
175. *WM* 22 Feb. 1845.
176. *GM* 54 (1854), 470; Doudney, *Retracings*, 151.
177. Cowman, *Making*, 82.
178. *GM* 53 (1853), 226; *Retracings*, 156, 160. Emigration from the area had begun before the famine: Cowman, *Making*, 71–2.
179. *Ireland*, 79.
180. Cowman, *Making*, 81.
181. Ibid., 76–8.

182 *The Bonmahon Infant, Embroidery, Printing and Agricultural Schools Co. Waterford* (included in the back section of B. Keach, *Tropologia* (London, 1856), 1.

183 NA ED 1/87/112/1A, 2; Cowman, *Making*, 100. It was held in the same location as the day school (Knockmahon Male). Three quarters of them (about 100 on the rolls) were 19 years of age. Held from 6 to 8 p.m., subjects covered included reading, writing, arithmetic, grammar, and geography.

184 *The Bonmahon Infant, Embroidery, Printing and Agricultural Schools Co. Waterford* (included in the back section of B. Keach, *Tropologia* (London, 1856), 1.

185 *Memoir*, 118; *Try and Try Again*, 161.

186 *PO*, 11.

187 *Try and Try Again*, 158.

188 For Sheffield: Doudney, *Retracings*, 127–9, 130–131; for Plymouth: *Retracings*, 136, 142–3; and for London: *Retracings*, 145. The Sheffield offer seemed timely since the lease on the house the family was staying in Annestown was nearly expired, with a growing family and more expenses which he was barely able to meet, and Doudney was against going anywhere else in Ireland, he enjoyed the sea situation as opposed to the city, but Bishop Daly declined to let him go. The relative quiet in Ireland allowed him the time to devote to the editorship of the *Gospel Magazine*: Ibid.

189 HC *A return of the number of churches in each benefice or union in Ireland* 1833 (400), xxvii, 22; *A return of the number of churches and chapels built in each diocese of Ireland since the 1st day of January, 1823* 1844 (190), xliii, 3 (also TCD Mss 2770–4/934); S. Lewis, *Topographical Dictionary of Ireland*, ii, 352.

190 Broderick, *Waterford's Anglicans*, 46.

191 Ibid., 359, 361, 366. See also the combined parochial figures: A. Stopford, *The increase and requirements of the Irish Church …* (1853), 108.

192 *Memoir*, 137; *Try and Try Again*, 161.

193 Emily Story, 4.
194 *Retracings*, 144, 160.
195 Ibid., 146.
196 *Memoir*, 145; *Retracings*, 137.
197 For the foreign crews: Emily's Story, 3.

Chapter 3

1 *GM* 56 (1856), 53.
2 *Ireland*, 60.
3 *GM* 57 (1857), 519.
4 R. B. McDowell, *The Church of Ireland, 1869–1969* (London, 1975), 17–18; Broderick, *Waterford's Anglicans*, 62–63.
5 *GM* 57 (1857), 519.
6 *A charge delivered by the Right Rev. the Lord Bishop of Cashel, etc at the visitation of the dioceses of Waterford and Lismore, Cashel and Emly July 1846* (Dublin, 1846), 20.
7 *Retracings*, 159, 161.
8 Ibid., 144.
9 *GM* 56 (1856), 54.
10 Ibid., 54.
11 *GM* 58 (1858), 235, a section of extracts from a new edition of the *Pictorial Outline of the rise and progress of the Bonmahon Industrial and Agricultural Schools* (1858).
12 Broderick, *Waterford's Anglicans*, 243–5.
13 *GM* 56 (1856), 54.
14 *GM* 52 (1852), 241.
15 *GM* 56 (1856), 53.
16 Ibid.
17 *Retracings*, 152–3.
18 Works such as Vitringa on Isaiah, Alting on Jeremiah, Caryll on Job, Lampe on John, Luther on Galatians, Owen on Hebrews, or Mede on Revelation.
19 *GM* 54 (1854), 364.
20 Ibid., 364–5.

21. *GM* 7 n.s. (1847), 179.
22. *GM* 54 (1854), 364–5.
23. *GM* 51 (1851), 205.
24. Ibid, 261, 300; *Retracings*, 152.
25. *GM* 51 (1851), 360.
26. *Retracings*, 153; *Memoir*, 147–8; Doudney, *Try and Try Again*, 163. He later reversed this decision and became a subscriber to Gill and other works issuing from Bunmahon: *Memoir*, 148.
27. *GM* 51 (1851), 360. This stance by some Baptists and Independents was later refuted by fellow adherents: Ibid., 407–8.
28. Ibid., 408.
29. Ibid., 624.
30. Ibid., 452.
31. Ibid., 550; *Ireland*, 26; *Retracings*, 154.
32. *GM* 53 (1853), 176.
33. *Memoir*, 151; *Retracings*, 158; *Credentials*, 301; Emily's Story, 18.
34. *Memoir*, 147.
35. *GM* 51 (1851), 550–551; 52 (1852), 241; *Retracings*, 154.
36. *Credentials*, 298–9.
37. Emily's Story, 13.
38. *GM* 51 (1851), 551.
39. Ibid. 52 (1852), 242; *Credentials*, 299.
40. Emily's Story, 13.
41. *Retracings*, 153.
42. The hotel was leased by Timothy Connolly from the College of Physicians, and though he had spent much on improvements, he surrendered his lease effective 25 Sept. 1849 (Connolly to Charles Farran, 8 Mar. 1849, petition of Timothy Connolly, 20 Mar.1849: RCPS 4/3/3/11); *Waterford News* 7 Nov. 1902, quoting same of 17 Oct. 1851: NLI Ms. 9497 No.22, p.16. At the time the premises was let to two separate families (*Try and Try Again*, 164).
43. *GM* 55 (1855), 141.
44. *GM* 51 (1851), 616-7, 624; 54 (1854), 109.

45 *GM* 52 (1852), 47.
46 *GM* 52 (1852), 242; *Credentials*, 299.
47 *GM* 54 (1854), 108; *Retracings*, 155.
48 *GM* 53 (1853), 227.
49 Ibid., 227.
50 Ibid., 227–8.
51 *The Bonmahon Infant, Embroidery, Printing and Agricultural Schools Co. Waterford* (included in the back section of B. Keach, *Tropologia* (London, 1856), 1.
52 *GM* 53 (1853), 228.
53 Cowman, *Making*, 80.
54 Doudney, *Try and Try Again*, 190.
55 *Ireland*, 28 quoting a correspondent from Kilmacthomas in *Waterford News*, 17 Oct. 1851.
56 *GM* 52 (1852), 46–7; *Retracings*, 156–8, 160.
57 *GM* 52 (1852), 47–8, 283.
58 Ibid., 47–8.
59 Ibid., 48, 283.
60 Ibid., 293.
61 Ibid., 242.
62 Ibid., 283, 400; *Retracings*, 163.
63 *GM* 52 (1852), 47.
64 Ibid., 52 (1852), 438.
65 Ibid. 53 (1853), 176; 54 (1854), 45.
66 Ibid., 226.
67 *GM* 54 (1854), 270.
68 *Credentials*, 302.
69 Ibid. 228; *Ireland*, 50.
70 As later recounted to him by his sons: *Ireland*, 11–12.
71 *GM* 53 (1853), 228.
72 Ibid., 52 (1852), 448.
73 Ibid., 47; 54 (1854), 365. Doudney acquired Greek and Hebrew fonts but whether by purchase or loan is unclear (*The Irish Book Lover* 32: 4 (1955), 83).

74 *GM* 54 (1854), 365.
75 *GM* 53 (1853), 226; *The Irish Booklover* 1 (1910), 97; *Ireland*, 48; *Credentials*, 487.
76 *Official Catalogue of the National Exhibition of the Arts, Manufactures and Products of Ireland, held in Cork 1852* (Cork, 1852). The only two exhibitors from Waterford under Class 16: Books, Paper, Printing, Stationary etc. were Cornelius Redmond (specimens of book bindings and a ledger) and Loughlace Sutherland, 3 New Street (specimens of book bindings). On the general background to the exhibition see A.C. Davies, "The first Irish industrial exhibition: Cork, 1852," *Irish Economic and Social History* 2 (1975), 46–59.
77 *GM* 52 (1852), 540; *Ireland*, 36.
78 J. Gill, *An Exposition of the Old Testament…* (London, 1854), vol. 4, "To Our Subscribers."
79 *GM* 54(1854), 109.
80 *Retracings*, 172. The living was in the patronage of the crown (Lewis, *Topographical Dictionary*, ii, 59). In 1849 its impropriate tithes were worth £34.12s. (ibid., 2nd ed. 1849, ii, 26). Kilcash had no church or parsonage and no resident Protestants, and the occasional one or two who came as police for the barracks located in the parish, were ministered to by the rector of an adjoining parish (*Memoir*, 166).
81 *WM* 24 Apr. 1855.
82 *WM* 7 July 1855.
83 *GM* 58 (1858), 68; *Credentials*, 512.
84 Hansard: HC Debates 12 June 1855 vol. 138 cc1909–10 (available online at http://hansard.millbanksystems.com).
85 *PO*, 24; *Memoir*, 161; *Credentials*, 302, 318–9; Emily's Story, 15. Proposals had been current from the time of Doudney's appointment to provide ground for the erection of a residence for him. His bishop, Robert Daly, had been in communication with the College of Physicians as early as 1848 as to the provision of such ground (C. Farran to J. Labbatt, 25 Apr. 1848: RCPI

4/3/3/11). However, this did not come to fruition until October, 1851 (see the exchange of letters: W.E. Steele to C. Farran, 28, [29] Aug., 18 Sept, 20 Oct. 1851 in Copy Letter Book, 1845-61(RCPI 2/3/2/3)). Doudney was regular in his payments of 30s for the glebe land (See #207 in RCPI 4/3/4/1/17 and #121 in 4/2/1/24).

86 Quoted in Cowman, *Making*, 82.

87 For a complete list of works printed in Bunmahon see: NLI Ms. 3966; *The Irish Booklover* 1 (1910), 98–100; *Memoir*, 152-4. For shorter pamphlets printed in Bunmahon see the advertisements in J. Gill, *The Cause of God and Truth* (1855), D. A. Doudney, *The Pictorial Outline* etc., ([1855]), and S. Rutherford, *Letters* (1857).

88 *GM* 53 (1853), 582; 54 (1854), 379–80.

89 *GM* 54 (1854), 269. It was available by July 1854: *Ireland*, 72.

90 Ibid., 270.

91 *GM* 54 (1854), 379–80.

92 *GM* 55 (1855), 46–7; *Ireland*, 73–4.

93 Ibid., 144.

94 Ibid., 341.

95 *GM* 56 (1856), 488.

96 *GM* 52 (1852), 544.

97 Emily's Story, 18.

98 Ibid., 544.

99 *GM* 55 (1855), 142.

100 *WM* 27 May 1856, 13 Jan., 8 Sept. 1857.

101 The work is undated. For dating to November 1855 see the notice in *WM* 24 Nov. 1855.

102 I owe this information to Des Cowman.

103 Doudney later claimed that *Old Jonathan* attained a monthly circulation of 15,000 before he left the area: Doudney, *Retracings*, 151.

104 HC *Report from the Select Committee on Postal Arrangements (Waterford etc.)*, 11 (1854–5), 71. Unless indicated otherwise details in the preceding section are taken from this source.
105 *Ireland*, 84–5.
106 *PO*, 16.
107 HC *Postal Arrangements (Waterford etc.)*, 11 (1854–5), 71–3, 173–4.
108 See *WM* 5 Jan., 9 Apr 1853, 4 Jan. 1854, and 9 Sept. 1856 (*The Irish Book Lover* 32: 4 (1955), 81).
109 *Credentials*, 340–41; Emily's Story, 15.
110 Ibid., 455–6.
111 Ibid., 456.
112 *PO*, 16; *Memoir*, 152.
113 *GM* 53 (1853), 176; Doudney, *Try and Try Again*, 170.
114 *GM* 58 (1858), 235.
115 Ibid., 237.
116 *Credentials*, 320.
117 *GM* 53 (1853), 226; *PO*, 16; *Memoir*, 152.
118 Church of Ireland Marriage Register, Stradbally, Co. Waterford. See also *WM* 24 Jan. 1852; NLI Ms. 9497, No.22, p.15.
119 *WM* 13 Jan. 1855: NLI Ms. 9497, No.22, p.17.
120 Lease from the College of Physicians, 2 Dec. 1857 (RCPI Estate Papers 4/3/2/43); *GM* 57 (1857), 519. The building still survives today adjacent to the former glebe house.
121 *GM* 57 (1857), 519.
122 *Ireland*, 93–4.
123 *Try and Try Again*, 191n.
124 *GM* 58 (1858), 231–2.

Chapter 4
1 *GM* 54 (1854), 519.
2 *GM* 56 (1856), 55.
3 *GM* 52 (1852), 134; *Ireland*, 33.
4 *GM* 52 (1852), 191.

5   Ibid., 52 (1852), 135, 192, 207, 244, 301–2, 390, 399, 496, 539–40, 543.
6   Ibid., 52 (1852), 134, 192; *Ireland*, 30.
7   *GM* 52 (1852), 443–4.
8   Ibid., 444.
9   Ibid., 191.
10 *Credentials*, 491–2.
11 *GM* 52 (1852), 301.
12 Ibid., 399, 444.
13 Ibid., 444–8.
14 Ibid., 444.
15 Ibid., 444–5; *Memoir*, 155–6. Although later encouraged to give an additional meal of stirabout, Doudney declined to consider it until he had sufficient funds in hand (*GM* 52 (1852), 541).
16 Emily's Story, 14.
17 *Credentials*, 493.
18 *GM* 52 (1852), 445.
19 Ibid., 445.
20 Ibid., 447, 496, 539.
21 *GM* 54 (1854), 45.
22 Ibid., 448.
23 *GM* 53 (1853), 175–7.
24 Ibid., 479.
25 Ibid. The treasurers' addresses are given in a preface to the *PO*.
26 Ibid., 144, 176, 326.
27 Ibid., 47.
28 *GM* 54 (1854), 46–7. There was nothing novel about giving a free meal to school children. In 1850, for instance, Lord Stuart de Decies provided a meal for 200 children at his schools in Villierstown (*WM* 6 Apr. 1850).
29 *Try and Try Again*, 176–7.
30 *GM* 54 (1854), 519.
31 *GM* 55 (1855), 538; 56 (1856), 55. About 50 was the average in May 1855: *The Bonmahon Infant, Embroidery, Printing and*

32 *Agricultural Schools Co. Waterford* (included in the back section of B. Keach, *Tropologia* (London, 1856), 1.
32 *GM* 56 (1856), 55.
33 *Credentials*, 320.
34 NA ED 1/87/5/2A.
35 *GM* 56 (1856), 56.
36 *GM* 57 (1857), 169; *Memoir*, 158–9; *The Bonmahon Infant, Embroidery, Printing and Agricultural Schools Co. Waterford* (included in the back section of B. Keach, *Tropologia* (London, 1856), 2.
37 *GM* 57 (1857), 169.
38 *GM* 56 (1856), 56.
39 Ibid.
40 Ibid.
41 For the foregoing: *Ireland*, 86–7.
42 *GM* 57 (1857), 169.
43 Ibid.
44 Ibid.
45 Ibid.
46 *GM* 58 (1858), 236.
47 *GM* 53 (1853), 330.
48 *GM* 54 (1854), 47–8.
49 *GM* 53 (1853), 330.
50 *GM* 54 (1854), 45.
51 Emily's Story, 14. The girls and young women wore the clothing they produced in the school to mass or to market: Ibid.
52 *GM* 55 (1855), 140; 56 (1856), 55; *Memoir*, 160; *Ireland*, 76; *Credentials*, 515. *The Bonmahon Infant, Embroidery, Printing and Agricultural Schools Co. Waterford* (included in the back section of B. Keach, *Tropologia* (London, 1856), 1, gives 5s.–8s. as the range of pay. The rates compare with an average weekly rate of 2s for work on the nearby dressing floors of the mining operation: Cowman, *Making*, 91. One source (Emily's Story, 15) claims the weekly amount were much more, at 10s. to 18s. per week.

53 *GM* 54 (1854), 45.
54 Ibid., 519.
55 Ibid.
56 *PO*, 4; *GM* 55 (1855), 144.
57 *GM* 56 (1856), 55; *WM* 7 July 1855.
58 *GM* 56 (1856), 55.
59 *GM* 58 (1858), 236; *Credentials*, 320.
60 Emily's Story, 15.
61 Ibid., 14.
62 *Ireland*, 17.
63 *GM* 53 (1853), 581. The system of treasurers did not materialize: Ibid., 54 (1854), 316.
64 *The Bonmahon Infant, Embroidery, Printing and Agricultural Schools Co. Waterford* (included in the back section of B. Keach, *Tropologia* (London, 1856), 1.
65 GM 53(1853), 581; 54 (1854), 315.
66 *GM* 54 (1854), 48, 315; 55 (1855), 538.
67 RCB Ms 718 Waterford Auxiliary Bible Society account book, 1846–1866, under date 1 January, 1858 in the amount of £4.11s.
68 *GM* 54 (1854), 44.
69 *Try and Try Again*, 181.
70 *GM* 58 (1858), 106.

Chapter 5

1 In writing this chapter I have made use of the following: D. English et al., *The Lion Handbook of Christian Belief* (London, 1988); A. McGrath, *The Blackwell Encyclopedia of Modern Christian Thought* (Oxford, 1993); P. Corish, *The Irish Catholic Experience: a historical survey* (Dublin, 1985); J.Baycroft, *The Eucharistic Way* (Toronto, 1981).
2 Brendan Kennelly, "The Irish: Priests and the People," in B. Kennelly (ed.), *Ireland: Past and Present* (Dublin, 1986), 107.
3 *The Book of Common Prayer* (Toronto, 1959), 700.

4   Printed in *Credentials*, 501–5. What follows, unless otherwise indicated, draws on this.
5   *GM* 52 (1852), 439; also in Doudney, *Ireland*, 41–3.
6   *WM* 3 Oct. 1856. What follows draws on this source. For other local reportage on differences in translation between the Authorized Version and Catholic versions (in this case a new edition by Duffy of Dublin), see *WM* 16, 23 Jan. 1858. For Mills: J. Crawford, *The Church of Ireland in Victorian Dublin* (Dublin, 2005), 171–4.
7   *Credentials*, 317. As it was he picked up the remnants which providentially provided him with the text for his sermon (ibid.)
8   *GM* 52 (1852), 438–440; 447. Doudney also reported on the burning of bibles by priests: Doudney, *Ireland*, 14.
9   *GM* 52 (1852), 447.
10 *GM* 52 (1852), 439; also in *Ireland*, 41–3.
11 *The Book of Common Prayer* (Toronto, 1959), 550.
12 In this section on communion I have found John Baycroft, *The Eucharistic Way* (Toronto, 1981) particularly helpful.
13 Baycroft, *Eucharistic Way*, 38–9.
14 *WM* 11, 18 Sept. 1850.
15 For the proceedings of the Synod of Thurles, see Corish, *The Irish Catholic Experience*, 195–7.
16 Connolly, *Priests and People*, 72.
17 D. O'Corrain & T. O'Riordain (ed.), *Ireland 1815–1870: Emancipation, Famine, and Religion* (Dublin, 2011), 192.
18 Connolly, *Priests and People*, 68–9.
19 Kerr, *Peel, Priests, and Politics*, 238–47.
20 Quoted in Connolly, *Priests and People*, 113.
21 Quoted ibid., 113.

Chapter 6

1   James Kelly, *Sir Richard Musgrave, 1746–1818: ultra-protestant ideologue* (Dublin, 2009).

2   T. Power, "Schools in Connection with the Kildare Place Society in County Waterford, 1817-1840," *Decies* 17 (May, 1981), 5–16.
3   Broderick, *Waterford's Anglicans*, 131–171.
4   Kerr, *Peel, Priests, and Politics*, 70n.
5   D.H. Akenson, *The Church of Ireland: Ecclesiastical Reform and Revolution, 1800-1885* (New Haven & London, 1971), 148–159.
6   D. Bowen, *The Protestant Crusade in Ireland, 1800–1870* (Dublin, 1978); I. Whelan, *The Bible War in Ireland* (Madison, WI, 2005).
7   *GM* 53 (1853), 176.
8   Broderick, *Waterford's Anglicans*, 76–82.
9   Ibid., 240–46.
10 These are the conclusions of D. Bowen, *Souperism: Myth or Reality? A study of Catholics and Protestants during the Great Famine* (Cork, 1970).
11 Broderick, *Waterford's Anglicans*, 252.
12 E. Broderick, "The Famine and Religious Controversy in Waterford, 1847– 1850," *Decies* 51 (1995), 11–24 at 18; idem, *Waterford's Anglicans*, 275–6.
13 *GM* 55 (1855), 438.
14 Ibid.
15 He does not appear to have been active in the various branches of the Irish Society, the Church Education Society, the Hibernian Bible Society, or the Protestant Orphan Society.
16 M. Moffitt, "The Society for Irish Church Missions to the Roman Catholics: Philanthropy or Bribery?" *International Bulletin of Missionary Research*, 30: 1 (Jan. 2006), 32–38.
17 Broderick, *Waterford's Anglicans*, 259–60.
18 *GM* 50 (1850), 286; See also Bowen, *Protestant Crusade*, 163–4, 205–6.
19 Bowen, *Protestant Crusade*, 205-6; Broderick, *Waterford's Anglicans*, 259– 262.
20 *GM* 50 (1850), 45–8, 133–5, 183–6, 235–6, 285–6, 380–82, 425–8, and 524–5. For Dingle see D.P. Thompson, *A brief*

account of the rise and progress of the change in religious opinion new taking place in Dingle and the west of the county of Kerry, Ireland (London, 1847).

21   Broderick, *Waterford's Anglicans*, 211–97.
22   *Personal recollections of the Right Rev. Robert Daly, DD, late bishop of Cashel at Powerscourt and Waterford by an old parishioner* (Dublin, 1872), 30.
23   Madden, *Memoir*, 93; for evangelical societies in Waterford see Broderick, *Waterford's Anglicans*, 229–37.
24   *The thirtieth annual report of the London Hibernian Society for establishing schools and circulating the Holy Scriptures in Ireland* (London, 1836), 23, 96, 108.
25   *The thirty-first annual report of the London Hibernian Society for establishing schools and circulating the Holy Scriptures in Ireland* (London, 1837), 19, 93; *The thirty-second annual report of the London Hibernian Society for establishing schools and circulating the Holy Scriptures in Ireland* (London, 1838), 93.
26   *Home proceedings of the Hibernian district of the Church Missionary Society, thirty-first year ending 31st December, 1844* (Dublin, 1845), 36–7. Annual meetings of the local branch continued into the 1850s: *WM* 25 July 1857.
27   *Thirty-ninth report of the Hibernian district of the Church Missionary Society for the year 1852…* (Dublin, 1853), 58. There were also collections at Stradbally (£4.5s.10d.) and Kilmacthomas (£1.17s.4d.): ibid., 58, 59.
28   *Forty-first report of the Hibernian district of the Church Missionary Society for the year 1854…* (Dublin, 1855), 42; *Forty-second report of the Hibernian district of the Church Missionary Society for the year 1855…* (Dublin, 1856), 42–3; *Forty-sixth report of the Hibernian district of the Church Missionary Society for the year 1859…* (Dublin, 1860), 76; *WM* 28 May 1857.
29   W. Marrable, *Sketch of the origin and operations of the Society of Irish Church Missions to the Roman Catholics* (London, 1852), 42.
30   *WM* 26 May 1857.

31 RCB Ms 718 Waterford Auxiliary Bible Society account book, 1846–1866.
32 Ibid., 22 January, 1855 and for 1 January, 1858 record the sale of books to the Bunmahon branch for £4.11s.
33 *WM* 11 Mar. 1848. There were also auxiliaries in Tramore and Portlaw: *WM* 1 Dec. 1857.
34 RCB Ms 182/1/1/7; 182/3/1; and 182/4/1.
35 RCB Ms 182/1/1/7, minute book, 1849–55.
36 *Personal recollections of the Right Rev. Robert Daly*, 32; *Memoir*, 124.
37 *WM* 5 June 1856.
38 *Memoir*, 124–5.
39 *WM* 26 July 1851.
40 *WM* 20 Feb., 20 Mar, 3 Apr. 1850, 12 Mar. 1851. Among the clergy who preached on these subjects were Rev. E. N. Hoare, Rev. Arthur Wynne, Rev. Edward Brien, Rev. W. Carson, and Rev. Edward Dalton.
41 *A Charge delivered by the Rt. Rev. the Lord Bishop of Cashel at the visitation of the Dioceses of Waterford and Lismore, Cashel and Emly* (1849), 4, 13 (extracts were published in *GM* 49 (1849), 477–80). However Luke 13: 1-5 warned against interpreting disasters as God's specific judgment on evil people.
42 *A Charge delivered by the Rt. Rev. the Lord Bishop of Cashel at the visitation held in the dioceses of Waterford and Lismore, Cashel and Emly* (1851), p.7, 12–3. Also printed in *WM* 4 Oct. 1851.
43 Cowman, *Making*, 50–51.
44 Ibid., 51.
45 *GM* 51 (1851), 551; *Waterford News* 7 Oct.1902 quoting same of 17 Oct. 1851: NLI Ms. 9497 No. 22 p.16.
46 *Waterford News*, 17 Oct. 1851 cited in *GM* 51 (1851), 551.
47 *Memoir*, 118.
48 Ibid., 118–9.
49 *Try and Try Again*, 159.
50 Cowman, *Making*, 57.

51. G. Flynn, "The Young Ireland Movement in Waterford, 1848: Part 1," *Decies*, 18 (1981), 44. Unless otherwise indicated, the following paragraph draws on this source.
52. G. Flynn, "The Young Ireland Movement in Waterford, 1848: Part 2," *Decies*, 19 (1982), 53–54, 55. Unless otherwise indicated, the following paragraph draws on this source.
53. *Memoir*, 130–131.
54. Ibid., 131; *Credentials*, 278–9.
55. *Memoir*, 132; *Credentials*, 279; Emily's Story, 6.
56. Cowman, *Making*, 54–5.
57. Ibid., 56.
58. Ibid.
59. *Ireland*, 16; *Credentials*, 284.
60. *Memoir*, 129.
61. Ibid., 129–130.
62. *Ireland*, 15–16; *Credentials*, 281–2.
63. *Memoir*, 134; *Credentials*, 283; Broderick, *Waterford's Anglicans*, 304–8.
64. *GM* 53 (1853), 227; *Ireland*, 50.
65. Ibid.
66. Ibid; *Ireland*, 27–8.
67. *Memoir*, 148; *Try and Try Again*, 164.
68. *GM* 52 (1852), 132.
69. Ibid.
70. Ibid.; *Ireland*, 31–2.
71. *GM* 52 (1852), 132–3. It was not unknown for Catholics to convert having read the Douay Version: see the case of John Kennedy of Nenagh: Ibid., 52 (1852), 442.
72. *GM* 52 (1852), 133.
73. Ibid., 133, 446.
74. *GM* 53 (1853), 176.
75. *GM* 52 (1852), 133.
76. Ibid, 242; *Ireland*, 34.
77. *GM* 55 (1855), 76.

78 *Ireland*, 30.
79 Ibid.
80 Printed in *Ireland*, 34–6.
81 *PO*, 20. For a further address similar in tone and content see *GM* 52 (1852), 243. Bible-reading by the people themselves was an important issue of controversy between Catholic and Protestant clergymen. In 1853–4, Doudney initiated a fund for a Bible Depository at Bunmahon, for this see: *PO*, 21; *GM* 54 (1854), 48; 55 (1855), 538.
82 *Ireland*, 34n.
83 Connolly, *Priests*, 124–5.
84 *The Bonmahon Infant, Embroidery, Printing and Agricultural Schools Co. Waterford* (included in the back section of B. Keach, *Tropologia* (London, 1856), 3.
85 *GM* 52 (1852), 192.
86 Broderick, *Waterford's Anglicans*, 308–311.
87 *GM* 52 (1852), 400.
88 Ibid.
89 Ibid.
90 *Ireland*, 39–41.
91 *GM* 52 (1852), 400.
92 Ibid., 445–6; *Credentials*, 494.
93 *Memoir*, 163. The incident is undated, but Doudney includes it shortly after his account of the erection of the new glebe house or parsonage, so it is datable to early 1854.
94 Mrs. [C.I.] Osborne, *Memorials of the life and character of Lady Osborne and some of her friends*, 2 vols. (Dublin, 1870), i, 122.
95 *GM* 52 (1852), 446.
96 Ibid.
97 Ibid.
98 *Credentials*, 494.
99 *GM* 52 (1852), 446. Despite opposition from the priests, the girls' embroidery school was also a success (*Memoir*, 159).
100 *GM* 52 (1852), 446–7.

101 *Credentials*, 305. Doudney reports that the priest had demanded the fee for saying the mass for the deceased, while Doudney's congregation had assisted her in her need (Ibid., 305).
102 *GM* 52 (1852), 447.
103 Ibid., 447–8. The dates and figures are as follows: August 17: 3 Protestants, 27 Catholics; August 18: 3 Protestants, 30 Catholics; August 19: 3 Protestants, 32 Catholics; August 20: 27 total.
104 *GM* 52 (1852), 445.
105 Ibid., 447, 539.
106 Ibid., 447; *Credentials*, 495.
107 *Ireland*, 45.
108 *GM* 52 (1852), 445–7.
109 Ibid., 447, 496.
110 Ibid., 133.
111 Ibid., 134; *Credentials*, 496.
112 *GM* 52 (1852), 539.
113 Ibid., 447; *Credentials*, 496.
114 *Credentials*, 497.
115 *GM* 52 (1852), 539.
116 Ibid., 539.
117 Connolly, *Priests*, 126.
118 Ibid., 126–7.
119 The text of the excommunication service is reproduced in *GM* 47 (1847), 350–53.
120 Connolly, *Priests*, 127.
121 *GM* 52 (1852), 326–7. Only the Veales are named: Doudney, *Ireland*, 69.
122 Ibid., 327. For his identity: Cowman, *Making*, 91; Power, *Parochial History of Waterford and Lismore*, 191.
123 *GM* 52 (1852), 326.
124 *Credentials*, 498.
125 *Ireland*, 52.
126 For both cases see *GM* 53 (1853), 326.
127 Ibid., 329.

128. *GM* 48 (1848), 326.
129. *Credentials*, 499.
130. Bowen, *Protestant Crusade*, 271–2.
131. *GM* 53 (1853), 326.
132. Connolly, *Priests*, 129–130.
133. *GM* 53 (1853), 328. The entire address is also printed in *Ireland*, 53–7.
134. Ibid., 328–9.
135. Ibid., 328.
136. Ibid., 330; *Credentials*, 505.
137. *GM* 9 n.s. (1849), 603.
138. *Ireland*, 37.
139. *Ireland*, 37–8.
140. Ibid., 37.
141. Ibid.
142. *Credentials*, 337.
143. Waterford Diocesan Archives: Bishop Nicholas Foran papers, Box B4, 1837– 1845. Printed notice in Latin of reserved sins, 27 Jan. 1852. Reserved sins were those for which only a superior confessor, in this case the bishop, could grant absolution.
144. *Credentials*, 316–7. For another case of awkward questions causing people to be uncomfortable and leading to emigration: *Credentials*, 317.
145. Ibid., 337–8.
146. Ibid., 338.
147. For the foregoing, see *GM* 48 (1848), 231–2; see also *Ireland*, 18.
148. *Ireland*, 30.
149. Ibid., 25-26. For criticism of the association of payment of fees with the dispensing of the sacraments, see D. O. Croly, *An essay religious and political on ecclesiastical finance as regards the Roman Catholic Church in Ireland* (Cork, 1834).
150. Ibid., 38–9.
151. Ibid., 76.
152. *Credentials*, 311.

153 *Ireland*, 109; *Credentials*, 312.
154 *Ireland*, 110; *Credentials*, 311.
155 Cowman, *Making*, 67.
156 *Ireland*, 18–19.
157 Ibid., 19.
158 *Ireland*, 38.
159 Corish, *Irish Catholic Experience*, 213.
160 *Ireland*, 52.
161 Printed in e.g. *Ireland*, 69–71.
162 *Ireland*, 71.
163 *GM* 54 (1854), 44.
164 Ibid.
165 Ibid.
166 Ibid.
167 *GM* 55 (1855), 140; *Ireland*, 77.
168 *GM* 55 (1855), 140.
169 *GM* 54 (1854), 518, 519.
170 *Ireland*, 76.
171 Power, *Parochial History*, 141.
172 *GM* 55 (1855), 140–141. The new chapel was in the planning and proposal stage at least as early as 1854: NA ED2/46/14 sub 14 August; Cowman, *Making*, 79.
173 *GM* 55 (1855), 141.
174 Ibid.
175 *GM* 52 (1852), 542.
176 Connolly, *Priests*, 49–50.
177 Waterford Diocesan Archives, Bishop Dominick O'Brien papers, box B6, 1855–1860: Cardinal Fransoni to Dr. M. Slattery of Cashel, 28 Nov. 1855; Corish, *Irish Catholic Experience*, 211.
178 *GM* 52 (1852), 542.
179 Ibid.
180 Ibid., 543.
181 *GM* 54 (1854), 42.
182 Ibid., 43.

183 Ibid., 44.
184 Ibid.
185 *Try and Try Again*, 185. Italics in original.
186 Ibid., 187.
187 Earl of Roden, *Progress of the Reformation in Ireland* (London, 1852); Bowen, *Protestant Crusade*, 185, 204–5; I. Whelan, "The stigma of souperism," in C. Poirteir (ed.), *The Great Irish Famine* (Cork and Dublin, 1995), 135–154.
188 *GM* 54 (1854), 45.
189 *Waterford News* 29 Sept.1854; NLI Ms. 9495 No. 9 p.3.

Chapter 7
1 Cowman, *Making*, 31-37.
2 NA ED 2/183/65 sub 30 Nov. 1859.
3 *Retracings*, 174.
4 See C. Kinealy, "The Workhouse System in County Waterford, 1838–1923," in *Waterford: History and Society*, ed. W. Nolan & Thomas P. Power (Dublin, 1992), 589; G. Crotty, "Kilmacthomas Union: the administration of poor law in a County Waterford workhouse, 1851–1872," Decies 64 (2008), 107.
5 Crotty, "Kilmacthomas Union," 117, 139–140.
6 *WM* 31 Mar.1855. Unless otherwise indicated what follows is dependent on this source.
7 *GM* 55 (1855), 336; *Ireland*, 79.
8 *GM* 55 (1855), 436.
9 *WM* 31 Mar. 1855.
10 *GM* 55 (1855), 337.
11 Ibid.
12 Ibid.
13 Ibid.
14 Ibid.
15 Ibid., 337–8.
16 Ibid., 338.

17 Ibid. At the point of writing, the original minute books of the Board of Guardians for Kilmacthomas workhouse do not survive, at least in public custody. However, receipt of the correspondence from Doudney dated 11 June, 1855 is recorded in an index book to the letter books: Waterford County Archives, Dungarvan: BG/KILTHOM/6.
18 *GM* 55 (1855), 338. This is likely the case reported on by W.H. Collingridge when he visited the area in late May, 1855: *The Bonmahon Infant, Embroidery, Printing and Agricultural Schools Co. Waterford* (included in the back section of B. Keach, *Tropologia* (London, 1856), 2.
19 *GM* 55 (1855), 338.
20 Ibid.
21 Ibid.
22 *GM* 52 (1852), 437.
23 *GM* 55 (1855), 339.
24 Ibid., 339–41.
25 Ibid., 341.
26 *Ireland*, 17; *GM* 55 (1855), 437–9.
27 *Retracings*, 163–4.
28 *GM* 58 (1858), 287.
29 *Credentials*, 505–6.
30 *GM* 58 (1858), 287.
31 *Credentials*, 319.
32 *Ireland*, 107.
33 Ibid., 17.
34 *GM* 58 (1858), 236.
35 *Ireland*, 43.
36 *Try and Try Again*, 235.
37 For what follows, see *Memoir*, 164–5; *Credentials*, 314–6.
38 *GM* 55 (1855), 436.
39 Ibid.
40 Ibid.

41 Ibid., 436–7; *Retracings*, 177 (which gives the date as Sunday, 26 August).
42 *GM* 55 (1855), 437.
43 Ibid., 440; *Retracings*, 178.
44 *GM* 55 (1855), 440.
45 Ibid.
46 Ibid.
47 Ibid., 437; *Credentials*, 309–310.
48 *GM* 55 (1855), 440; Emily's Story, 26.
49 Emily's Story, 26.
50 *Ireland*, 70.
51 *GM* 55 (1855), 440.
52 Emily's Story, 26.
53 Ibid. For his prior Protestant status see *Decies* 8 (1978), 27.
54 *Credentials*, 310.
55 Emily's Story, 26.
56 Connolly, *Priests* 55; J.A. Murphy, "The support of the Catholic Clergy in Ireland, 1750–1850," *Historical Studies*, ed. J.L McCracken, 5 (1965), 103– 121.
57 Quoted in Kerr, *Peel, Priests, and Politics*, 31; see also *GM* 55 (1855), 510.
58 Connolly, *Priests*, 272–3.
59 See Ibid., 88–9; E. Larkin, "The devotional revolution in Ireland, 1850–1875" *American Historical Review* 77 (June 1972), 625–52 and D. W. Miller, "Mass attendance in Ireland in 1834" in *Piety and Power in Ireland, 1760–1960*, ed. S.J. Brown & D.W. Miller (2000), 158–180. While Miller's research has modified the previously inflated percentages advanced by Larkin, nevertheless the figures for the south-east exceed those for other areas.
60 *Decies* 8 (1978), 25.
61 Connolly, *Priests*, 90–91.
62 Ibid., 93, 96.
63 *Credentials*, 319.
64 *GM* 54 (1854), 519.

65 *PO*, 24; *Retracings*, 180.
66 *Retracings*, 181.
67 *GM* 56 (1856), 380.
68 Ibid., 486.
69 Ibid., 486–7.
70 Ibid., 487.
71 Ibid.
72 Ibid.
73 *GM* 57 (1857), 169.
74 Ibid., 488.
75 *GM* 56 (1856), 488.
76 Ibid.
77 Ibid.
78 Ibid.
79 Ibid., 603.
80 *Retracings*, 182.
81 NA ED 2/183/18.
82 For details see NA ED 2/46/14 sub 9 Dec.1853, ED 2/46/17, ED 2/183/65, ED 86/109/1; Cowman, *Making*, 53.
83 The appointment from 1 November 1855 of an Edward Kelly as a monitor in the Knockmahon male school was approved in December 1855: NA ED 2/183/18 sub 28 December.
84 *GM* 57 (1857), 334.
85 Ibid., 335; *Credentials*, 387: *Memoir*, 170; Emily's Story, 25.
86 Emily's Story, 25.
87 *GM* 57 (1857), 335; *Credentials*, 387-8; Emily's Story, 25.
88 *Ireland*, 88; *Credentials*, 388. Copy of the letter is included in Doudney to Lord Lieutenant, 25 May 1857 (NA CSO RP/1857/4759).
89 *Ireland*, 88; *Credentials*, 388.
90 *Ireland*, 88–9; *Credentials*, 388–9.
91 *Ireland*, 89; *Credentials*, 389; Doudney to Lord Lieutenant, 25 May 1857 (NA CSO RP/1857/4759).
92 *GM* 57 (1857), 336; *Retracings*, 185; *Ireland*, 89; *Credentials*, 389.

93 *GM* 57 (1857), 336; Doudney to Lord Lieutenant, 25 May 1857 (NA CSO RP/1857/4759).
94 *Retracings*, 185; *Credentials*, 390.
95 *Ireland*, 89–90; *Credentials*, 390.
96 Emily's Story, 25.
97 *Ireland*, 90; Cowman, *Making*, 93.
98 Emily's Story, 25.
99 See *WM* 5 Jan. 1849, 9 Mar., 10 Apr., 27 Apr. 1857.
100 Cowman, *Making*, 57–60.
101 Emily's Story, 25.
102 Ibid.
103 *GM* 57 (1857), 336; *Memoir*, 171; *Credentials*, 390.
104 *Ireland*, 90; *Credentials*, 390.
105 Emily's Story, 25.
106 Doudney to Lord Lieutenant, 25 May 1857 (NA CSO RP/1857/4759).
107 NA CSO RP1857/5065. This paragraph is based on this source.
108 NA CSO RP1857/4782.
109 NA CSO RP1857/5065. This paragraph is based on this source.
110 *GM* 57 (1857), 337; 58 (1858), 285; *Ireland*, 90; *Credentials*, 390. Kelly was accorded space in the columns of the *Waterford Mail* to announce his acquittal: *WM* 11 June 1857.
111 *GM* 58 (1858), 286; *Memoir*, 170–71.
112 Emily's Story, 25.
113 *Ireland*, 90.
114 Emily's Story, 25.
115 *GM* 58 (1858), 285.
116 *Retracings*, 186.
117 Ibid. This would have been before June 15 the date of the diary entry.
118 *Ireland*, 92; *Credentials*, 393. Given the context of the letter, the lessons for the day, i.e. Psalm 71, Joshua 10, and Mark 14, turned out to be singularly apposite: *Credentials*, 394.

119 *GM* 57 (1857), 403; *Credentials*, 412. The letter contained a drawing of a coffin.
120 *Ireland*, 95; *Credentials*, 412.
121 *Retracings*, 188.
122 On this aspect see Stephen R. Gibbons, *Captain Rock, Night Errant: the threatening letters of Pre-Famine Ireland, 1801-1845* (Dublin, 2004).
123 *Credentials*, 466–8.
124 *Memoir*, 173.
125 *Credentials*, 455.
126 *Retracings*, 191.
127 Ibid.
128 Ibid., 193.
129 Ibid., 187, 189.
130 *GM* 58 (1858), 106. Italics in original.
131 *Memoir*, 147.
132 *Retracings*, 174.
133 Ibid., 184.
134 Emily's Story, 16.
135 *GM* 55 (1855), 178.
136 Ibid., 336.
137 *Credentials*, 335.
138 *Memoir*, 122–3.
139 *Credentials*, 165.
140 *GM* 55 (1855), 141.
141 Ibid.; *Ireland*, 76–7.
142 *GM* 55 (1855), 144.
143 *GM* 54 (1854), 379; *Ireland*, 68.
144 I. Whelan, "The Stigma of Souperism," in C. Póirtéir (ed.), *The Great Irish Famine* (Dublin, 1995), 135–154.

Chapter 8

1 *Retracings*, 191.
2 *Try and Try Again*, 196.

3 *Credentials*, 494.
4 *Try and Try Again*, 183.
5 The entire is conveniently printed in *Ireland*, 98–109. The delay in explaining his sudden departure may have been occasioned by the non-arrival of documents which he needed to quote from. These had not yet arrived by the time of his contribution of 22 May: Ibid., 105.
6 *Ireland*, 106.
7 Ibid., 107.
8 Ibid.
9 Ibid., 105.
10 Ibid. In 1853 he had seven children living: *Retracings*, 167. Some of them were the victims of scarlet fever in 1855, for instance: *Retracings*, 178.
11 *Ireland*, 102.
12 *Retracings*, 164.
13 *GM* 55 (1855), 140.
14 *Retracings*, 177, 191.
15 *Credentials*, 339–340.
16 Ibid., 334. The person concerned (unnamed but likely Clifford) was clearly irresponsible, instanced in the case of his reaction when a ship went aground: Ibid., 335.
17 *Retracings*, 187–8, 191; *WM* 13 May 1858. He had been taught by the village teacher in Bunmahon and was subsequently tutored for entry to Trinity College Dublin: Emily's Story, 13. He was later appointed to a curacy near Carlisle: *Retracings*, 207. For daughter Emily's experience see Emily's Story, 5–6, 11– 13, 18–24.
18 *GM* 58 (1858), 232.
19 Ibid., 240. The letter is dated 9 April [1858]; see also *GM* 58 (1858), 441; *Ireland*, 104.
20 *PO*, 239.
21 *GM* 58 (1858), 237.

22. *The Bonmahon Infant, Embroidery, Printing and Agricultural Schools Co. Waterford* (included in the back section of B. Keach, *Tropologia* (London, 1856), 3.
23. *GM* 56 (1856), 620.
24. "Decay of Proselytism in Bunmahon" in *Catholic Telegraph* 9 Aug.1856; NLI Ms 9497 No.22 p.19; *Irish Book Lover* 32: 4 (1955), 81; *Credentials*, 509–514.
25. *GM* 56 (1856), 54, 486–8.
26. *GM* 57 (1857), 519.
27. *Try and Try Again*, 224, 226.
28. *GM* 56 (1856), 54; *Credentials*, 319.
29. *GM* 55 (1855), 436; *Retracings*, 178. During the Crimean war all naval personnel including the local coast guard had to be prepared to be called for service, and a local man, Attridge, lost his life in action: Emily's Story, 17.
30. *Try and Try Again*, 182.
31. *Retracings*, 180; *Ireland*, 95.
32. *Memoir*, 174; *Credentials*, 455.
33. *GM* 58 (1858), 23; *Ireland*, 99; *Try and Try Again*, 197.
34. *GM* 55 (1855), 436.
35. *Ireland*, 99.
36. *Try and Try Again*, 197.
37. *GM* 55 (1855), 142. It had been his practice to be absent in England preaching charity sermons and raising funds, and for other reasons, during the course of his ministry in Monksland: *Retracings*, 132, 139–140, 166, 171, 178–9.
38. *GM* 55 (1855), 538; in December he received £50 as a loan: *Retracings*, 178.
39. *WM* 14 Feb. 1856.
40. *GM* 57 (1857), 112.
41. *Credentials*, 494.
42. *Try and Try Again*, 203.
43. *GM* 55 (1855), 46.
44. Ibid.

45 *GM* 55 (1855), 341; *The Bonmahon Infant, Embroidery, Printing and Agricultural Schools Co. Waterford* (included in the back section of B. Keach, *Tropologia* (London, 1856), 3.
46 *GM* 58 (1858), 232.
47 *Try and Try Again*, 196.
48 *GM* 58 (1858), 232.
49 *Retracings*, 169. Doudney did not expect the bishop to be favourable: Ibid., 169.
50 Ibid., 172.
51 Ibid., 170, 173–4.
52 *Credentials*, 324; for the identification of clergy in the following section I am dependent on Cotton, Leslie, and Rennison, *Clergy of Waterford*.
53 *Credentials*, 324.
54 Ibid.
55 Ibid., 325.
56 For the foregoing paragraph, *Credentials*, 325.
57 Ibid, 326.
58 Ibid., 326–7.
59 Ibid., 327.
60 Ibid., 328. Smith lasted less than a year in Stradbally for in November 1856 he was made precentor of Waterford and chaplain to Daly (*WM* 15 Nov. 1856), and it continued to suffer from short-term appointments, e.g. Smith's replacement, Rev. R. Tottenham, resigned in June 1857: *WM* 4 July 1857.
61 Ibid., 328.
62 Emily's Story, 26.
63 *Try and Try Again*, 235.
64 *GM* 58 (1858), 287.
65 Ibid., 232–3, 287.
66 P. Lee (or Leo) was Doudney's successor in Monksland: Cotton, Leslie, and Rennison, *Clergy of Waterford*, 128, 168, 308; *Thom's Directory* 1859 p.687. At an ordination service in the Cathedral in December, 1857 a Patrick Lee was made a deacon (*WM* 22

Dec. 1857), while in May 1858 Rev. P. Leo was appointed to the curacy of Monksland and Bonmahon (*WM* 27 May 1858).

67 *Ireland*, 112.
68 *WM* 8 June 1858. This refusal was also prominent in his daughter's account of his reasons for leaving: Emily's Story, 26.
69 *WM* 5 June 1858; NLI Ms 9497 No.22 p.18; *Credentials*, 340, 455.
70 *WM* 8 June 1858.
71 *Try and Try Again*, 193–4.
72 *GM* 58 (1858), 287.
73 Ibid.
74 As cited in *The Irish Booklover* 32 no. 4 (1955), 82.
75 *Credentials*, 459.
76 Ibid., 482. For instance Rev. William Henry Krause, minister of Bethesda Episcopal Chapel, Dublin.
77 Broderick, *Waterford's Anglicans*, 225–7; *Credentials*, 482.
78 Ibid., 483. They were Prof. Foley (Rev. Daniel Foley, Professor of Irish at Trinity College Dublin), and Rev. John Morgan, later Dean of Waterford: Ibid.
79 *Try and Try Again*, 221.
80 *Memoir*, 175. The congregation later sent Bishop Daly an address lamenting Doudney's departure, which Doudney later received a copy of and to which he suitably replied: Ibid., 176.
81 *WM* 13 May1858: NLI Ms 9497 no. 22 p.18.
82 *WM* 5 June 1858; *Irish Book Lover* 32: 4 (1955), 81–2.
83 *WM* 5 June 1858.
84 *Memoir*, 161; Emily's Story, 18.
85 Indenture between David A Doudney and Robert Heron, 5 Apr. 1861 (RCPI 4/3/2). The amount was £51.
86 *GM* 58 (1858), 240, 534.
87 He was still contributing to the *Gospel Magazine* as late as February, 1858 but by July he was writing from Plymouth, by September from Southampton, and by October from Bristol: *GM* 58 (1858), 64, 12, 177, 393, 494, and 541.

88 *GM* 58 (1858), 234.
89 *Emily's Story*, 4.
90 *Ireland*, 112.
91 *WM* 24 Aug. 1866; NLI Ms 9497 no. 22 p.17.
92 *Memoir*, 138.
93 *WM* 5 July 1861.
94 Ibid., 15 Aug.1864; *Credentials*, 195; *Retracings*, 249–251. He commented on "The removal of those who in my late parish so opposed [me], was most marvelous and humbling." (Ibid., 250).
95 *Retracings*, 284, 382–3.
96 NLI Ms9497 no. 22 p.17.
97 *Memoir*, 226; *Retracings*, 296.
98 *Memoir*, 193–6, 197–8; *Emily's Story*, 3.
99 Ibid, 198–9.
100 Ibid., 243–4. She was buried in Southsea and he was buried beside her in 1893.
101 Ibid., 231. His youngest son Arthur died in Samoa in the South Pacific in 1891: Ibid., 266–71.
102 Ibid., 225–6.
103 Ibid., 246. For his son, Charles's, recovery from rheumatic fever, see Ibid., 251.
104 Ibid., 245, 247. They had two children but both died young (Ibid., 247). In 1864 Edwin was determined, to Doudney's dismay, to join the Confederate army as a surgeon in the civil war between North and South in America (*Retracings*, 252); and in 1867 he went to Australia (Ibid., 298). Another son, Arthur, chose the seafaring life going to India initially (Ibid., 300).
105 Ibid., 252–4.
106 A. F. Pollard, 'Doudney, David Alfred (1811–1893)', rev. I. T. Foster, *Oxford Dictionary of National Biography*, Oxford University Press, 2004. Doudney maintained his interest in writing pastoral and religious works right up to the time of his death. For his works post-1860, see under "D. A. Doudney" in J.F. Kirk *A supplement to Allibone's critical dictionary of English*

literature, vol. 1 (1895). There were only six subscribers with Irish addresses listed in the *Memoir* (283–290), none of them from Waterford.
107 *Credentials*, 515. This was a departure in other respects as typical sermons in chapels were based on the catechism: Corish, *Irish Catholic Experience*, 210.
108 Cowman, *Making*, 96; Broderick, *Waterford's Anglicans*, 274.
109 Ibid., 96; Broderick, *Waterford's Anglicans*, 264 n.343.
110 Broderick, *Waterford's Anglicans*, 265.
111 Ibid., 265–6; Cowman, *Making*, 96.
112 *Parochial History of Waterford and Lismore During the 18th and 19th centuries* (Waterford, 1912), 141.
113 Corish, *Irish Catholic Experience*, 210–11.

Chapter 9
1 On this aspect, see Thomas P. Power, "Of No Small Importance:' Curricular Change in the School of Divinity, Trinity College Dublin, 1790-1850" in Thomas P. Power (ed.), *Change and Transformation: Essays in Anglican History* (Eugene, OR, 2013), 140–183.
2 *Emily's Story*, 4.
3 *Credentials*, 318.
4 Quoted in John Crawford, *The Church of Ireland in Victorian Dublin* (Dublin, 2005), 87.
5 *Memoir*, 272.
6 Ibid.
7 *Ireland*, 73.

BIBLIOGRAPHY

Manuscripts

Dublin
Royal College of Physicians of Ireland
Estate papers relating to Co. Waterford

National Archives of Ireland
Board of National Education (ED series)
Famine relief papers (RFLC series)
Osborne Deeds (D 6086, D 6088, D 5998 and D 6091
    D 6186, 6214)
Chief Secretary Papers: NA CSO RP1857/4759, 4782, 5065.

National Library of Ireland
Ms 657 Minutes and proceedings of the Hibernian Mining Company
Ms 9497 No.22 O'Casaide

Private Collection
Emily's Story (copy in the possession of Julian C. Walton, Seafield,
    Bunmahon, Co. Waterford).

Representative Church Body Library
Church Education Society, Committee Proceedings
Ms 182 Sunday School Society for Ireland

Ms. 138/6/4 Architectural drawing of Bunmahon church by James Pain, 1830
Ms 718 Waterford Auxiliary Bible Society account book, 1846–1866

Trinity College Dublin
Mss 2770–4 (incorporating Mss 2490–91) Ecclesiastical commissioners for Ireland

Waterford County Archives, Dungarvan, Co. Waterford
BG/KILTHOM/6 Board of Guardians Records (Kilmacthomas): Index to the letter books

Waterford Diocesan Archives, Waterford
Papers of Bishop Nicholas Foran
Papers of Bishop Dominick O'Brien

Parliamentary Papers
Hansard: http://hansard.millbanksystems.com
HC *Papers relating to the state of the established church* 1820 (93), ix.
HC *An account of the salaries and emoluments of the different curate in each and every benefice in Ireland* 1833 (721), xxvii,
HC *A return of the number of churches in each benefice or union in Ireland* 1833 (400), xxvii.
HC *Reports from commissioners on the employment of children (Mines)*, xvi (1842).
HC *A return of the number of churches and chapels built in each diocese of Ireland since the 1st day of January, 1823* 1844 (190), xliii.
HC *Appendix to 16th Report of the Commissioners of National Education (Irl.)*, xxv (1850).
HC *Report from the Select Committee on Postal Arrangements (Waterford etc.)*, 11,1854–5, (445).

Contemporary Works

Annual reports of Church Education Society for Ireland (from 1840 onwards).

Bagenal, Philip Henry. *The Life of Ralph Bernal Osborne* (London, 1884).

Bell, Robert. *Some thoughts on the past history and present position of the question at issue between the adherents of the government system and the supporters of scriptural education* (Dublin, 1850).

The Bonmahon Infant, Embroidery, Printing and Agricultural Schools Co. Waterford (included in the back section of B. Keach, *Tropologia* (London, 1856).

Croly, D. O. *An essay religious and political on ecclesiastical finance as regards the Roman Catholic Church in Ireland* (Cork, 1834).

[Daly, Robert]. *A Charge delivered by the Rt. Rev. the Lord Bishop of Cashel at the visitation of the Dioceses of Waterford and Lismore, Cashel and Emly* (Waterford, 1849).

[Daly, Robert]. *A Charge delivered by the Rt. Rev. the Lord Bishop of Cashel at the visitation held in the dioceses of Waterford and Lismore, Cashel and Emly* (Waterford, 1851).

[Daly, Robert] *Substance of a speech delivered by the Bishop of Cashel etc in the House of Lords, 17th June 1843 on presenting petitions on the subject of National Education* (Waterford, [1845]).

[Daly, Robert]. *A charge delivered by the Right Rev. the Lord Bishop of Cashel, etc at the visitation of the dioceses of Waterford and Lismore, Cashel and Emly July 1846* (Dublin, 1846).

[Daly, Robert] *A charge by Robert, Lord Bishop of Cashel and Emly, Waterford and Lismore delivered on the 25th and 30th of July and 1st of August, 1861* (Dublin 1861).

Doudney, D.A. *Ireland: its priests and its people* (London, 1892).

Doudney, D. A. *The Credentials, Call & Claims of the Christian Ministry with details of the author's labours in Ireland during a period of eleven to twelve years* (London, n.d. [c.1883]).

Doudney, D.A. *Retracings and Renewings or Gleanings from a journal extending over nearly half a century* (London, 1878).

Doudney, D.A. *Try and Try Again* (London, 1864).

[Doudney, D.A.] *A Run Through Connemara: by the editor of the "Gospel Magazine"* (Dublin, 1856).

[Doudney, D.A.], *Recollections and remains of the late Rev. George David Doudney* (London, 1866).

Doudney, D. A. & H.O. Adams. *Memoir of the Rev. D. A Doudney, D.D.* (London, 1893).

Eight report of the Church Education Society for Ireland being for the years 1846 and 1847 (Dublin, 1847).

Foley, D. *A missionary tour through the South and West of Ireland, undertaken for the [Irish] Society [for Promoting Scriptural Education]* (Dublin, 1849).

Foley, D. *An English-Irish dictionary: intended for the use of students of the Irish language* (Dublin, 1855).

Foran, N. *Report of the total temperance society founded at Mount Sion in the City of Waterford on the 10th day of November 1839 by the Rt. Rev. Dr. Nicholas Foran* (Cork, 1840).

Forty-first report of the Hibernian district of the Church Missionary Society for the year 1854... (Dublin, 1855).

Forty-second report of the Hibernian district of the Church Missionary Society for the year 1855... (Dublin, 1856).

Forty-sixth report of the Hibernian district of the Church Missionary Society for the year 1859... (Dublin, 1860).

Gill, J. *An Exposition of the Old Testament...* (London, 1854).

Godkin, J. *Ireland and Her Churches* (London, 1867).

The Gospel Magazine and Protestant Beacon (1846–1860)

Home proceedings of the Hibernian district of the Church Missionary Society, thirty-first year ending 31st December, 1844 (Dublin, 1845).

Irish Catholic Directory (Dublin, 1850, 1860).

Kane, R. *The industrial resources* of Ireland (Dublin, 1844).

Key to the Catholic Ecclesiastical map of Ireland (Dublin, 1859).

Lewis, S. *Topographical Dictionary of Ireland*, 2 vols (London, 1837).

Madden, Mrs. H. *Memoirs of the late Right Rev. Robert Daly DD, Lord Bishop of Cashel* (London, 1875).

Marrable, W. *Sketch of the origin and operations of the Society of Irish Church Missions to the Roman Catholics* (London, 1852).

Official Catalogue of the National Exhibition of the Arts, Manufactures and Products of Ireland, held in Cork 1852 (Cork, 1852).

Osborne, Mrs [C.I.]. *Memorials of the life and character of Lady Osborne and some of her friends*, 2 vols. (Dublin, 1870).

Personal recollections of the Right Rev. Robert Daly, DD, late bishop of Cashel at Powerscourt and Waterford by an old parishioner (Dublin, 1872).

Retrospections of Dorothea Herbert, 2 vols. (London, 1929–30).

Roden, Earl of. *Progress of the Reformation in Ireland* (London, 1852).

Stopford, A. *The increase and requirements of the Irish Church …* (Dublin, 1853).

The thirtieth annual report of the London Hibernian Society for establishing schools and circulating the Holy Scriptures in Ireland (London, 1836).

The thirty-first annual report of the London Hibernian Society for establishing schools and circulating the Holy Scriptures in Ireland (London, 1837).

Thirty-ninth report of the Hibernian district of the Church Missionary Society for the year 1852… (Dublin, 1853).

The thirty-second annual report of the London Hibernian Society for establishing schools and circulating the Holy Scriptures in Ireland (London, 1838).

Thompson, D.P. *A brief account of the rise and progress of the change in religious opinion now taking place in Dingle and the west of the county of Kerry, Ireland* (London, 1847).

Thom's Directory 1859.

Transactions of the central relief committee of the Society of Friends during the famine in Ireland in 1846 and 1847 (Dublin, 1852).

Waterford Mail, The

Modern

Akenson, D. H. *A Protestant in Purgatory: Richard Whately, Archbishop of Dublin* (Hamden, Conn., 1981).

Baycroft, John. *The Eucharistic Way* (Toronto, 1981).

The Book of Common Prayer (Toronto, 1959).

Broderick, E. *Waterford's Anglicans: Religion and Politics, 1819–1872* (Newcastle-Upon-Tyne, 2009).

Burtchaell, J. "19th Century Society in County Waterford" *Decies* 31 (1986), 35–42.

Connolly, S. J. *Priests and People in Pre-Famine Ireland* (Dublin, 1982).

Corish, P. *The Irish Catholic Experience: a historical survey* (Dublin, 1985).

Cowman, D. "Survival, Statistics and Structures: Knockmahon Copper Mines, 1850-78" *Decies* 46 (1992), 10–20.

[Cowman, D.], "Life and Work in an Irish Mining Camp c.1840: Knockmahon Copper Mines, Co. Waterford" *Decies* 14 (May, 1980), 28–42.

Cowman, D. & D. Brady (ed.). *The Famine in Waterford* (Dublin, 1995).

Crawford, J. *The Church of Ireland in Victorian Dublin* (Dublin, 2005).

Crotty, G. "Kilmacthomas Union: the administration of poor law in a County Waterford workhouse, 1851–1872" *Decies* 64 (2008), 105–148.

Davies, A.C. "The first Irish industrial exhibition: Cork, 1852" *Irish Economic and Social History* 2 (1975), 46–59.

Flynn, G. "The Young Ireland Movement in Waterford, 1848: Part 1," *Decies*, 18 (1981), 41–49; Part 2, 19 (1982), 53–60.

The Irish Booklover 1 (1910), 32: 4 (1955).

Gibbons, Stephen R. *Captain Rock, Night Errant: the threatening letters of Pre-Famine Ireland, 1801-1845* (Dublin, 2004).

Kelly, J. *Sir Richard Musgrave, 1746–1818: ultra-protestant ideologue* (Dublin, 2009).

Kennelly, B. (ed.), *Ireland: Past and Present* (Dublin, 1986).

Kerr, D. *Peel, Priests, and Politics: Sir Robert Peel's Administration and the Roman Catholic Church in Ireland, 1841–1846* (Oxford, 1982).

Kinealy, C. "The Workhouse System in County Waterford, 1838–1923," in *Waterford: History and Society*, ed. W. Nolan & T. P. Power (Dublin, 1992).

Larkin, E. "The devotional revolution in Ireland, 1850–1875" *American Historical Review* 77 (June 1972), 625–52.

McDowell, R. B. *The Church of Ireland, 1869–1969* (London, 1975).

McDowell, R. B. & D.A. Webb, *Trinity College Dublin, 1592–1952: An academic history* (Cambridge, 1982).

Mhic Mhurchu, D. "Phillip Barron: Man of Mystery," *Decies* 2 (May, 1976), 10–15.

Miller, D. W. "Mass attendance in Ireland in 1834" in *Piety and Power in Ireland, 1760–1960*, ed. S.J. Brown & D.W. Miller (2000), 158–180.

Moffitt, M. "The Society for Irish Church Missions to the Roman Catholics: Philanthropy or Bribery?" *International Bulletin of Missionary Research*, 30: 1 (Jan. 2006), 32–38.

Murphy, J.A. "The support of the Catholic Clergy in Ireland, 1750–1850" *Historical Studies* ed. J.L McCracken, 5 (1965), 103–121.

Nolan, W. & T. P. Power (ed.) *Waterford: History and Society* (Dublin, 1992).

North, J. E. "David Alfred Doudney: An Unsung Hero of the Christian Church." *The Journal of the Church of England (Continuing)* no. 19 (Apr. 2001), 15–21, no. 20 (Aug. 2001), 7–15.

O'Connell, M.R. (ed.). *The Correspondence of Daniel O'Connell*. 7 vols. (Dublin, 1973–).

O'Connor, Emmet. *A Labour History of Waterford* (Waterford, 1989).

O'Corrain, D. & T. O'Riordain (ed.), *Ireland 1815–1870: Emancipation, Famine, and Religion* (Dublin, 2011).

Power, P. *Parochial History of Waterford and Lismore During the 18th and 19th centuries* (Waterford, 1912).

Power, T. "Notes on a Forgotten Co. Waterford Religious House," *Decies* 9 (1978), 28–33.

Power, T. "Rev. David Alfred Doudney and Educational Establishments at Bunmahon, Co. Waterford, 1847-58." *Decies* 10 (Jan. 1979), 6–19; 11 (May, 1979), 26–34.

Power, T. "Schools in Connection with the Kildare Place Society in County Waterford, 1817–1840" *Decies* 17 (May, 1981), 5–16.

Power, Thomas P. *Land, Politics, and Society in Eighteenth-Century Tipperary* (Oxford, 1993).

Power, Thomas P. "'Of No Small Importance:' Curricular Change in the School of Divinity, Trinity College Dublin, 1790-1850" in Thomas P. Power (ed.). *Change and Transformation: Essays in Anglican History* (Eugene, OR, 2013).

"The Village of Kill," Decies (1978), 19–43.

Whelan, I. "The Stigma of Souperism," in C. Póirtéir (ed.), *The Great Irish Famine* (Dublin, 1995), 135–154.

Widdess, J.D.H. *A History of the Royal College of Physicians of Ireland, 1654–1963* (Edinburgh, 1963).

Reference

Bell, P. *Victorian Biography: a checklist of contemporary biographies of British men and women dying between 1851 and 1901* (Edinburgh, 1993).

Burtchaell, G. D. & T U. Sadleir, *Alumni Dublinenses* (London, 1924).

Cotton, H., J.B. Leslie, & W.H. Rennison (revised and updated by I. Knox), *Clergy of Waterford, Lismore, and Ferns: Biographical Succession Lists* (Dublin, 2008).

Kirk, J. *A supplement to Allibone's Critical Dictionary of English literature and British and American Authors* (London & Philadelphia, 1908).

Oxford Dictionary of National Biography ed. H. C. G. Matthew and Brian Harrison (Oxford, 2004).
Nineteenth Century Short Title Catalogues ser.ii, phase 1, 1816–1870, vol. 12 (Newcastle-upon-Tyne, 1988).
North, John. *The Waterloo Directory of Irish Newspapers and Periodicals, 1800–1900* (Waterloo, 1986).
Idem., *The Waterloo Directory of English Newspapers and Periodicals, 1800–1900*. 20 vols. (Waterloo, 2003).

INDEX

All place names are in Co. Waterford unless indicated otherwise. Information in the Endnotes has not been indexed.

Adams, Henry 46
agricultural school 99, 106-110, 113, 204-5, 228, 249
Alcock, Rev. James 72
America 64, 96, 97, 113, 114, 124, 141, 163, 174, 175, 204, 212, 228, 239
A Pictorial Outline of the Rise and Progress 91, 92
Ardmore 149
arminianism 215
Arminius, Jacob 215
Astley, England 104
Atkinson, Robert K. 46, 48
Attridge, James 46
Australia 64, 174, 239
Auxiliary Bible Society 114, 149

Ballinarrid 26
Ballinasissla 28
Ballingarry, Co. Tipperary 219
Ballylaneen 38, 39, 42, 50, 78, 160, 162, 168, 173, 176, 179, 183, 187, 195, 201, 202, 209

Ballyristeen 39
Bandon, Co. Cork 148
Baptists 2, 23, 75
Barkla, William 46
Barron, Sir Henry Winston 154
Barron, James 41
Barron, Phillip 54
Bateman, Edward 46
Bateman, John 46
Bath, England 104
Bedfordshire, England 104
Bell, Kate 242
Bennett, James 46
Beresford family 135, 140, 184, 209
Beresford, Lord George 140
Bernal-Osborne, Ralph 44-47, 49, 60, 152
Bible, The
 -Douay-Rheims Version 113, 119, 122, 158, 171, 172, 190
 -King James Version 90, 121, 122
bible repository 113-4

315

Birmingham, England 104, 113
Blewit, Benjamin 46
Brackin, J.H. 210, 211
Bristol, England 236, 240, 241, 253
Brixton, England 112
Brown, John 87
Bunmahon/Knockmahon
   -emigration 28, 61, 64-5, 114, 186, 200, 225, 241, 248
   -famine 48, 57-63, 68, 133, 136, 142-3, 151, 153, 163, 186, 200-202, 219, 246-8
   -housing 12, 27, 30, 32, 34, 39, 247-8
   -literacy 51-3
   -living conditions 32-5
   -population 35-6, 39-40, 52, 54, 62-4, 67, 70, 79, 153-4, 169, 184, 200-201, 247-8, 250
   -rental 26-7, 30-35, 62
   -schools 40-51
Bunmahon Bible Fund 114
Burgess, J.J. 77, 97
burials 20, 172-3, 176-7
Burke, Rev. J. 94
Butler, family of, earls of Ormond 27
Butlerstown 37, 211
Cahill, Catherine 183
Cahill, Rev. Daniel William 181
Cambridge, University of 55, 56
Canada 195, 227, 239
Cappamore, Co. Limerick 146
Cappoquin 211
Carden, family of 12

Carlisle, Earl of 86, 234
Carlisle, England 241
Carrick-on-Suir, Co. Tipperary 93, 196
Catholic emancipation act (1829) 40, 138
Chant, John Barret 97
Church Education Society 42, 43, 45, 99
Church Missionary Society 149
Church of Ireland 38-45, 55, 67, 70, 75, 84, 116, 123, 138-43, 147, 150-51, 182, 194, 215, 223, 243-4, 246, 248-9, 253
Christian Brothers 135, 140
Clashmore 43, 49, 104
Clifford, Herbert I. 147
Clonmel, Co. Tipperary 40, 43, 86, 155, 222, 231, 234, 235
Clunes, James 46
College of Physicians of Ireland 58, 61-63, 77, 91, 93, 98, 101, 239
Collingridge, William Hill, 6, 64, 76, 78, 82, 87, 91, 93, 98, 100, 208, 228, 238, 239
Comeragh 150
Condon, Anne 186-8, 191
Condon, Bridget 187-9, 191
Condon, Catherine 187, 191
Connemara, Co. Galway 141, 146, 147, 182, 183
Connolly, Timothy 77
conversion 2, 3, 141, 145-8, 152, 181, 183, 192-5, 206-7, 209, 219, 245, 248, 250
Coombes, James 46
Coombes, John 46

Cork City 85, 114
Cork, Co.29, 30, 54, 68.
Cornwall, England 28, 29, 30, 39, 64, 67, 137, 152, 156
Coughlan, Catherine 188-90
Courtenay, Miss 56
Cowell, George 113, 114
Crimean War 227
Cuba 57
Cuddy, Maurice 52
Cuppaige, J.E. 99
Curnew, Richard 46
Curry, William 46
curses 161, 168, 197, 249

Dallas, Rev. Alexander 183, 223
Dalton, Rev. Edward 94
Daly, Robert, Bishop of Cashel 46, 49, 55-6, 60, 70, 73, 78, 94-5, 120, 138, 141, 146-52, 164, 176, 184, 223, 225, 231-6, 237, 243-6, 248, 252
Devonshire, Duke of 232-3
Dickson, Fr. 244
Dingle, Co. Kerry 141, 147, 148, 182
Doddridge, Phillip 2
Donegal Co.56, 214
Donoughmore, Lord 55
Doon, Co. Limerick 141, 145, 146, 219
Doudney, Alice 241
Doudney, Arthur Searle 11, 241
Dudney, Augustus Montague 241
Doudney, Bourne Hall 10
Doudney, David Alfred jun. 11, 77

Doudney, David Alfred sen.
-conversion 2-3
-family bereavements 10-11, 17, 241-2
-marriage 10, 11, 241-2
-ordination 7, 16, 23, 237
-printing trade 7-9
-threatening letters 185, 206, 210-15, 219, 220, 222, 223, 238, 244, 253
Doudney, Edwin 241, 242
Doudney, Eliza (nee Durkin) 1, 73, 111, 178
Doudney, Emily 23, 67, 86, 102, 111, 197, 198, 207, 208, 209, 211, 234, 241, 249
Doudney, Rev. George D. 53, 57,
Doudney, George William 11
Doudney, Helen 241
Doudney, John 2
Doudney, Mary Jane 10
Doudney, Sarah 10
Doudney, Sarah sen. 2
Dover, England 104
Draper, Jane 10
Draper, Rev. Bourne Hall 10
Dublin City 58, 63, 122, 134, 139, 155, 210, 217, 232
Dun, Sir Patrick 57
Dunfoy, M.G. 97
Dunfoy, William 46
Dungarvan 37, 61, 93, 95, 149, 154, 186, 189, 210, 230, 232, 233
Dunhill 55, 56, 202
Dunlewey, Co. Donegal 56
Dunmore 149
Durden, Rev. Thomas Garde 42
Durkin, William 11

Eddy, Peter 46
Edmondson, Rev. George 38
Ellis, Edward 146
embroidery school 14, 106. 110-113, 178, 186-91, 193, 196, 204-5, 217, 222, 225, 249, 250
England 1, 15, 16, 23, 25, 31, 73, 76, 78, 94, 95, 96, 100, 104, 111, 141, 145, 147, 149, 155, 157, 163, 179, 205, 209, 212, 214, 216, 218, 223, 226, 228, 230, 235-8, 240, 244, 249
English, Richard 41
Esmonde, John 162
excommunication 118, 165, 166-71, 173, 178-9, 184, 185, 214, 249, 251

Fawcett, Rev. Benjamin C. 232
Farran, Charles 61, 62
Fitzgerald, Mary 183
Foley, Rev. Daniel 55, 56
Foran, Nicholas, Bishop of Waterford and Lismore 35, 37, 38, 164, 165, 169, 173, 176, 179, 196
Forsythe, G. 210
Fry, Mary 183

Galway Co.142, 219
Gardenmorris 26
Giles, O. 95
Gill, Francis 46
Gill, James 46
Gill, John 73-5, 78, 80-81, 85-7, 94-8, 153, 218, 223, 227, 228, 249
Goodwin, Thomas 97, 226
Gospel Magazine, The 4-7, 16, 55, 74, 76, 87, 89, 90, 93-5, 97-8, 100-104, 110, 145, 147, 162-3, 197, 215, 218, 221, 223, 225, 226, 228-9, 235, 240, 242, 252
Greek 16, 85, 123
Guilcagh 55

Hawke, Helen 52
Hawker, Robert 74, 87
Hebrew 73, 85
Hely-Hutchinson, Richard 162
Herbert, Dorothea 25
Hewlett, Rev. Arthur 5
Hibernian Bible Society 149
Howe, James 41

Inch, Benjamin 46
Inch, William 46
Independents 75
infant school 99, 100-106, 110-111, 113, 118-9, 166-67, 169-70, 178-9, 188, 190-91, 195-6, 200, 203-5, 223, 225, 249-50
Inislounaght (or Abbey), Co. Tipperary 24, 231, 235
Irish language 53-7, 113, 122, 148
Irish Society for Promoting the Education of the Native Irish through the Medium of their own Language (Irish Society), The 55, 56, 145, 148, 194, 236, 243

James, William 46, 47, 155
Jesuits 74, 244
Jocelyn, Robert, earl of Roden 5, 150, 240
Jowett & Mills, London 8
justification by faith 124-6, 132

Keach, Benjamin 87, 88, 205, 228, 229
Kelly, Bridget 206
Kelly, Edward 195, 206-09, 219
Kelly, Mary 48, 208, 210, 223
Kelly, Michael 48, 196, 204, 207, 208, 210-11, 253
Kerry Co. 55, 141, 146, 147, 183
Kilbarrymeaden 25
Kilcash, Co. Tipperary 86
Kilduane 28
Kill 25, 26, 36, 38, 39, 41, 58, 63, 156, 176, 179, 201, 202, 209
Killeen, Lawrence 97
Killeen, Mary 97
Kilmacthomas 25, 48, 58, 60, 93, 94, 95, 150, 153, 186, 188, 230, 243, 251
Kilrossanty 95
Kilvemnon, Co. Tipperary 219
Kinsalebeg 95, 218
Kinsman, Richard 46
Knocklofty, Co. Tipperary 55

Lancashire, England 104
Lane, John Doudney 4, 7, 17
Lane, Kitty 183
Lathbean, John 46
Lee (or Leo), Rev. Patrick J. 149, 235, 239, 243

Lismore 37, 149, 186, 232,
Liverpool, England 96, 114, 195
London, England 3, 4, 8, 9, 13, 23, 65, 66, 73, 75, 76, 77, 78, 80, 81, 82, 84, 87, 88, 91, 93, 100, 104, 110, 112, 115, 148, 150, 152, 159, 163, 185, 207, 208, 227, 229, 232, 233, 236, 238, 239, 240, 241
London Hibernian Society 148
Lynch, Laurence 152, 168

MacConmara, Donncha Ruadh 54
Mackesy, Rev. William 43, 49
Mahon, River 25-26, 32, 35, 50, 231
Malcomson of Portlaw 188
Manchester, England 104
mass, the 54, 127, 132, 161, 173-5
Mathew, Theobald 35, 36
Maunsell, Rev. Richard 24, 43, 222, 234
Maynooth College 37, 38, 45, 122, 135
Mayo Co. 141, 142, 183, 219
McCarthy, Rev. D. 122
M'Crea, William 46
McDonagh, Thomas 30
McGrath, Rev. John 41
Meagher, Thomas F. 154, 155
Michigan, USA 64
Mills, Rev. Thomas 122, 123
Mining Company of Ireland 27, 31, 39, 58, 64, 97, 239
Monksland, parish of 15, 23-27, 38, 41-45, 49, 52, 64, 66, 67-71, 95, 99, 100,

148-50, 176, 191, 215, 221, 230-31, 234-5, 238, 240-41, 243-4, 253
Moore, W.S. 106, 107, 108, 109, 110, 205
Morgan, Rev. John 94-5
Moriarty, Jack 16
Morrissey, Patrick 36
Musgrave, Sir Richard 139, 184

Nangle, Rev. Edward 183,
National Board of Education 41-44, 46-8, 50-51, 99, 106, 107, 185
Newton, John 90
Newtown 38, 39, 41, 58, 179, 201
Newtown Anner, Co. Tipperary 40, 141, 148
New York, America 239
Nixon, Rev. Alexander 214
Nottingham, England 96, 103, 104
Oakham, England 104
O'Brien, Dominick, Bishop of Waterford and Lismore 37
O'Connell, Daniel 37, 45, 140, 141, 155, 198
Old Jonathan or the District and Parish Helper 91, 93, 94, 97, 226, 240
O'Neill, Rev. Francis 199
Ormsby, Rev. Edwin 15, 22
orphan house 202, 203
Osborne, family of 27, 39, 48, 66, 68, 141, 246, 247, 248
Osborne, Lady Catherine 27, 36, 40, 41, 43, 44, 46-8, 50, 51, 148, 163
Osborne, Catherine Isabella 28

Ostend, Belgium 4
O'Suilleabhain, Tadhg Gaelach 54

Pallasgreen, Co. Limerick 146
Parker, Rev. J. 95
particular redemption 237
Petherick, John 36, 39, 41, 45, 48, 60, 68, 152, 155, 175, 185, 198, 199
Plymouth, England 56, 66, 104, 221, 241
Pollard, Jane 52
Pope, Samuel 46
Portlaw 108, 149, 188, 211
Portsea, England 2, 11
Power, Rev. James 36, 41, 48, 59
Power, Joseph N. 187
Power, Lorenzo 42, 58
Power, Nicholas Mahon 162
Power, Rev. Michael 42, 50, 51 106, 160, 164, 168, 178, 179
Power, Rev. Roger 39, 48, 179, 180, 201, 243
Power, Rev. Thomas 42, 43, 45, 47, 49, 59, 60, 104, 246
Power, William (father of Thomas?) 49
Power, William (Poor Law guardian) 187, 188, 190, 246
Power-O'Shee 38, 246, 262
Power-O'Shee, John 41
Power-O'Shee, Richard 26, 27, 33, 262
Predestination 180, 215, 243
priest, role of 4, 20, 22, 118-9, 127, 129, 132-7, 139-40, 147, 156, 158, 162-7, 168-76, 178-84, 192, 195-203, 220, 250-52
priesthood of all believers 126, 133

printing school 73-94, 96-8, 102, 105, 111, 157-60, 165, 172, 178, 179, 180-81, 197, 204-5, 217, 225, 227-8, 236, 239, 250, 252
proselytism 20-21, 142-4, 146, 154, 193, 204, 206, 219, 250-51
Purdy, Richard 58

Quakers 27, 60
Quin, Thomas 42

Ralph, William 46
Redemptorists 243-4
Redmond, H.E. 211, 216
Reynolds, Thomas 46
Richards, John 41
Ridley, Nicholas 159
Ring 72
Roche, Rev. George Tierney 231-2
Roman Catholic Church 4, 22, 38-9, 43, 116, 118-22, 125-7, 130, 132-3, 135-6, 139, 144, 152, 166-7, 176-7, 180-82, 200-01, 244, 247-50, 252
Rutherford, Samuel 87
Ryan, James 97

sacraments
  -baptism 127, 134, 181, 202,
  -communion 126-133, 174, 181, 201
Sandes, Stephen Creagh, bishop of Cashel 44
Sandford, Rev. William 14, 20, 22, 219
Shaftesbury, Lord 86
Shankill 262
Shaw, Charles 173

Shaw, Rev. William Elliott 61, 95, 218, 232-3
Sheehan, Rev. John 60, 140
Sheffield, England 66
Sibree, Peter 25, 217
Slattery, Thomas 42
Sligo Co. 142
Smith, Rev. Richard H. 95, 233
Society for Education of the Poor in Ireland (Kildare Place Society) 139
Society for Irish Church Missions 141, 145, 163, 243
souper/souperism 142-4, 146, 152, 157, 219, 250
Southampton, England 2, 3, 4, 8, 10, 104
Southsea, England 242
Stradbally 38, 39, 42, 50, 60, 71, 93, 95, 149, 150, 168, 176, 177, 179, 187, 209, 211, 224, 230, 231, 232, 233-4, 235, 237, 244, 246, 266
Stuart, Henry Villiers 135, 140
suicide 126, 185, 206, 208, 211, 217, 253
Sullivan, John 42
Sullivan, [Mr.] 176
Sunday School Society for Ireland 149
Surrey, England 112
Suttons, Reading, England 108
Swansea, Wales 28, 57

temperance 27, 35-8, 39, 179, 201, 247
Templemore, Co. Tipperary 6-7, 12-24, 69, 143, 153, 219, 240, 246, 247, 248

321

Templeree, Co. Tipperary 49
Templevrick 25-6, 28, 50
Thirty-Nine Articles of Religion 90, 117
Thurles, synod of 51, 134-6, 160, 181, 197, 202
tithe 139-40, 199
Tobin, Julia 191
Tobin, William 209
Tollymore, Co. Down 150, 240
Toplady, Augustus 90
Trench, Power le Poer 147
Trinity College, Dublin 55, 56
Tunbridge Wells, England 112

Veale, Biddy 167, 195
Veale, Rev. James 36, 39, 41
Veale, Larry 167
Veale, Michael 175
Veale, Norah 195

Walker, Dr. George 39, 41, 63, 157
Waterford and Lismore, diocese of 37, 38, 42, 94, 134, 147, 218, 238
Waterford Auxiliary Bible Society 114, 149
Waterford Auxiliary Relief Association 60
Waterford City 35, 42, 45, 135, 140, 149, 150, 154
Watts, James 239
Way, Mary Ann 76
Wesleyan Methodists 64, 67, 68, 137, 152, 215, 252
West, John 46
West, Bithia 97
Wexford Co. 156, 224

Whately, Richard, Archbishop of Dublin 44
Whitefield, George 90
Whitney, H. 115, 215-6
Wilkinson, Rev. N. 95
Winsford, England 104
Woodcock, William 46
Workhouses 144, 165, 185-90, 198, 202, 251
Wyse, Thomas 140
Young Irelanders 154-5

About the Author

Born in Waterford, Ireland, Thomas P. Power is a member of the faculty of Wycliffe College, University of Toronto, Ontario, Canada.

www.ingramcontent.com/pod-product-compliance
Lightning Source LLC
Chambersburg PA
CBHW061426300426
44114CB00014B/1561